Treasure of the Vanquished

Treasure of the Vanquished

A Novel of Visigothic Spain

Bernard Reilly

COMBINED BOOKS
Pennsylvania

PUBLISHER'S NOTE

Combined Books, Inc., is dedicated to publishing books of distinction in history and military history. We are proud of the quality of writing and the quantity of information found in our books. Our books are manufactured with style and durability and are printed on acid-free paper. We like to think of our books as soldiers: not infantry grunts, but well dressed and well equipped avant garde. Our logo reflects our commitment to the modern and yet historic art of bookmaking.

We call ourselves Combined Books because we view the publishing enterprise as a "combined" effort of authors, publishers and readers. And we promise to bridge the gap between us–a gap which is all too seldom closed in contemporary publishing.

We would like to hear from our readers and invite you to write to us at our offices in Pennsylvania with your reactions, queries, comments, even complaints. All of your correspondence will be answered directly by a member of the Editorial Board or by the author.

We encourage all of our readers to purchase our books from their local booksellers, and we hope that you let us know of booksellers in your area that might be interested in carrying our books. If you are unable to find a book in your area, please write to us.

For information, address:
COMBINED BOOKS, INC.
151 East 10th Avenue
Conshohocken, PA 19428

Map by Lizbeth Nauta.

Library of Congress Cataloging-in-Publication Data
Reilly, Bernard F., 1925-
    Treasure of the vanquished : a novel of Visigothic Spain/by Bernard Reilly.
        p. cm.
    ISBN 0-938289-27-6
    1. Spain—History—Gothic period, 414-711—Fiction. I. Title.
PS3568.E4845T74 1993   93-5476
813'.54—dc20   CIP
Combined Books Edition 1 2 3 4 5

First published in the USA in 1993 by Combined Books and distributed in North America by Stackpole Books, Inc., 5067 Ritter Road, Mechanicsville, PA 17055; 717-796-0411 or 1-800-732-3669

Printed in the United States of America.

Treasure of the Vanquished

BAY OF BISCAY

Oviedo •

Narbonne •

Lugo •

Leon
• Astorea

Zamora •

Visev •

Palencia •
Segovia •

Saragossa •

Barcelona •

Salamanca •

Avila •

Tarragona

Toledo •

Merida •

Corboba •

Seville •

Guabalete

Algeciras •

------ Tarik's Campaign of 711 & 712

·········· Musa's Campaign of 713 & 714

Major Mountain Ranges

Spain in the 8th Century

Prologue

During the late spring of the year 711 A.D. a Muslim army of perhaps 10,000 men crossed the Straits of Gibraltar from North Africa to invade the Iberian peninsula, then ruled by the kings of the Visigoths. The last of these Germanic warrior-kings, Rodrigo, marched hastily south to meet the invaders at Guadalete, south of modern-day Medina Sidonia, before they could penetrate to the vital portions of his kingdom. In the resulting battle there, the Visigothic army was crushed and King Rodrigo himself vanished from history. He was not captured but his body was never found. Almost two hundred years later a Christian chronicler reported the discovery of an epitaph recording his supposed burial at Viseu in modern Portugal.

The victor of the battle of Guadalete was the Arab freedman Tarik, who then undertook a most audacious march north into the heart of the Visigothic Iberian kingdom. His exact itinerary is still a matter of some little debate among historians but its major outlines are clear nonetheless. First he passed up the valley of the Guadalquivir River and north to the old Visigothic royal city of Toledo where he was able to seize the royal treasure. Then he marched northeast, around the end of the Guadarrama Mountains, and swept out onto the great northern *meseta*, or plain, of the Duero River. Meeting little resistance there, he moved as far west as León and Astorga before turning south to regain Toledo by way of Zamora, Salamanca, and Segovia. Nowhere was there report of another pitched battle but Tarik's situation would have been precarious in the extreme had he faced a disciplined and determined enemy.

The Muslim general had reported his initial victory to his patron and superior Musa ibn Nasr, the governor of Muslim North Africa. During the spring of 712 Musa led another Muslim army of about 15,000 to 20,000 men across the Straits and marched north to Mérida, where some Visigothic forces were attempting to organize a defense. The Muslim siege of Mérida was difficult and lasted from the fall of 712 to the spring of 713 before finally forcing the surrender of the city. Shortly thereafter Tarik and Musa joined forces at Toledo and the fate of the Visigothic kingdom was sealed. By 720 A.D. the Muslim invaders had even penetrated north of the Pyrenees and consolidated their hold about Narbonne. A dozen years later, in 732, another raiding force based there was just barely defeated at Poitiers in the valley of the Loire River by the Carolingian leader, Charles Martel, who thereby put an end to the Muslim thrust into Western Europe.

Nevertheless a Muslim power had taken shape in the Iberian peninsula that would endure, with varying fortunes and extent, until the final reconquest of Granada by Ferdinand and Isabella in 1492. The remains of the palaces, fortresses, and mosques erected by Islam still dot the Iberian countryside and cities. Despite this material splendor, the sway of Islam in Iberia was more often than not unstable.

In part this was due to the fact that the conquest took place less than a century after the death of the prophet Muhammad in 632 A.D. The very religious content of Islam was only incompletely developed and its political and social implications even less so. Moreover, the great bulk of the army that Tarik led into Iberia was comprised not of Arabs but of North African Berber peoples whose grasp of Islam was as limited as it was new. They themselves had only been overrun by Arab armies in the preceding half-century. Large numbers of them were still either outright pagans or still Christians, who were divided from their Arab leaders by language, custom, and religion. In Tarik's army many of them would largely have been either mercenaries or adventurers pure and simple.

Musa's army seems to have been composed of a much larger contingent of Arabs but it also had its Berber auxiliaries. Before thirty years had passed Muslim Iberia experienced a major revolt of Berber against Arab. In theory the Ummayad caliphs of Damascus in distant Syria ruled all of these unlikely subjects, but actually their authority was never consolidated in Iberia. Within a half-century Muslim Iberia was independent.

The first Muslim generals, or *emirs*, had to create an Islamic Iberian society with the most slender resources and from the most variegated human materials. Their extraordinary success is a commentary upon the debility of the Visigothic society that they displaced. In the two preceding centuries in the peninsula the Visigoths had retained much of Roman law, the Roman Christianity, and the Roman economy that they had found there. Themselves originally a minority of scarcely 10% of the 4 million inhabitants of Iberia, they ruled the indigenous population almost as a military garrison. How substantial their authority ever was, beyond the limits of the towns and their fortified villas, is difficult to determine. It is clear, however, that it stopped well short of the primitive and pagan hill-peoples, Asturians, Cantabrians, and Basques, who lived among the mountain chains of the Pyrenees and the Cantabrians and along the littoral of the Bay of Biscay to the north.

Moreover, the Visigoths were badly divided among themselves at the time of Tarik's appearance in the peninsula. Rodrigo, their king in 711, was regarded by some as no more than a usurper. His rivals, the sons of the deceased King Witiza, went over to the Muslim side at Guadalete and were subsequently pensioned off with a substantial portion of the former lands of the Visigothic crown. One son, Agila, seems to have enjoyed a nominally independent but tributary kingdom around Narbonne until 720 A.D. Certainly many of the Visigothic magnates signed treaties with the Muslims that permitted them to keep their estates, religion, and even some subordinate but public authority, in return for an annual tribute. Although the religion of Islam eventually spread widely among the conquered peoples of Iberia it is likely that the Mozarabs, Christians living subject to Muslim rule and participating in the social and economic life of the conquerors while retaining their own religion and law, always continued to make up the majority of the population.

Quite separate from this ordinary development is the figure of Pelayo. A Visigothic noble, he appears in the chronicles of the late ninth century as the organizer of armed resistance to Muslim rule. In 719 he managed to defeat a Muslim expeditionary force at Covadonga in the heart of the Cantabrian Mountains. From that beginning, a Christian kingdom of Asturias was gradually constructed during the following century. The Spanish still regard the miraculous victory at Covadonga as the starting point of their nation. The process is mysterious still but, by one means or another, Pelayo was able to form a motley assemblage of refugees and primitives into a single people, united under one king and the one Christian religion, and to fire them with the will to resist Muslim control.

In 1858 a small flood in the region of Guadamur, some 15 kilometers southwest of Toledo, eroded a section of cemetery and disclosed the presence of a hoard of Visigothic jewelry, votive crowns, and liturgical objects, hidden in the ground since the Muslim conquest. Most of this so-called treasure of the Guarrazar has since passed into the possession of the National Museum of Archaeology in Madrid and to the Cluny Museum in Paris.

Chapter 1

Behind him, in the royal city of Toledo, points of flame showed among the rooftops. Half-turning on his pony, he could see them, but the night breeze carried the screams which accompanied them away to the southeast. The sorry nag labored steadily towards the southwest under the double burden of the man and his treasure.

Pelayo cursed. Softly, monotonously, like a refrain, a dirge, the words jolted from him as his mount's feet felt irregularly for footing among the rocks of the night. "Christ. Oh, Christ! God! Oh my God! For Christ's sake!" At each motion of the animal the sweat from the bunched, red hairs of his armpits coursed a little lower down his sides. The wind from the Guadarramas was chill as it reached him. He shivered in his own sweat and plodded on.

Now and again he reined in the ridiculous little animal to listen. He heard no sound but the labored breathing of the beast under him. The young man was large of bone and heavily fleshed, as redheads sometimes are. His warrior harness was soaked with sweat. The weight of the man, his sodden leather, and gold in the sack across the hindquarters were too much for the little pony which half-trotted through the night.

Pelayo knew that they were back there, somewhere. That they must follow him. Those Africans! Tall, lean, brown men who loped across rock and scrub without effort, who clenched their bows and spears together in one hand as they alternately trotted and jumped through the low bush, forcing his poor pony towards its death. And still they had breath enough to shout to each other and cry down the quarry.

He could hear nothing now of that ululation and yelping but he knew that a pursuit had been, or would be, mounted. They would catch him, drag him down. His death would be like his brother's. No warrior's death but a bloody degradation! It would come and catch him as the slaughter of a pig, or a dog, and he raging ineffectually against it. For he would be unable to touch them, match them—only to feel the pain and the shame. Even like King Rodrigo perhaps? Was the king still alive?

"Oh my God, why did I run? Why run, and run, and start, and plunge away until your heart is bursting inside you? And your gut is so tight and knotted that you can taste your own bile in your throat! Can it be that bad? Stop and die!" He was haranguing himself and his fates, his God, the luckless, damned providence which had left him here. "Why did I run? Oh God, my brother, my own brother! I left him! I didn't help. I hid. I ran. Oh Christ, I left him there!"

The world had come apart so suddenly. A lousy little rebellion! A lousy little raid! And the king marched south—and disappeared. They said he had died in the battle. They said that he escaped. They said that he was moving to raise another army but those damned Africans spread over the land like locusts, like vicious little badgers. All the heroes were dead, dragged down like fat cows in their own blood. It couldn't be stopped! No one could do it!

They had come up so suddenly. The bad news had come before, of course. No courier—but news. And behind it, them! King Rodrigo was dead, slaughtered! He was beaten but had escaped! He was making his way north of the Guadarrama, in disguise, to raise a new army! A fugitive king, a defeated king, and the hope of the Gothic nation. Nobody believed it. It was all over, done, ruined, dead. As dead as the old gods!

The day of the gray wolf! All the warriors dead, all the great chiefs gutted, all the women raped, all the children brained! And those brown ants, lice, all over them! Picking at the wounds! Eating the brains! Jabbering their nervous, jerky words and slinging the shields of dead chiefs over their backs.

Everybody believed it. No one believed it. It was hope. It was a chance for life. His brother believed it. Like a chief and a king's man, he had reacted as he had so often before. The treasure of the royal chapel, which was his charge, must be saved for the king. It must be taken to him, for the chiefs of the northern plains had little feeling for Rodrigo. Counts and dukes, they called themselves. They dressed themselves in Roman finery and styled themselves Roman officers and governors but they were a rabble of warriors in a long-conquered land. The king must not come to them as a defeated man, without resources. He must have that booty of a thousand raids and fights, long since cast into golden crosses and jewel-heavy crowns, which adorned the royal chapels of Toledo. It had glorified God and mollified the saints. Now it could support a hundred more campaigns. Now the king needed it and they would find him and get it to him. Such a task was the duty of the men of the king's house.

Together they had gone through the dark little streets to one of the royal chapels. There was no guard and no priest there. No one was any longer where he was supposed to be. The city itself was strange and alien in the moonlight. Only the stars were familiar.

They took only the finest stuff. The rest of it might be reconquered with luck and God's favor. They stripped the stuff down as fast as they could. The place was dark and they left it that way, for they had no desire to attract looters. The treasure had never been meant to be moved and some of it got smashed in the breaking loose of it. No time for scrambling after bits and pieces! Load the bag!

It was noisy as hell and the brothers crossed themselves repeatedly. God might or might not understand the need to rob him and the noise could raise the spirits of the dead. It was an unlucky business at best. The thought of the curses of the saints raised the hackles on both their napes. They crossed themselves again and finished it up, there in the hot, dark interior.

Pelayo strained under the sack as he moved through the little door into the street. His brother would have to refasten it, against the faint hope that what remained would be respected by other, less loyal looters—or would find protectors against those others.

Only a few paces up the street, he had heard it. The shouts! Shouts in no language he knew. They were here. Here in the royal city! Getting to the roof of the nearest house was a nightmare. Lifting that goddamned bag with his legs trembling from the weight and his lungs burning! Not having sense enough to let go of it. Heaving up one step after the other. Knowing that his brother could hardly carry his part of the burden and yet would never leave it. His brother! Where the hell was he?

He was just coming out of the chapel. Just fastening the heavy door as the bastards entered the little square—a good dozen of them. Turning he readied his great axe and shield, the instinct of the old soldier. He was heavy like Pelayo but the rusty hair of his chest and head was liberally grayed. His arm behind the axe could still cut away opposing shield and arm together to leave a dead man at second stroke if the fight gave time for finishing. But his wind was gone. Too fat, too old, he couldn't pin them, even in the little square. They were hard too, those African tribesmen, but lean and young. Their feet slap-slapped on the packed earth as they avoided the brief charges.

In the end it became a game for them. They laughed and called to one another, taunting him. Their arrows found him, one by one. He could not cover his legs and so was backed finally against the chapel door, whose recessed arch protected his flanks. But he had taken two arrows in one thigh and another in the calf of his other leg. The archery contest continued in leisurely fashion as the massive arms, drained of blood, slowly gave in to the weight of axe and shield. He bawled curses at them, called them boys and bastards, cowards and no men. They giggled excitedly now and aimed for his upper arms and shoulders. At last, bristling with a dozen arrows, he fell heavily. Drawing back the great head by the tangled, faintly reddish hair, they cut his living throat like a hog's.

Pelayo watched from the roof. His brother never so much as glanced about for him, never called for him. A second axeman in that square, a second sword? But King Rodrigo must have his gold. So his brother must have thought. Or did he hope, with his lungs burning and the sweat bursting through his eyebrows to nearly blind him, did he hope that brother would rally to brother? Risk his king for his own flesh?

Pelayo pressed close against the roof. He had been blooded. He was no child. But he could not move. He wanted to run but he watched it out in terror. He wanted, finally, to be sick but in a frenzy of fear he fought back the betraying noises. It never occurred to him either to enter the struggle or to reproach himself. King Rodrigo and the king's gold piled beside him were utterly forgotten.

Simply, those jeering, lithe, angular forms terrified him. Like warrior spirits, like valkyrie, they were invincible and deathdealing. They fought without passion yet with playful precision. He hid.

Again and again the terrible details of that little scene returned to his mind as he pushed on through the night. Each time the terror within him rose to a new pitch. From the sickness in his stomach, it became a constricting tension in the muscles of his back and shoulders, an awful pressure in the back of his skull; it threatened to immobilize him. A slackness, a shuddering helplessness, dissolution lay just out there beyond the fringes of his hysterical self-control. Savagely he forced the horse on. They could not but follow. If not now, not yet, surely when daylight revealed to them the full import of what had transpired in that little Toledan chapel. After the scattered street fights, after the women, after the wine, the first casual collection of trophies, someone would survey the scene. Scent the loss. Would drive the initially reluctant victors to a new chase. Once begun, the sport and its challenge would take them. Perhaps it had begun already!

Riding and listening, listening and then riding once again, he gradually became aware that the pony was faltering. The load was too great, the ground too broken. Half lame and exhausted, the little beast was nearly done. Strangely, the new desperation of his situation steadied him. As the pace decreased, as each of his urgings elicited less and less response from his mount, he dully began to plan. For the first time now, he dismounted and began to half lead and half pull the animal, stumbling in the dark. It was clearly too late to do more than coax a little more distance out of it.

But the ground had been flattening out, bit by bit. He had skirted, carefully, a little cluster of huts which gave no sign of life. Not even a dog or a cock. Now he came suddenly on a small oratory. A solid little church whose priest had doubtless fled, perhaps with the villagers. Just beyond it lay a cemetery to the edge of which he now led the pony. He stopped by a grave. The granite cover looked loose and he must dispose of the gold. Perhaps it would be safe. Perhaps he could return for it. He hardly cared except to get rid of that weight, that drag.

The notion of the hunt, rising within him, raised anew the thrill of terror. Urgently he wrestled off the granite slabs, straining at the weight. He must not break them. The faint stench that met him was familiar from a dozen battlefields. Too frightened to do more than curse weakly, he wrestled the pony towards the sarcophagus and tipped the heavy sack into it.

Relieved of its load the broken beast moved briefly, away

from the smell of old death, and shuffled in the dirt. Now Pelayo must wrestle the grave coverings back into place. He was alarmed at his own weakness as he did so.

Pelayo considered his predicament and necessities briefly. His line of flight from Toledo had been dictated by the possibilities of the night but it had been fortunate. Unless his scrabbling through the river Tagus had left clear traces, they would search for him at first towards the north. The whole Gothic world was fleeing north. That he had gone roughly west would buy him time but now he must turn north to reach the mountains where a man afoot was less easily found. And when the conquerors found no traces of a man with treasure to the north of Toledo, they would spread their search to the east and west. Even if they did not pick up his trail itself, he must reach the mountains before that search spread across the open flats to the north of him. Especially must he find a place to cross the Tagus before the dawn.

But what if they did pick up his trail? What if it led them here? If they found the treasure, the hopes that he would be carrying yet more of it would spur the search. He would be marked. He had done all that he could to conceal it but an old woman could read in the dirt that the pony had stopped here a while. He would give them some explanation of that. It was a poor one but nothing else suggested itself. Not far from the animal he dropped his pants and emptied his bowels.

Now he mounted the poor beast again. It stood immobile and broken but he must not leave it here to give them reason to search. And he must ride it to explain his taking it farther. Savagely he kicked it and dug the point of his dagger's scabbard into its hindquarters. Reluctantly the animal broke into a slow walk and they swung around towards the north. Only the desperation of his will and the brutality of his treatment kept it in motion over the next hour. When it finally collapsed and went down, he was ready and got clear of its fall easily, even in the dark. Then he drew his knife across its throat and struck out for the Tagus on foot.

Just before full dawn he reached the river and, in the half-light, was able to cross. The river was low and full of shallows. He could not swim and so he leapt and plunged from one to the other crossing the divided branches of the current by main force. On the north bank, in the cover of a small copse, he lay down and slept.

Later, try as he might, he could never really recall the incidents of the next few days. He traveled by night unless the cover was good but it seldom was until he reached the foothills. Food was no problem for the fields and the villages were often deserted and, where they were not, no one was disposed to challenge night noises. When he could, Pelayo took melons for he had no water or a means to carry it and he dared not approach the wells. His feet were in ribbons from the rocky soil and the weight of his own body. He sweated continuously by day and shivered by night. He was reaching exhaustion but he dared not stop. He saw no one. He heard nothing. Once or twice, fitfully awake and panting in the afternoon sun, he saw dust trails.

But he knew they were there, back there. Searching, crossing and recrossing his trail, they would find him. His fear had redoubled when he awoke without his horse. The distance was so great. Alone under the great arch of the blue sky, he felt small and dwarfed. The mountains seemed farther away each time he looked at them. His path ahead must be blocked a dozen times each day by their little bands. If only he could find a few warriors of his own kind. To die alone, helplessly, when they came on him, suddenly, as they had in that little square. Dragging him down, full of arrows, to meet the knife. And no chance against them. Oh God, God!

That was how it happened. He had plunged on, reaching the foothills, and then the mountains themselves. There he had stuck to the high ground, away from the valley trails that they would be searching, using. He feared the shepherds who could give news of him, a Goth in warrior's gear in full flight. It was night and moonlit, and the shale gave to his step. He was too exhausted to recover his balance. He rolled over and down the steep slope, his shield bouncing down before him. Arms and legs spread out, grasping for purchase, he found only insubstantial brush whipped past him by his own growing momentum. And then the crash! Rolling, turning, he dropped over the edge onto a rock below. The impact of it on his left side drove the air out of him as the ribs gave. He gasped desperately to recapture it while the pain shot through him. He still had not recovered it when consciousness slid away from him.

About ten o'clock in the morning, he awoke. Slowly his eyes began to focus and he saw, almost beneath his nose, a solemn little caravan of ants, each of them bearing its own fragment of burdens. Instinctively his head jerked back and pain thrilled through him. Aah! He laid very still, waiting for the gradually diminishing ebb and flow of it to still, and watched the tiny procession vanish beyond his eyebrows. As the pain settled down to a variety of aches and throbbings, his eyes searched out the rich green pine boughs to his right where the mountainside fell away again and left them framed against the valley below and the blue morning sky not yet bleached by the sun. In it he could see two hawks circling. It was all very far away from him and quite insubstantial, like a reflection in a pond.

He lay in the center of a small trail along the mountain. Underneath his chest was a rock, worn smooth by many feet, that would have killed him had it been sharp or more pointed. Atop it lay his three cracked or broken ribs. He felt the pressure of it as he breathed as shallowly as possible and the pain eddied about the lower left of his chest. He would have slid to the right but he was afraid of what new possibilities of anguish that might open up. Without moving, looking below his right armpit and down along the line of his right leg, he could see his right ankle and foot. The leg itself was a mass of cuts and scratches but they looked blue. By staring at his foot very hard and concentrating with his mind on its sensations, he could distinguish finally a special area of throbbing hurt which began somewhere below his right knee. The effort was too much, he lost ability to focus either mind or eyes, he fainted.

It must have been about three in the afternoon when he awoke again. He ached so that individual pains were hard to separate. His head throbbed dully and the glare of the sun hurt his eyes. Even with his lids closed the fierceness of its rays painted their interior a light, reddish color. But the ever present breeze among the pines was chill with the threat of the coming evening. The deserted sky was faded to the palest of blue tints, looking translucent, almost like a crystal.

Pelayo was just conscious of the wetness under him. The sweat baked out of him by the rock ran down its side to make brief mud beneath. Most of all he was thirsty. He was being fried alive. He could see the dried salt on the leather shoulder-strap of his harness. His sword and scabbard were a searing iron against his left leg. Cautiously he twitched the calf muscle and it moved without pain. Braver, he rocked the whole leg and the scabbard shifted and the heat subsided.

Just above the level of his brow on the path, lay some of the loose shale he had carried down with him last night. Using his fingers as feet, he inched his right arm towards them. Fumbling among the pebbles he chose a smaller one. Bringing it back to his face, he put it in his mouth. The latter motion shifted his body slightly from the rock moving the broken ribs and forcing his right knee against the earth. Pain shot through him, across his chest and up through his groin from his right leg. For a moment, he was cold from pain and weakness and then the heat came back. He was conscious of the heat of the pebble burning his dry tongue and mouth but he shifted it from side to side and, slowly, reluctantly, a little saliva came. He rested and sucked.

Now, he thought, he must get away from the rock and the sunlight. Towards the right side of the trail the pines threw a little shade. Employing his right elbow as a lever he began to inch his body towards the shade. As he dragged his chest off the rock, dropping it an inch or two onto the dirt of the trail his left side exploded into fiery darts of agony. His right leg protested in minor chorus. He thought that he would be sick but the contractions in his stomach found nothing to expel. He dropped his pebble at the sudden thought that he would choke on it, then found it again after the heaving subsided. Slowly he reached the blessed shade with his upper body. He pulled his legs into it by inching forward. He used his left leg simply to push his strengthless, tortured right one deeper into the shade. Finally, he reached with his right arm to grasp the left one, which had been trailing uselessly, pulling it up and out of the sun. Again, he thought that he would faint but the dizziness faded and the pulsating pressure at the base of his brain again asserted itself.

From his present position he could see down the steeply sloping mountainside to yet another trail, or a lower reach of the one he lay on. Along it, he slowly comprehended, moved a small knot of five or six men whom he could see, now and again, through the slender trunks of the pines. As he watched their deliberate progress, for they examined the sides of the path they were taking as well as the portion of it just before them, he determined that it was them. The Africans! The breeze carried away their conversation but there was no mistaking their gestures and movements. Above them, on the hillside, he could just see his shield, caught on a bit of scrub. It reflected the sun like a semaphore. If the stones about it shifted, if the breeze bent the scrub too energetically, it might bound down before them like a betraying cartwheel. Any movement of his might dislodge pebbles that would run down the slope to ring off it like a signal bell.

With unconsciously muted breath, he watched them, watched them proceed up the far end of their trail and beyond the angle of his vision. Despite his side, despite his leg, he then raised himself on his right arm and looked about. If their path led up to his, he was dead. His panic gave him strength. Ahead of him the path was but a narrow rut in the hillside. No cover there. Fighting off the pain and dizziness, he pushed himself over and up into a sitting position.

There was surprisingly little blood on the ground or himself. His right ankle was swollen grotesquely and a mottled blue-black in color. But the leg was obviously not broken and the ankle might not be. His left arm seemed sound. Aiding and lifting it with his right one, he tucked it inside his harness strap. His left side screamed at him but at least that arm was part of him again.

Positioned as he was, he could see a point at which the trail widened, where the mountain drew back into the sheer granite of itself, leaving some room for a growth of hardy scrub and pine below the face of rock. With his knife, Pelayo carefully cut off a small plant just below the level of the ground and smoothed over the betraying butt. Turning himself around with his good arm and leg, he now began to lift and push himself back down the path. Every couple of feet, he stopped and brushed the ground he had just covered into some appearance of natural disarray. In this fashion, he finally reached the mountain's recess.

At its deepest, it was not more than six or seven feet. He pushed into it until his back rested against the granite and let the bush drop. All his pains were numbered and familiar now and he suffered and tolerated them, enjoying the slightly damp support of the rock at his back. He could see, sick at heart, that the cover was not adequate. No one could fail to see him from the path unless they were blind and drunk. And he remembered his shield. They could not miss it from above as they had from below. There was no escape from them, even in the mountains. There was no place to run, no stratagem prevailed. They were fated to conquer and his guts would rot in this corner. A prickling of horror ran up his nape.

Drawing his sword, he lay it across his thighs. With the fingers of his right hand he probed the flesh of his chest, searching and finding the spot where a blade could slip through to the heart, returning to it yet twice again to be sure. With his knife then he made a small cut at the proper place. It would have to be done quickly. Better to do it himself when they came. No hope. He pushed the dagger blade into a patch of moss close to his right hand and waited. He stared out, beyond the brush, at a small patch of sky which he did not see. All his awareness now was concentrated in his ears, as he listened for their approach. The dagger's pommel was smooth to his palm.

When or how long he slept, he had no idea. He awoke to the dark and a starry sky. By turns he was hot and cold. His body throbbed miserably. His head was light for want of food and his mouth like dry wool. He turned his head and pressed his cracked lips to the slightly damp rock. He pulled up some patches of moss and licked them for their faint wetness. He tried chewing some of the leaves of the shrubs about him for liquid but they were bitter and acid to the taste, so he found himself another pebble and worked it furiously about his mouth. The sharp edge of the cold wind and the damp of night started him shivering uncontrollably but he could get no moisture from it.

For the first time in days, perhaps years, he tried to pray. "God, don't let me die here! God, have mercy on me! Lord, let me escape!"

And in a calmer vein, "Let me find some companions to help me. To get away to the north. I'll find a place in Toulouse, in Narbonne, beyond the Pyrenees, and become a man of prayer, a monk. I'll build a church. I'll spend my life in your service. I'll do penance for the desertion of my brother.

"Christ, what could I do? There was no chance. You know that I'm no coward. You know that I have served my king, your anointed, and carry his scars. But they were too many, and hardly human. Our king was dead. We wanted to help him but it was no use. Was it your judgment, Lord? Is it your will to give up the whole Visigothic people to the knife? Should I have fought that? Can any of us do anything but bow to your will? If you make us corpses, or slaves, or fugitives, what can we do?

"Yes, I was afraid. Yes, my guts turned to water. Yes, I ran. I want to run again. Where are you, my God? Am I the only one left to worship you? The palaces are gutted. The cities are burning. The fields and houses are deserted. The enemy, the African, is everywhere. God, don't let me die here. I'll build you a church, only don't let me rot. Mend my bones. Make me well. Get me out of this. Please."

He fell silent. The night noises were all around him. Pebbles rolled somewhere. An animal coughed. The wind whined in the pines. Nothing was still, everything was moving. Only he sat motionless against the cliff, dagger in his hand. There was no one. His people were gone, vanished. King Rodrigo, a phantom. God was gone. His brother, dead. A deserted land, a vast, aching loneliness. He touched his body. It seemed hardly part of him. It only hurt him. There was nothing, nothing. Eventually, he slept.

Pelayo was hardly awake when the rage overtook him. At first, he had been surprised and glad that he was alive, pleased that the misery of his body had receded so greatly. As he fashioned a clumsy crutch from a pine bough, it had grown on him. As he struggled along the trail with the green branch bending unpredictably and now and again dropping his bulk on his ankle which sent long spears of pain up through his thigh, it worked itself into a storm. As the exertion began to exacerbate his hunger and his thirst, it took possession of him.

Inanimate objects became enemies. A fox darted across the path. He could have killed it.

"Bastard!"

Its sin was agility. The birds sang in the morning branches, unconcerned and unperturbed.

"Sons of bitches!"

The sun laid its heat upon his back.

"God damn!"

He had a profane litany, equal to each experience as he progressed. He knew the unreasonableness of it. That only provoked him further. He would have slashed with his crutch, sword, dagger, but he would have fallen. Why was he alone, hurt, helpless? He knew that the answer was them, the Africans, but he declined to give it. He could not give or accept it because his terror of them remained. He was afraid to turn his anger on them. He wanted to kill something, someone, but he knew that, if they should appear, his anger would drain away and leave only naked fear. That knowledge provoked him even more.

"Cowards, whoresons, gutless wonders."

That for the whole nation of the Visigoths who had vanished from the earth. That for the peasants who had vanished from their fields into the hare holes of the earth.

On and on it went, getting him, sliding, slipping, sweating, down off the mountain.

Just before twilight he reached the field. A rivulet had quenched his thirst and cooled his ankle, but his hunger remained. A cultivated field! And beyond it, a peasant's hut. No animals, no people. Frightened off and hiding like everyone else. Warned by the turmoil of his stomach, he ate slowly, grinding the flesh of the melon between his teeth and savoring the flavorsome wetness. Two of them and a handful of withered beans. He did not dare move. In his condition, to sleep anywhere but in the hut was impossible. No one moved after dark in the mountains anyway.

He stood in the low doorway, almost blind in the dark. Gradually the outlines of a low pallet emerged on his right. As he moved towards it a bundle of rags exploded into motion.

"Christ!"

The adrenalin shot through him. The rage returned. Propelling himself with his good left leg, dropping the crutch, he grasped the bundle in the middle, his bulky body carrying both crashing down upon the pallet. His catch was still and small. Underneath him lay a woman. He could see her small, dark face, impassive, a peasant. Someone who had not fled but was still part of it all. Someone to pay. A bitch who would betray a warrior if she had escaped—or put a knife into him if she dared. All his anger had an object now, all the fright, and weariness and fear of the past days.

Roughly he pulled the rags away from her loins. Pinning her with his torso, he fumbled at his own pants. She lay absolutely quiet, unresisting, unmoving. He shoved her legs apart and thrust himself into her. Still no protest. He began to rock back and forth, enjoying even the faint pain that his exertions extorted from his own body when coupled with the sweetness that surrounded him. But the toll of the past days had been too great. He could not finish it. He knew it. He was too tired.

Humiliated, he looked at her. Behind that expressionless face, those unreadable black eyes regarding his, this low born bitch was laughing at him. Furious, he thrust into her as roughly as he could, reaching, probing, searching, for something he could hurt. Now he was watching her. Except for an almost imperceptible, backward arching of her head, the slightest opening and tightening of her lips, she gave no acknowledgment of his purpose. Rather, exhaustion stopped him. Unmanned him.

He looked at her, this time questioningly. She knew!

"They hurt me more."

Flat, matter of fact, it was what he already knew. Them! Even here! Even so! The new masters! And she flaunted it in his face! They had beaten him and all his kind. Even the peasants knew it and had changed their masters. She had beaten him too. She had endured them both and they had been crueler, fiercer, harder.

With something like a sob, he began to strike her. Except

to turn her face slightly at each blow, she suffered that too. Heavily he slapped at her, bringing blood from her nose and mouth. He would have beaten her to death if he had not, at last, pitched down over her, unconscious.

Chapter 11

She was moving about the hut when he wakened. A little charcoal glowed in the center of the room. Noticing him she picked up a small bowl and came over to sit down beside the pallet. With her thumb and two fingers she formed the brown, mealy stuff in the bowl into little balls, stuffing them, in turn, slowly into his mouth. It smelled a little of oil and wine. Bits of bean clung chopped among the barley. He chewed slowly and forced himself to swallow. He was feverish and half-sick.

Her face, the lips and eye, were swollen and bluish, under the skin, along the entire left side of her face. From beneath bushy, black brows, the dark eyes regarded him with quiet curiosity. No other emotion was visible on her face. His eyes sought his sword which leaned against the wall and the dagger which lay by it, and her eyes followed his.

"It seemed hardly worth the doing," she said. "Anyway, you seem to want to die."

Her fingers brushed the cut on his chest, over the heart, with an easy familiarity. The faintest flicker of a grim smile moved across her bruised lips, as she resumed pushing the little balls of barley into his mouth. When he turned his head away, she rose without a word and then finished the contents of the bowl herself. Silently, she left the hut without a further glance. He discovered then that his cuts had been cleaned and oiled.

At dusk she re-entered the hut. From a variety of jars in the far corner, she mixed some more of the cereal. Cutting a small melon, she gave him several small chips and then fed him the barley mixture. He was light-headed and hot. The room and the objects in it floated strangely in the twilight. Seeing his neck muscles jerk, she ceased to feed him and finished the small meal herself, still seated by his bed.

Then, quite simply, she removed her clothing. She was small and dark, like all the natives of the land. He was easily two heads taller than she. Her arms were slender but firm and her shoulders well-muscled in the way that shows continued, physical labor. Her breasts were small and firm with the slight sag and enlarged nipples. She had suckled children. The abdomen, more than gently rounded, and the buttocks which were well-fleshed and a bit flattened towards the bottom indicated more than one childbirth. Her thighs were thick and getting heavy while her calves were muscular, almost masculine in their development. Pelayo had seen dozens like her. Young wives to the peasants, working alongside their men until disease, or childbirth, or war and rape killed them or broke them, leaving a few, blackened crones to tend infants and pots.

She lay down beside him and drew the bedclothes over them. He was shaking uncontrollably now with fever and the satiated hunger and exhaustion of the past days. Half-turning she drew him to her, turning his bulk with small effort. Her warmth and gentle smoothness absorbed his tremors and her hands stroked his back gradually quieting and relaxing his muscles. With his cheek against her breast and his hand resting on her thigh, he drifted off, safe and fully at rest for the first time in a week.

For three days, this routine was unvarying. Then the fever left him. Pelayo sat outside the hut in the sun, watching her work. Feet spread apart, she chopped steadily at the dried wreckage of the past summer's bean field, breaking the stems and mixing them into the brown earth, preparing it for a future sowing. She backed down the row towards him, bending now and again to shake loose a stubborn root. Her peasant shift was dark with the sweat of her back along the line of her hips. From time to time she went to drink at a small, mountain rivulet which rushed off towards some flatter land along one side of the field. He joined her there, walking stiffly.

"Where is your husband?"

"Over there in the earth—by the trees."

Following the line of her arm, he saw three small stones beyond the field and just in front of a grove of pines. Before one of them there was a irregular depression, not yet filled with needles or brush. It was a man's length.

"They didn't kill him then?"

"The Africans? No, he died in the spring. He got sick doing the early planting, a fever, and never got better. I laid him there beside his sons."

"They didn't kill you either, nor burn the hut, nor even take your food."

"No, they didn't. But then, I didn't resist them. There were three hens and a good rooster that they fancied. Luckily the hogs were off rooting somewhere."

She had looked at him closely before she replied. Now she could see his annoyance at her words, so she returned to her hoeing. Sulkily, Pelayo resumed sitting in the sun and idly watched her rhythmic motions. Only slowly did their implication dawn on him. My God, she intends to stay here!

In the evening, as they ate, he asked her about it.

"You are not going to leave here?"

The idea clearly had not occurred to her and his implied presumption that it should have nettled her a little.

"No. Where should I go? This is my land and my crop. I have a house and the pigs are around somewhere. My husband and my two children are in the earth here and one day I will be too."

"But you will work the land by yourself?"

"If I have to, I have before."

"But the Africans will come back."

"I expect so. But they don't seem to be farmers or mountain folk so they probably won't stay. There is not much to steal."

"Next time they may kill you."

"Possibly. I'll hide if I have a chance."

"At the very least they'll rape you."

She regarded him steadily now, showing just a trace of amusement.

"I'll avoid that if I can. But I've been raped before."

He lapsed into silence, Her manner hardly allowed either anger or penitence although he felt both in some measure. But she was unwilling to let the conversation drop. It was a long time since she had enjoyed the luxury. He was conscious for the first time of a weakness in her. She asked almost teasingly, "You will go north, my brave redhaired warrior?"

"Yes."

"To find your own people?"

"Yes."

"And because the others are hunting for you."

It was a statement and he was startled by it. She could see the consternation in his face.

"Oh, they asked about you. There were five of them in the search party. Their description was pretty good and they seemed quite serious about finding you although, when I first saw you, you hardly looked dangerous—or valuable."

Again the half-mocking note. She seemed to regard him as a child.

"What did they tell you about me?"

"They just described you, nothing more. They said that you were a Goth and a warrior—probably dangerous. They said that anyone who helped or concealed you would be killed by you or them."

He would have preferred to sit and think about that but she wanted to talk still, and gave him no respite.

"Where would you expect me to flee? To your people? They have never been mine, or my people's people. Among the old folk, the story tellers say that the land was ours before the Goths came, before the Romans, before the people who came before the Romans, and whose name is forgotten. You hunted over it, fought over it, taxed it, but it remained to us just as it did with all the others. So it will be with the Africans too.

"Should I leave my own land to go and live, a landless slave, among your people? You think that the Goths are the best of masters? Or should I cease to be an honest farm woman to become the concubine of a noble warrior? I am too old for that. And surely your fellow Goths would laugh at you. Or would you marry me and make me a Visigothic princess?"

Her quiet scorn left him no answer. Yet somehow, he was not surprised that she should not be afraid of him. He was not even surprised that he was not angry at her audacity, this peasant woman. He even argued with her.

"But you can't work this land alone forever. Where will you find another husband alone here in the hills? Will you take one of the Africans?"

"That is possible. A woman never knows. Perhaps they don't marry Christians. Perhaps they don't farm. But even a little piece of good land draws those who do and lack it. Someone will come. Hopefully he'll be healthy and I and my children will die and be buried on our own land."

Now Pelayo was angry. Why he was not entirely sure. Her composure and her confidence unsettled him. His world was gone, destroyed, and her's seemed unaffected and intact. It was outrageous.

"Look, all five of them raped you. You did not resist. Another man will come along and rape you and, if he is willing, you will probably marry him, share your land with him, bear his children. That is what you expect, wait for?"

"Would it have made a difference if I had resisted? Except that I should be dead, my virtue preserved? And how do men deal with a woman alone? Or a lone woman with men? My husband and I worked for a good two years here before we had the price of a priest for marriage. You don't know country life. At least, you don't know the farmer's side of it. One does what one can, but more usually what one must."

"And after such a life, you will join your husband and children in death and heaven? You think that God will have you?"

"From what the priests say, God has a poor opinion of women. Perhaps he has a little concern about them. In any event, I am as good as the world permits me to be. I say my prayers. If God expects much more, then there will be precious few in heaven."

He knew that he had not shaken her. He had hurt her a little maybe, but nothing more. And she kept reducing him to helpless silence. Again, she had made him feel like a child, prattling. Still she wanted the talk to continue. She was not finished and returned to the original tack, but gently.

"Are you sure that there is anywhere to go? Are your people gathering to the north or are they just running aimlessly? The Africans who passed through here did not seem to expect danger on the northern plains."

"No. I am not sure. How could I be? Does anyone know what to expect, even of tomorrow? I will try to find my king and my people. If they have gone north of the Pyrenees, so will I. What else can I do? Here I must be a dead man since I will not be a slave."

"Perhaps not. You could join them. Become a Muslim. They will need warriors, men to enforce the taxes as always. Many of your people will do that."

He knew that it was true. Visigoths had plotted to bring the Africans into the country. Visigoths had fought with them against King Rodrigo. But he dared not tell her of the treasure. He could not tell her of his brother. He would not tell this peasant woman that fear, and shame, and pride blocked that path for him, not loyalty or faith. It was easier to sound stupid than to meet her question.

"I will not desert my king."

"You could stay here for now. Become stronger. The northern plains will be in an uproar now. Everyone rushing about. We are out of all that here. There is food enough for two. Your ribs will mend and people seldom come here. Winter will fill the passes and people will settle down. In the spring you will know better what you must do."

"I am not a farmer."

"I am."

He had responded sulkily, yet he knew that he would do it. More, although he knew that she was entirely capable of making the same offer to another, that she would have, he was still pleased that she had made it to him. She wanted him to stay. It could cost her life, she should have waited for someone else, but she wanted him to stay. Touched and flattered somehow, for the first time he responded to her as a person rather than a problem.

"What is your name?"

"What would you like my name to be, noble warrior?"

"No. Come now, what is your name?"

"It is the name that my lord Pelayo would wish me to have."

For the first time, she used his name, learned from his delirium. She used it to soften her refusal, he knew. It claimed a relationship that she knew he had already accepted and, at the same time, set a limit to it. There was that part of her, of her life's past, that she would not open to him. At least, not yet. It annoyed him that she should set the terms between them but it was useless to persist. He could kill her but she would not tell him.

"I think that your name must be Elena."

"My name is Elena, my lord Pelayo."

Chapter III

In the following weeks Pelayo did not become a farmer. He merely sat and watched Elena work. As his strength returned, he began to make wider and wider circuits of the surrounding area. First he explored the little valley, hardly more than a wide passage in the mountains, until he knew every foot of it, every bird's nest and rabbit burrow. Then, he crossed and crisscrossed the mountainsides above it. He searched out every depression and cave, every footpath and goat run. Every position from which one could watch the entrances to the valley was known to him. He could finally have found his way about their little retreat in total darkness. That was as he wanted it.

But, as Elena had said, no one came. The cry of the birds as they circled above the pines, the howl of the wolf at night, the soft tinkling of the spring water forcing its way down through the iced rocks, the wind brushing through the trees—all became sharp and distinct against the vast silence of their background. It seemed as if his ears had taken on a life of their own. For long periods he stood on the slopes, listening, sorting out, identifying. It was a soothing study but it was more than that too. He was entering nature, breathing with it, adapting to it.

King Rodrigo and his court, Toledo, his life among his Gothic kinsmen grew steadily more distant from his consciousness. The Roman experience of his people faded too. His Latin became more and more the patois that Elena spoke.

He was beginning now to sense the meanings, the style, of the old songs of his Gothic forebears among the forests of the Baltic, told to him by his nurse in childhood.

He never regained the fatty excess that had been flushed away by the heat of his sickness. New muscle grew and his skin darkened. Elena watched the process in silence and with growing pleasure. She trimmed his beard and plaited his hair. With obvious relish, she watched him eat. Like a young lion, she thought and the thought awakened old currents in her.

One morning before he was fully awake she disappeared from the hut. When she reappeared she was carrying a hunting bow and a quiver of arrows.

"Here," she said, "your ribs are fully healed now and you can draw it. We will have meat for the winter."

He examined it in silence. He was piqued that she still knew the valley better than he had come to. He would not have thought that anyone could have hidden an object so large as this from him.

"It is not much of a bow."

His obvious delight at the present, and the gentleness of his tone, took any possible sting out of the statement. She took it as teasing and responded in kind.

"A mere hunting bow, my lord, not a warrior's gear."

"The bowstring is good but some of the arrows will have to be rewrapped and feathered."

"I knew that you would miss your attendants, lord."

"On the whole it will suffice because I am such a good shot."

"I will try not to tire of the gutting and skinning."

"So your husband was a hunter as well as a farmer."

"He was many things, as I remember him."

She turned the banter to food and after eating they went out, she to the field and he to the hunt.

He was, in truth, an excellent shot. If the bow was light, it was still limber and the arrows were passably straight. Moreover, the experience of the past weeks now stood him in good stead. He knew the animals' runs, almost every one, their foraging and hunting habits. Some of them he almost knew individually. He could hear now their hesitating withdrawal at his approach. With all his skill with the bow, he needed this knowledge for his size made taking cover difficult.

He took two hares easily, with only three shots. The arrow that missed though disappeared among the shale and, search as he did, he could not find it. His exasperation suggested to him the essential silliness of hunting very small game with a bow. Seated on a rock he gutted the rabbits, fat for winter. He cast back in his memory of his boyhood days trying to recall the fine points and details of the traps he had set then. Doubtless Elena would know something about them too.

In any event, the smell of blood on him would make further hunting difficult that day so he returned to the farm. Although she straightened her back and arched her eyebrows at his early return, Elena was pleased with the rabbits. Pelayo spent the late afternoon seeking the proper sapling boughs, tying up traps with clumsy fingers, and designing triggers for them. He worked at it a long time, his memory slowly reviving and his hands remembering habitual positions. Elena's curiousity was aroused. She cut short her work and watched him for a time. Then, retreating into the hut, she reemerged with some strong, thin leather thongs from some recess. Afterwards, she sat down and began to flay the rabbits, all the while watching him.

The following morning Pelayo spoke to her about one of the ideas that had been forming in his mind.

"The hare was good last night."

"Yes, fat and tender. It was a long time since I'd tasted rabbit."

"But such a small valley as this one could be quickly hunted out if we are to eat meat regularly. Besides, in a day or two all the animals will know that there is a hunter here. They will get harder to take unawares."

"True."

"We will make traps for the winter, when I cannot range farther afield but, in the meanwhile, we must be careful not to kill too much in the valley."

"Where are you going?"

"Where is there to go? To the next valley, to the next mountain, and to the valleys and mountains beyond."

"Today?"

"Yes, I think today. But only to the next valley this time. I will be back by night."

"And will you memorize that valley too?"

She had surprised him again. The thoughts that he hid from himself she found.

"Is that such a bad thing to do? The hunter must know the country."

"Or the hunted? Forgive me, my Pelayo, for by day now you are a fine figure of a warrior. But by night you still dream terrible dreams and sweat and shake in my arms without waking. Your wounds are healed but defeat is still in your bones and, with it, some terrible dread. You still wait for them, the Africans, to come for you and to hunt you to the death."

"Sometimes I dream, yes. And they may come. I was a great noble and could make a fair prize for them."

It was true. He often saw the little square in Toledo, his slaughtered brother, remembered that terrible flight. He did not tell her that he was not always asleep when she comforted him but feigned it. He wanted, needed, her soothing him at those moments as she would a child. The momentary urge to tell her of the ground of all his fears, he fought back. She knew that the moment was over, had passed. He got up and went out, taking the bow and quiver.

Pelayo climbed to the top of the closest little pass and then to the top of the mountain which formed one of its sides. From there he could see, better than he ever had before, the next small valley. It seemed uninhabited and probably was. Who could live there? The pines along its floor seemed unbroken by fields. There was no smoke, no huts. Only silence.

Elena was right. He had planned in his mind a hundred strategems over the little ground where they lived. A dozen places of quick refuge where he could hide. Places from which they could be surprised, where he would know the land and they would not. It was the best that he could do then in his weakness and not knowing about the bow. Well, now he could do better. He would repeat the same process in a hundred other valleys and on a hundred other mountains. It would take an army to catch him.

Slowly he began his descent. He worked first along the side of the mountain. Animal trails were everywhere and none of men. He surveyed the valley floor from new angles and saw nothing. He estimated the possible lines of ascent to the ridge and where a possible crossing would bring him out in their own valley. Dropping farther down the slope, he was able, at last, to reach the point at which it debouched, through a narrow ravine, into another yet beyond. As he entered the ravine the hairs on the back of his neck lifted and the muscles of his loins tightened. He walked lightly and without effort. But there was nothing. He briefly scanned what lay beyond and then returned through the ravine. A perfect ambuscade!

Pelayo worked around the head of the valley, opposite whence he had come. The ravine seemed the only outlet. This wall rose sheerly. The further into the center that he worked, the more he was sure that it was uninhabited. There seemed to be no running water, which doubtless was part of it. He did find the smallest of springs and quenched his thirst and refilled his skin bottle. Not far from the spring he found the remains of a fire but it was months old.

By mid-afternoon it had become apparent that he would find no one but, as his concentration was relaxing, broadening, he suddenly became aware that his advance was pushing some large animal ahead of him. His hunting instinct rose. He stopped and listened—and so did it. He smiled and could have laughed. All else was forgotten. He moved gently off to one side, working towards a large outcropping of granite which stretched off, gradually diminishing, some thirty feet or so. Part way down it, he hitched himself up on his belly to a natural saddle and looked for the beast he was hunting. He missed it at first for he was looking in the wrong direction, off to his left. As his head swung round in puzzlement, there it was. The boar was poised, looking intently towards that point at which Pelayo would have rounded the spur if he had completed his circuit.

His heart danced within him. That was a pig! Very slowly he nocked an arrow and drew the bowstring. The animal started at the strum of the bowstring so that the arrow did not go exactly home but missed the heart. Wheeling to face his assailant, the boar started to charge in the same instant. Pelayo stood hurriedly and shouted encouragement.

"Come on, pig! Come on you great, black bastard! Ayah!"

He loosed another arrow over the great shoulders, aiming for the gut behind and below the heaving forequarters but the shot angled off a rib. Feet away from the spur, the front legs of the animal buckled and its incredible speed carried it, skidding along on the lower jaw, over the intervening distance to crash into the rock. He leapt down beside it, plunging in and twisting the dagger to find the heart. But the exertions of the boar had already done the job, working the arrowhead of his first shot against that organ. It was dead before his knife touched it.

With the elation of the hunt slowly cooling in him, Pelayo worked to sever the great head. That done, he heaved the decapitated carcass up on the rock to let the blood drain from it. It was a fair kill. Smiling he paced off the distance. Elena would have the full story. She would be pleased at the quantity of meat but more pleased with him. He would tell the story carefully over some wine and on a very full stomach. Later he began the long carry out of the valley and over the pass.

Chapter IV

Before the heavy snows flew, Pelayo had mapped the wild country about them. His head was full of its peaks and springs, its cliffs and paths, its valleys and forests. In every place he was familiar and secure. Often he was gone for days. He lived off the dying autumnal land, eating its roots and shrivelled berries mixed with the dried meat and beans which Elena had prepared for him.

From time to time he saw someone. Once or twice he watched shepherds who were gradually husbanding their flocks to lower country. He felt the ache then to talk to them. He wanted to know what they knew, what was happening, what had happened, but the fear always restrained him. They were Elena's people. Dark as he had become, his size and his flaming hair would tell them immediately of his stock. And when they dropped further down the mountains and entered the flatlands? Who would they talk to then? It was easy to avoid them since they were so intent on their own business, their own thoughts. Like all the world! He stayed upwind of their dogs and watched and followed them until he had some idea of their routes also.

In the extreme north of his range, at the edge of the northern plain, he lay on a bluff one day and surveyed its stretch towards the north. Below him a small pack train of fifteen burros or so labored north and east. He examined it closely and it told him a little. The drovers were of Elena's race, small dark men. The owner, seated on a horse, came behind. Probably a Jew, Pelayo thought morosely. They would not weep over the passing of the Visigoths. Then there were eight of the Africans. They moved on foot with a long stride which matched the pace of the pack animals without strain. They talked and laughed as they moved in a small knot near the center of the column. They carried spears and bows and hide shields. Only two of them had metal shields, likely taken from Goths. He saw no battle swords.

The sight, and its memory later, was a weight on his spirits. From it he could read the establishment of a fairly regular order in the land. Pack trains moved again and peasants and merchants went about their business. Like the plains to his south, the northern flats belonged to the Africans. Certainly there was not perfect peace in the land for the caravan had to have an armed escort. He could not tell whether the goods it carried were army supplies or simple trade goods. But the guard that protected it would have been proof against no more than casual robber bands. Clearly they had reason to expect an attack by nothing more serious. Where were the Goths? Had they surrendered the whole of the northern plain to the Africans? He felt terribly alone again and trapped here in his mountains.

Returning from this, the most extended of his reconnaissances, Pelayo come upon a bear. A stupid animal intent on one last meal before retiring to some cave for its rest. He stalked it easily and put three arrows into it before the beast knew itself in danger. Glaring at him, it coughed out its life. It would be a homecoming present and hurriedly he covered the remaining distance to the hut to tell Elena.

She smiled at his coming as well as at the news of the hunt.

"We will sleep warm this winter under his skin. "

She collected some food and the two of them set off for the small clearing in which he had surprised the animal. There they ate in festive spirits while Pelayo recounted what he had seen, where he had been. They were both exhilarated to be again in one another's company and even the coldness of the wind did not chill their happiness. Afterwards, lashing the bear's paws around a pole which Pelayo cut, they carried their prize back to the hut.

The depth of winter came and the round of activities lessened for them both. Even when the leaden sky did not drop snow they slept later in the mornings and went to bed earlier. The food was sufficient, supplemented as it was by an occasional rabbit from the traps. Elena had slaughtered and dressed one of the pigs during the fall and his body hung, cured, close to the roof. It became thinner and thinner as they whittled away at it. The snow made the birds careless and desperate too so that Pelayo was able to snare some lean partridge.

It was an agreeable time, a lazy time, for the strangely matched pair. The intimacy and affection which had grown between them in the fall now ripened into full love. They both knew it and yet seldom, except in passion, spoke of it. To name it would be an embarrassment since it was such an unlikely thing. Carefully they kept their pasts from one another, unspoken, unspeakable. Reminscence could bring only pain and contradiction of their present lives. They dwelt in the present, savoring one another's companionship and strength, for each one of them knew too that it could not last.

That winter was a comfort. It enforced that leisure which each had desired to have for the other. It shut them in upon each other securely. The weather isolated them from the world of man and the world of work alike. What they would never have planned for themselves was forced upon them. Whether they lay warm and dreamy under the skins or moved about outside in the blinding snow, there was time for smiles, time for caresses, time for soft words and gentle embrace. The magnificent translucent sky, the dark green of the pines, the gleaming icicles, their valley was a frozen playground. They wondered at the sharpness of their own perception of all this. They laughed for no reason and as suddenly fell silent for no reason. They clung to each passing day and each night and crossed the bounds between them, dreamlike, freed of all necessities but that of their love.

The poignancy passed into pain. Each blissful day of winter hastened the threat of spring. Their Eden melted day by day. Increasingly, when they made love, Elena shed that reserve which nature and the peasant life had made her second nature. She reached for him eagerly and pressed her hands urgently along his buttocks, pulling him down into her loins, locking her calves behind his. She bloomed, suffused with passion, into a second girlhood wearing winter flowers in her dark hair. In February she was with child but they never spoke of it. It lay between them like a faint threat. A fulfillment and a promise of the impossible. She was radiant but now, when they were surfeited with lovemaking and lay quietly listening to the gentle drip of the ice, tremors passed through her strong body and he had to brush his hand along her cheeks to assure himself that there were no tears.

"You will have to leave."

"We both will have to leave."

"That is impossible, Pelayo, my land, my life is here. I do not know another way."

"But you cannot plant it now, not enough of it. For a time you will not be as strong as you were. What you could sow would not last you through the next winter."

"I shall have to try. What else could I do?"

"When the spring comes we will take the food that remains and go north to find my people."

"Oh Pelayo, where are they? How will you find them? Your enemy is to the north as well as to the south. Can we walk through them going—where? Can you pull a woman through them? I have no wish to die nor for you to die for me."

"We shall have to try. In the spring it is likely that they will come into the mountains again. There will be others that have taken refuge like me and the Africans will want to clear the land of them. It will be a summer of fighting here or, at least, of hunting and running fights. With luck, I can stay clear of them but I could not leave you. There is no hope here now. Someone would kill you anyway. Even if you want to return later, you must leave your land in the spring unless you want to be buried in it before fall."

"What if we should reach your people, Pelayo? What could I do but disgrace you. Wherever they are, they will be a nation at war, your Goths, trying to reestablish themselves on some land, conquering my people and their masters. You will lead in that attempt. Your blood is noble, you are young, brave, strong. Would they accept you with a peasant wife, older than yourself, big with child? You know how such matters are regarded by the Visigoths. Their fine ladies would laugh at you, at me, and their men would follow suit. You will be a great conqueror or find a warrior's death. For me there is no place in it."

He knew the truth of what she spoke. For his people, marriage to a peasant was a disgrace, a bad joke. He knew also his own weakness. Coming in like a straggler, a pregnant peasant woman in tow. And how if they had heard, somehow, of his flight? His desertion? But he could not leave her here. Even if she were not killed, the thought of her being appropriated, casually, by another peasant, or Goth, or African was a prospect he could not bear, a memory he would not live with. He would not leave Elena to his brother's fate. He answered without conviction.

"We shall have to do it. Any other course is sure death."

"You could go."

"I will not leave you."

Now she wept. Holding him frenziedly, she wept. He had never seen her helpless, weak, and he tried awkwardly to soothe her, serving that function which she had so often performed for him. He felt confused and inadequate.

"Pelayo, my love, can't we both stay here? Perhaps they will not come. Perhaps your people will come down from the north. There may be great battles on the northern plains and they will have no time to look for you. You can hunt. You won't have to farm. I am strong when you are with me and we can eat less than last summer. If we can get through another summer, the following spring—who knows? The world may have changed. They may be gone. At least the child will be born and I can work again with my full strength. Or we can leave then if we have to."

"But if they do come, what then?"

"You can hide in the hills. They can't surprise you and they can't catch you. I can be the peasant woman and before long now no man will be interested in me."

"They will want to know who is the child's father and where he is. One way or another, they will try to find out, Elena."

There was no answer to that. She fell silent, clinging very tightly to him. They did not speak of it again. Instead, they lived a little more recklessly, a bit more urgently. The two of them ate rather better than they should have if their stocks were to carry them through to the next harvest. They drank rather too deeply of the wine if it were to last the season. Quiet and passivity grew in them as they both waited for some event, some occurrence which would point out a possible course of action for them. They could not conceive an initiative of their own which would promise them some real hope but they would not surrender their hopes. And so they waited for a sign, an omen to give them direction.

When the spring opened, Pelayo resumed his explorations to the north. He spoke of finding the best trails and the safest ones for their journey. He carefully repaired all of the arrows and worked his sword and dagger to a fine edge. He had Elena make them both two additional pairs of sandals and she had worked rapidly and steadily at it. At the same time, when he returned from his surveys, each time he perceived that something more had been planted, that another field had been opened. Elena smiled at his questioning looks. She said that, being a peasant woman, she couldn't help it. The land needed to be sowed in the spring and she would not feel right to neglect it. If they would not see it ripen, another would and he would be welcome to it. If no one came, the birds and the rabbits would attend to it. But for herself, she felt better doing the planting just as she had always done, or helped to do, since she was a little girl. Pelayo knew what she wanted. He knew that they must leave quickly. But they did not start and time passed.

And then one day, descending the trail from the small pass at the head of the valley, he became increasingly uneasy. His long sojourn with nature, his newfound empathy for its moods and movings, had sensitized him to the threat of danger and violence. A small sick feeling began to form in the pit of his stomach as he started, automatically, to pick his steps in hunter fashion. His pulse heightened and a prickling sensation played along his shoulders. He saw no one. Elena was not in the field. In the early afternoon sunlight, he moved along just within the tree-line, circling behind the hut.

He came upon it from the back, stepping around and through the doorway suddenly, in one continuing motion, dagger in hand. Elena was on the pallet. She looked very small, and very old, and gray. Her mouth was slightly open and her head tilted back and to one side. Her stomach and abdomen were thick with blood from wounds in her chest. She was dead.

The African had been examining the contents of the storage jars. He judged correctly that there was no time to reach his knife as the two of them hurtled together in the gloom of the hut. His instantaneous reaction, and Pelayo's hesitation at the sight of the bed, gave him a hand on the latter's knife arm as their other palms met. They stood, after the first shock of contact, chest to chest and leaning slightly towards one another. Their feet felt carefully in the dirt for purchase. There was no play for maneuver. They were fully engaged from the first second. To shift position more than a fraction of an inch was to risk being overborne while unbalanced. It could not be other than a test of sheer power and determination.

Pelayo could feel the strength of his opponent. The man was lighter than himself but half a head taller. His grip on the knife arm was solid and hard on the wrist, keeping the dagger point well out from his side. With his right arm he pressed steadily against Pelayo's left one, seeking to force it backwards and to break his balance. They strained together, forcing more and more power into their shoulders, their forearms.

Pelayo felt the evenness of their resources and knew a momentary panic. It had become a contest of sheer endurance. The first one of them to falter would be dead in seconds. He could not feel nor sense any slackening in the pressure applied by his opponent. All of his own blind fury at Elena's death, all of the closely-channelled fear of his own imminent death, had not given him the strength to overbear his enemy. They remained locked, muscle against muscle, committing more and more of their reserves to merely maintain the contest. Pelayo strained to the effort, his head pressed close against the other's cheek, and strained, and strained again, without feeling any effect or lessening of that steady pressure. His anger and frustration must have an outlet.

Turning his head slightly, he began to search for the African's jugular with his teeth. The enemy's greater height made him vulnerable now to this terrible attempt. His skin was like leather but he could not force down his jaw or head to protect his neck. Pelayo's teeth searched for a grip, unable to break the skin directly, and looking for some purchase, some way to grind and tear. His hate flowed into the effort.

He could feel the tremors begin. He pressed more closely and bit more savagely. The sheer bestiality of it had snapped some nerve within his enemy, who now wanted only, irrationally to escape the contact of those teeth. Pelayo had been waiting and threw his body forward now, using his smaller frame as a lever, breaking the African out of position after position as he tried desperately to reestablish his balance. As the latter's back hit, finally, the post of the far wall, still trying to recover, Pelayo crouched slightly and drove his right knee into the man's groin. Twice more he repeated that action. His enemy lost his grip on the knife arm. He began to double. Pelayo drove the dagger into his left side, under the ribs. The grip on Pelayo's left hand fell away. The African slid to his knees while Pelayo's left hand found his hair. Holding him upright, against the post, methodically Pelayo stabbed him, twice in the throat below the Adam's apple. Then, dragging him sideways, Pelayo stabbed him twice more in the rib cage, kneeling over him while he died.

He knelt there, trembling, as the rage left him. He fought off the desire to hack at the body, to dismember it. Slowly he grew empty. He knew that there might be others but the knowledge left him unmoved. After a long time he rose and grasped his former opponent by one heel. He dragged the body from the hut and dropped it finally in the little stream by the field. He could feel nothing; but somehow, somewhere in a dark recess of his being, a second death for his enemy, by drowning, was grimly satisfying.

There was no question as to where Elena's grave would be. She would be buried in her own land, beside her husband and children, as she had wanted. With her own hoe Pelayo opened up her grave, using his sword on roots and to pry out rock. When he had deepened it sufficiently, he brought out her body. Already it was stiffening slightly and the face was that of no one he knew. He laid it gently in the grave and covered the face with a fold of cloth. Only then did she become familiar again. His love!

The law forbade it but he placed her hoe by her side. The priests believed such things to be pagan but they knew nothing of such love. The hoe was simply hers and part of her. It should lie with her. With his hands, scrabbling now in the dirt, he covered her. He moved faster and faster, for the actual doing of it was terrible. Finally done, he moved off to find the boughs for a small cross. She would have wanted a cross. He had considered removing the stones from the others, for fear of graverobbers, but rejected the idea because of the impossibility of concealing them adequately. Perhaps a cross was the best protection.

After he placed it, Pelayo knelt, splay-legged, at the side of the little mound. It was finished. His beloved, his wife, his son to be, were all dead. He could think of her as his wife now, to himself. He could acknowledge here the son which the autumn would have seen. But they were gone. Against his will, his memory prompted him of the times when he had dreamed himself free over the past months. It reminded him of his own impatience at the absurdity and impossibility of their love and, from time to time, his day-dreams about escape from its demands. Now he was free. Oh, God! The pain!

You could not say that he wept. It was just that he shook, uncontrollably. Not just his muscles but his inner organs, heart, lungs, stomach, were seized by those recurring, worsening spasms. Some part of him wondered if he were going to die. Some part of him decided that it did not care.

"My God, why didn't we leave?"

"God, why did he come here? Why now? Why not six months ago? Why not when I was here?"

Why would he have killed her? He seemed alone. Just rabble, a deserter, he had no purpose. Why kill her? He had nothing to learn from a pregnant peasant woman. Pelayo knew—Elena had resisted the African. She had not wanted to die. She never had. She only died because, out of love for him, she would not surrender herself. This woman, who had never told him her own name, had died for him.

"God, have mercy on her!"

"Christ protect her, keep her, forgive her! Forgive me!"

She had saved his life. She had fed him. She had worked for him. She had held his body. She had been the womb in which he was reformed.

Elena had always been so much stronger. He had often been angry with her strength and his own weakness. She had been so pleased with him, so proud of him.

He was drained, numb. Moving woodenly in the dark, he put together his gear. The sword he would wear. He packed the food that would travel best. Two shirts and a light skin for sleeping. Extra sandals. Flint and steel. A water bottle and a wineskin. With his dagger and bow and quiver, it was enough. It was more than he had come with.

Pelayo knelt and fired some thatch at the door of the hut. The flames moved swiftly up the seasoned beams. They illuminated the body of the African, stiff in the creek. Pelayo moved away from the growing heat. The roof roared, and glowed, and collapsed inward in a shower of sparks and embers. Pelayo shouldered his equipment and moved up the valley into the dark. From the top of the pass he could still see the glowing embers.

Chapter V

There were three of them proceeding up the trail so Pelayo stalked them carefully. They were all Goths and warriors. The oldest was a veteran of about forty-five, tall and thin; he carried a throwing spear and wore a knife. There was a beefy boy of about twenty who had Pelayo's own coloring. He was armed with a bow and a knife. But the leader of the group was clearly the extraordinary figure who strode ahead in the lead. He was of only middle height but he was broad, with a great barrel of a chest and biceps muscled like a peasant's thighs. On top of a bull neck sat a very large head, swarthy and wreathed in jet black hair and beard. He wore a leather cap and full warrior's gear: shield, sword, dagger and throwing spear. They moved easily, sweating in the afternoon sun and obviously expecting no challenge.

Pelayo stepped into the trail a short distance behind them. It had been easy. They clearly were new in these mountains.

"Hold right there! Don't turn around! Don't move!"

The series of short, barked commands froze the three. They caught the military ring. It was another Goth. The boy with the bow half turned, involuntarily, and Pelayo thought that he was going to have to kill him.

"Stand still, boy," growled the leader.

"What do you want with us, soldier?"

"I'm recruiting this afternoon. I want you all, I think. Now lay down your arms carefully and move down the path to that flat rock and sit on your legs. Don't turn around."

"Who are you to disarm us?"

"Do what I said. If you want to die like warriors with weapons in your hands, you can right now. If you want to live to serve a chief, put them down."

They had been preparing to turn on him. He could see that. But the words were just right. They were familiar ones, spoken with authority and a dangerous urgency. The dark one caught it and his shoulder muscles relaxed. He let the spear fall from his hand.

"Put them down. Do as you're told."

The other two obeyed almost automatically. They left their weapons there and went down the path to the rock. The boy and the old warrior sat down as they had been told but their leader slowly and deliberately turned to face Pelayo, folding his arms across his chest. Pelayo, with the arrow at full nock, was tempted to release it but the man's eyes held his. There was no flinching in them. Defiance, muted, spoke out of his whole posture and impassive face. While Pelayo hesitated, the man sat down facing him, carefully, on his legs. As the man stooped, Pelayo covered the distance between them. He slacked the bow string and drew his sword in the same motion. The leader of the three followed all this closely with his eyes. He examined Pelayo's motions and balance, his sword and dagger hilts, his gear, his bow and, finally, his face.

"So there was only one of you."

"I am alone. I have been. Now who are you three?"

"We are warriors, as you can see. The old one is Euric. The kid is Teudemiro. I am Fruela. I'm their leader. I picked them up in Córdoba. We're going north to find a chief worth a fight."

"Tell me some more. How is it that you're not dead—or slaves?"

"Because we're lucky. Because we're tough. I damn near got myself killed at Guadalete when the Africans trapped us.

The king led us into that trap and then, like a fool, tried to break off the fight—or run—when it was going badly. Lucky he didn't kill us all but some of us on the wings managed to fight clear after the main body was butchered."

"King Rodrigo is dead then?"

"He couldn't be anything else. They said that he changed into ordinary warrior's gear when the fight got hot but he was with the center. Nobody got out of that. So you weren't there, lord?"

Pelayo ignored the question, with its implication.

"You said you came from Córdoba."

"We did. I made it there after the battle and these two were part of the garrison. The Count who commanded it was a good man. We couldn't hold the city for there were too many of Witiza's bunch there. They would have opened a gate or just stabbed us in the back. So the Count pulled us out of it to a church outside the walls where we stood the bastards off. We bought a lot of respect with the sword there. It was a good position. We held it for almost three months.

"Then the Count strolled over to them one night and arranged our surrender. Everyone kept his weapons and his land, if he had any, especially the Count. There was some kind of tax arranged but we walked out of that church like warriors, not like slaves. It was a pretty job."

"It was so good that you didn't stay with him. Why?"

"A lot of reasons. The Count was a hard man to please and I don't take to garrison life much or farming either for that matter. Not much excitement and not much loot. Then too, the Africans are not going to let the Count keep as large a war band as before—no matter what he thinks. There will be less pay and fewer men or they won't be able to control the land and, from what I heard, this Arab Tarik plans to do just that. Besides, we were on Rodrigo's side, not Witiza's. Things always go worse for the losers sooner or later. We decided that we could do better going north to see if any one had any fight left in them. To find a new chief."

"Witiza's family is back?"

"Sure, the whole tribe. The boys are getting their lands back but they'll have to whistle for their daddy's throne. Fat landowners they'll be, but not kings. His girls are wiggling their asses at the Arabs already, like all the other great ladies. They know who the masters are."

"How do the Africans get along with the Arabs?"

"They take orders. The Arabs are a proud bunch, real aristocrats. The Africans are just herdsmen and hill people. They're mean fighters but not chiefs or governors. They'll take orders so long as the Arabs are giving them our lands. Anyway, they're mostly Muslims, whatever that is."

The information that this sardonic Gothic warrior was giving him reopened the larger world to Pelayo for the first time in months. His spirits alternately rose and fell as he pondered it. It was not so changed as he had feared. There were Goths like these. There were other chiefs, like the count of whom he spoke. If Rodrigo was dead, a new king could be elected. The Africans were not invincible. The world he had known was still there. With enough men and the treasure— he thought of it suddenly for the first time in months.

The knowledge sickened him. He had acted like a frightened boy. He had panicked. Run away. Deserted his brother. He and Elena could have made it north, only his fears had prevented them, killed her. One lousy African! But the experience of the past fall and winter would not leave him. The thoughts that came to mind angered him. How would he have appeared to these warriors whom he now regarded? A Gothic noble with a pregnant peasant for a wife! How would that world regard him. Arab masters with African warriors and Gothic ladies for mistresses? Gothic nobles jostling to keep their men and lands. Soldiers searching for a chief to follow. And he, Pelayo, who had run away alone and hidden in a mountain shack with a farm woman.

Still, he would not reject her memory. She had saved his life. She had loved him. And he had loved her. Icily, he hated the men in front of him for what they would have said, or thought. He hated the whole, stupid Gothic nation with its pride, its self-satisfied arrogance and witless superiority. But most of all he hated the Africans and their Arab leaders because they were the masters now. It was their world that would not have accepted Elena or himself. It was their doing that finally destroyed her.

Fruela watched him closely as he had watched chiefs before. He was a chief, a noble, this big redhead. A fighter, he had trapped them nicely. He could kill them yet if that quiet rage stirring inside him turned into a wild, blood lust. Fruela had seen them before, those great lords who thought too much, who could fight like madmen sometimes and at other times couldn't make up their minds to take a shit. He didn't trust them. They were too complicated. They threw away the lives of good warriors on dreams or their own vanity. The priests flattered them and used them to make a fat living. Their women led them around like puppies in their first heat.

Pelayo, in turn, was conscious of the brawny warrior's gaze and he sensed something of insolence and faint contempt in it. He would make a tough fighter, this Fruela would. And the others would follow him. They had already.

"This is where we begin then."

"My lord, we don't know you."

It was put surprisingly politely, but the black-haired soldier was challenging his right to lead, was holding back his little band.

"I am Pelayo, a noble of King Rodrigo's court. My family holds land in the northwest, in Galicia. I am a chief and a warrior, as you have reason to know."

"You were not at Guadalete, lord."

"Some of us were left behind at Toledo, to safeguard the court and keep the populace loyal."

"We have heard that there was no resistance at Toledo."

"No, there was no fighting, only rout and panic. When the news came of disaster in the south every old woman in the city started to scream. The garrison ran off like scared boys. Witiza's people began to threaten their enemies openly, in the streets. It was not a city to defend then."

Pelayo knew how partial was his telling of the tale and so did they. Such things it would have been his duty to prevent. They could not know the extent of his failure and he would not tell them.

"Toledo is a very strong city, lord."

Fruela again!

"No city defended by rabble is strong. I came here, to the mountains, to wait for the Goths to regain their manhood. Since some of you have, now we can begin."

"We thought to go farther north, lord."

"You no longer have a choice. We begin now and we begin here. I have chosen the ground. You can give me your hand."

The decision must be made now. Pelayo stood over them, sword in hand. They would accept his leadership or he would kill them. At least he would kill Fruela. It would probably not be necessary to kill the other two. Without Fruela they would not have the will to resist him. How loyal were they to him, he wondered? Still, he wanted the big-chested warrior. He was a fighter. He would be useful for the plan already half-formed in Pelayo's mind.

Fruela read the determination in this noble's stance. He could gauge the tension in the sword arm. The wild bastard would kill him alright. There was something strange about this lonely Goth. He must have spent the winter alone in these mountains, brooding over something. It was a funny business. Perhaps some devil had hold of him. Still, the whole world was crazy anyway. And it was a hell of a way to die, sitting like a fat cow, unarmed in the middle of a sheep track. He would try it for a while. Slowly, deliberately, he extended his hand to meet the other's grasp.

"Alright—done! Stand up and get your weapons."

They rose slowly, pounding their feet on the path, getting the blood to flow in prickling streams. They were all relieved to be out of the shadow of death. They were pleased but confused. The initiative belonged to Pelayo.

"Get your gear. We can begin now."

"What will we do, lord?"

"Kill Africans."

That they liked, even Fruela. No nonsense but a straight, plain answer. Pelayo built on it.

"There will be more Goths coming north through these hills. There must be dozens of others scattered through them now. We will recruit them as I've recruited you. In a month, we'll have a war band to respect. But first, we must have proper weapons. We'll need full gear: shields, swords, spears, bows for every man. Those we get from the Africans."

They were armed now. Pelayo was ostentatiously off-guard. They must accept his leadership freely for he could not compel it continuously. They could kill him and they knew it but they had pledged themselves. He was a noble too. He looked like the most convincing chief that they had seen in months. More, he had aroused their interest for he obviously had a plan. Still, Fruela spoke for the group, on which he had prior claims which he had no intention of giving up.

"How do we do that?"

The affected politeness, and with it the reserve, of negotiation was gone. It was a blunt soldier's question that asked for a sensible soldier's answer. It asked for, and expected, direction but it made the enterprise common.

"All spring and summer the caravans will cross these mountains, north and south. Some will skirt them. The way the times are, each one of them will have an escort. I've seen some of them already. Nothing much, a few Africans and a string of mules. We kill the Africans and take their weapons so that every one of us will have full gear and extras. It will be easy at first. They don't expect much trouble if you can judge by the way that they travel. They're careless. Later, when we've picked up a few, word will spread and it will get tougher but by then there will be more of us.

"But remember that it is the weapons that we're after. No mercy to the Africans and no prisoners. We don't need slaves and we don't need survivors to come back looking for us. There will be no booty and no women either. We need to build a war band, not a barracks."

The boy, Teudemiro, glanced sidelong at the old veteran. Fighting without prospect of loot was a strange notion. But the veterans, Euric and Fruela, understood. Putting together a warband came first. If they could form a large enough one, the loot would follow. That's the way that the world ran. A step at a time and no fool's mistakes.

"What do we do with Goths who won't join us?"

"They get the same choice that you got," said Pelayo with a tight smile.

"What do we do when the Africans come after us? Enough flies and one makes a fly swatter. These caravans are going to be missed."

"We run. There'll be no heroics and no treaties. You can be famous warriors later when we're strong enough for it. Treaties are chains for the weaker party. We stay smart and free.

"I know these mountains better than the shepherds do. So long as we can travel light, no one can catch us and we can ambush any force small enough to keep up with us. It would take a full-size army to track us down properly and, from what you say, I don't think that the Arabs have one to spare right now. If they did, they wouldn't have had to make terms with your count.

"We live off the caravans and the mountains. You'll drink well if you fight well. You'll eat well if you learn to hunt well. There is plenty of game if one knows how to find it."

"That's well and good for the summer, but what do we do when the winter comes?"

"By the fall we'll either be a war band or we'll be dead and rotting. If we're not dead, we will be strong enough to march north and claim my estates by the western sea. We'll build a county—or a duchy—or maybe a kingdom. The Suevi made a kingdom there not so many generations ago."

It was brave talk for a chief and three warriors. They liked it though. He had a plan and he had all the answers. They had a sense of purpose and they liked the idea of being in at the beginning. Christ, it would be something to tell one's children—something for the bards to sing about! Even the old life, before the Africans came, hadn't offered a chance like this. The best you could do then was to enlist under some chief who was in on some plot against some king, or pretender, or some pretender king's supporter. Whether it worked or not, you were still a damned soldier even if a live one. This was a new thing—clean. It might be that this Pelayo was crazy. They would see that soon enough. The first few fights would tell. For now they were docile and slightly exhilarated.

As for Pelayo, he did not care. They were his for the present and he would use them as he told them. It might work and it might get them all killed. Most probably it would be the latter. But while he lived, he would command. He would command and those who would not accept his leadership he would kill. The Goths would accept him, damn them, even if it was too late. As for the Africans and the Arabs, they would die in such numbers as he could manage. He had never met an Arab. They had never terrified him, driven him in headlong flight, murdered his lover and son-to-be; but they had ordered all that. They still did. He would slaughter them all. Or they would kill him. But the greater the band he led, the bloodier the price that they would pay. In his mind he regarded the prospect evenly, with a savage satisfaction. In his own mind, he was already dead.

Chapter VI

The first fight was very easy. Pelayo, as he would almost invariably in the future, chose the place. It was a small ridge on a comparatively easy path running north and south over the mountains. They had followed the tiny caravan for a day. There were twenty donkeys laden with goods of some kind and a guard of five. A fat, swarthy merchant usually rode in the middle with a young boy, a captive of some sort, riding the donkey just ahead of him, his feet tied together under the animal's belly. Three drovers busied themselves with keeping the animals moving and checking their loads, making the camp at night and cooking the meals. Three of the guards ordinarily walked behind the last of the donkeys, over whose pack they had slung their hide shields and bows. Their spears they used as walking staffs or, occasionally, to prod one of the drovers.

The leader customarily rode the lead donkey, talking easily to the young man of about seventeen years, who strode alongside. He was instructing him, pointing out the land, commenting on the progress of the group. The two of them were evidently the privileged members of the guard. They both wore good swords of Gothic make and boasted metal-faced shields of the same origin. The young man carried his, shifting it from arm to arm as the weight became bothersome in the growing fatigue of the day. The older man let his hang across his back by its strap. Lashed to the next donkey just forward of its pack was a long pouch of leather from which five javelins protruded. They were never far from his reach.

Pelayo waited until the very late morning was beginning to verge into afternoon. Enough of the day's trip had passed for its monotony to begin to dull the watchfulness of the guard. They were bored and hungry, urging the donkeys and their drivers to find a spot for rest, and so prompting disorder in the column which increasingly demanded their attention. The ground to their left sloped down sharply over a shaley surface. To their right it rose more gently to a small pine grove at their rear. Fifty feet ahead of them, Pelayo stepped around an outcropping of rock and drove an arrow three-quarters through the chest of the mounted warrior.

The beast carrying him stopped suddenly and the dead body fell heavily, resting a moment on the edge of the trail, and then sliding with increasing speed down the slope, shield banging alongside. The young man had involuntarily moved a pace backwards to avoid the falling body. Now he half-crouched, covering himself with his shield and drawing his sword. A half-panicky, sidelong glance told him that the javelins were out of reach while ahead Pelayo moved closer, arrow nocked, angling for a clear shot.

At the rear of the column, the guards threw themselves toward the donkey carrying their shields and bows. From the grove above Teudemiro fired twice in seconds. One arrow struck the hindquarters of the donkey causing it to begin to kick frantically, and hampering comically the desperate efforts of the guards to retrieve their shields and bows. The other caught one of them in the shoulder, driving him back against the beast and further frightening the animal. At the same time Euric and Fruela broke from the pines and rushed down the grade. Fruela, in the lead and bellowing at the top of his lungs, plunged straight down. Expertly he deflected his opponent's spear with his shield. His own javelin, propelled by his impetus and those great biceps, passed through the hastily retrieved hide shield of his enemy just below the arm and pierced his stomach. Releasing the embedded weapon, Fruela drew and chopped with his sword, almost severing the man's head with the blow.

Euric had come down at a half-trot, bounding from side to side, for lack of a shield, to cover himself against the other's spear, unable to cast his own for fear of leaving himself defenseless. Above on the slope Teudemiro shot twice more to keep the African occupied. The latter knew that he was lost. He backed along the line of animals, followed carefully by Euric, as Fruela rushed up the opposite side of the animals to reach his back. Finally, he broke up the slope towards Teudemiro who was armed only with the bow. Euric let him go a good eight paces before he threw. His spear took the man in the side and he pitched forward on his shield. It was scarcely worth Euric's cutting his throat.

At the sound of Fruela's charge, the boy in the front of the column had lost his head. With his dead chief still coasting down the slope, he had begun to run back towards his fellows, keeping close to the donkeys and their packs to make hitting him harder. Pelayo's arrow took him in the kidney and he fell, screaming. Pelayo stabbed him under the shoulder blade as he hurried to the rear but the fight there was over by the time he reached it. Fruela had just brushed aside the dagger of the man whom Teudemiro's arrow had struck and stabbed him down.

Through the fight, the merchant and the young prisoner had sat very still. They tight-reined their donkeys on the narrow path and made themselves as small as they could. The muscles of their bellies were very taut and hard. They peered from side to side, moving to secure better cover as the movements of the combatants dictated. Now they watched in silence as the victors dispatched the last of the guard and then stripped them of their weapons. Teudemiro slid down the slope to the dead leader's body where he retrieved his sword and shield. Then they suffered themselves to be herded along and down the trail to a small hollow, leaving the bodies of their guards forlornly alone on the slope behind them.

In the hollow, the band held their council of victory. First they examined the cargo of the caravan. Most of it consisted of ordinary enough trade goods: pottery, cloth, cheap jewelry, agricultural tools—things for which they had no use. What they could use fell into simple categories. There were dried fruits and olives which would relieve the monotony of their diet for some weeks. There were four donkeys loaded with wine jars, the disposal of which they began on the spot. Another beast was loaded with the most significant prize— the sacks he bore were full of iron arrowpoints. Doubtless they were intended for some garrison. To the little group of warriors they were beyond price. They would mean food and victory for weeks.

Their armament had grown significantly in other ways too. To Pelayo and Euric went the iron shields. Teudemiro had to content himself with one of the hide shields but he had a sword at last as did Euric. In addition there were two extra hide shields, three bows and full quivers which the guards had never had a chance to get into action and no less than seven spears. Over the next week they were to happen across four more Gothic stragglers in the hills for whom this armament was to supplement the odds and ends that they carried. It provided weapons for the boy too. He could not have been more than fourteen years. When they cut him off the donkey he had taken his place in the little knot of other prisoners without a word but holding aloof from them. His clothes were good linen. He was fair and blond, obviously of good blood. Now, having examined the pack train and decided on its disposition, they called him out.

"Who are you, boy?"

"My name is Sunna and I am a Goth like yourselves."

"You were a prisoner. Where were they taking you?"

"They were taking me to Salamanca. My father, Bodo, is

count in Palencia and they are negotiating with him. Some of his men are in Salamanca to see that I am still well."

"Hoo! We've grabbed off some old bear's cub. That will make pretty news up north," broke in Fruela.

Pelayo addressed the boy again, "Who is doing the negotiating with your father?"

"The Lord Tarik who commands the Africans. He had me sent from Córdoba."

"Do you know this Tarik, Fruela?"

"Only what the boy says, Pelayo. He's the leader and a first-rate fighter. After he beat us he drove straight on for Toledo, never giving much of a chance for us to reorganize. It was only a detachment of his that took Córdoba. He must have kept seven or eight thousand men with him. He left maybe that many more scattered around the south. We'd heard that he moved north from Toledo pretty quick and, from what the boy says, he has. It's a courageous move and he could be hanging from the end of a long, thin rope.

"He'll be sore as a scalded pig when the boy disappears. If he has the time, there could be search parties out. It makes our plans pretty chancy."

"They'll find nothing. In any event, it's done. If the boy's ours, there will be no treaty with his father. That will make trouble for both of them and trouble is our bread for now. Later on, Fruela, we may make our own terms with this Count Bodo."

Pelayo turned to the boy.

"You look strong enough to draw a bow, Sunna. You will join us as a warrior now. We're building a band by killing Africans—like today. No treaties for them and no refusals from Goths. By fall, when we are stronger, we may march north and you may see your father if you're in luck. Before then you will be a man."

The young man took the extended bow and quiver and passed over to the party of the victors. Instinctively he placed himself between Euric and Teudemiro, avoiding looking directly into the sardonic gaze of Fruela.

"What do we do with the drovers," asked Teudemiro.

The young warrior was flushed and a little drunk already with the wine. He wanted to assert his prior membership in the group in the face of this new youth who was dressed so finely and who was obviously his better in the great world. Euric spoke mildly, half reflecting, as though to no one in particular.

"Likely they're slaves. We could recruit them."

"How much good did you ever see slaves do on the battlefield?" asked Fruela. "All they do is eat rations and run away with the weapons you give them. We'd spend all our time watching them. But we can't let them go either. The first African who picked them up would get news of us before we're ready just by cutting a few holes in their skins. I say we cut their throats. Simple and neat."

Pelayo felt the flush in his own cheeks. Fruela was pushing things towards his own conclusion, taking the lead. He felt his anger towards the stocky Goth, towards all the Goths and their drunken arrogance. He looked at the drovers closely for the first time. One man in his forties and two maybe in their thirties. They were obviously slaves from their dress. They were natives, Elena's people.

"No."

He put it as simply and baldly as he could. He wanted it just that harsh and humiliating. He looked coldly at Fruela as he said it, ignoring the others, and tried to give the appearance of easy relaxation. His own assurance had to be his weapon now. Fruela's neck swelled at the unexpectedness of the rebuff and his arms half-rose involuntarily but he was confused. He was stung at this sudden rebuke but he didn't understand why it had happened. The fight had been satisfying, the ambush perfect, the division of the spoils sensible. Now what? He waited to see and the others were surprised.

"They won't make soldiers, that's true. And we don't need slaves. So we let them go."

"And what if they tell their story to the Africans, to Tarik, or to Count Bodo?"

"How many freed slaves are going to talk to counts and generals? When did one of these natives ever tell you anything that you believed, Fruela, whether he was slave or free? When did they ever tell a Goth anything but what they wanted him to know? You think that it will be any different between them and the Africans? What did you do when you really wanted the truth out of one of them? You put them to torture. So would Bodo or Tarik. You think that they'll walk up to those great men and ask for that?

"No they'll run away and lose themselves. It'll be easy. There must be more fugitives than farmers all across the land. If they finally do get caught, it will be by somebody who wants a new slave and who likely won't inquire too closely about where they came from. Even if they did, by then we'll be well away or dead."

Pelayo delivered himself of all this in the most sarcastic and mocking tone he could muster without losing his self-control.

Fruela was amazed and unable to react as the torrent of scorn poured over him. What was it all about? What the red-haired whoreson was saying was true enough, but why take a chance? What difference did a few lousy slaves make? They had just become battle-brothers. It had gone very well and now the bastard was humiliating him in front of the slaves and that fat slob of a merchant as well as the others.

He's mad. Some devil has his wits. They are all like that, those fine nobles but this one has some particular devil gnawing at his head. Something happened to him—him and his liar's tale about Toledo. A winter in the mountains alone. He must be possessed by some ice-spirit.

Fruela would have killed him, wanted to, vowed silently that he would. But his confusion robbed him of the fine edge of rage that he needed for it. He knew too that this strange noble was a formidable opponent. Besides Pelayo knew the country. And somewhere he had estates and a powerful family. At least, if that was not a lie too. What would the others do? Put a spear in his back? The fight and its success had enhanced Pelayo's authority over the little group and diminished his. Fruela did not trust himself to speak. He didn't know what to say. One day I'll kill you he thought. I'll spread that fancy brain all over the blade of my sword.

Pelayo had turned to the eldest of the drovers who had stood, watching the clash, impassively.

"You are slaves?"

"We are, lord."

"Slaves of this trader?"

"Yes, lord."

"Well, you're free now."

"Your pardon, lord?"

"What?"

"Could you give us a writ, lord? Some proof of our freedom? No one loves a runaway."

Pelayo was startled and so he stared at the man. The kingdom in ruins, the invader everywhere and this one wanted judicial proofs! Someone behind him tittered, half out of nervousness and half from the wine. The boy likely. He had spoken to them of conquest, a county perhaps, and now an old slave asked by what right he freed them. To kill him for it would be to admit Fruela was right. Bluff would not do it either but he could hardly claim to act in the king's name. There was no king.

He turned to the merchant who watched him with fear in his eyes.

"These men are your slaves, old one?"

"Yes, lord. "

"What is your name, trader?"

"Aaron ben-Ibrahim, lord."

"You are a Jew, then?"

"I am, lord."

"But those men are not Jews."

"No, lord, they are not Jews."

"Then they are Christians?"

"Everyone who is not a Jew is a Christian. Everyone was before the Muslims came, at least. "

"Tell me, Jew, what is the law about a Jew holding Christian slaves?"

"It is forbidden, lord, under pain of losing half one's property."

Euric guffawed drunkenly at this and the boy, Teudemiro, joined him. Pelayo addressed himself again to the older slave.

"You and the others are Christians?"

"Yes, lord."

"Then you could not be this man's slaves legally. You are as free now as you have always been. And half of this Jew's property is yours because he unjustly tried to enslave you."

"That is what the law says, lord. But for the poor man, the law was mostly blind."

"Well, you are fortunate now that we live in days when the law is enforced strictly. Each of you can take four of the donkeys and the trade goods on it. That's the law. Still, I would advise you to go north and that mostly by night. This Jew will have friends in the south. If you stay here, we will have to kill you for we are at war as you see. Should you get far enough north without being robbed you may be able to sell that stuff and become honest men."

Pelayo's tone was light and mocking but there was an intentional undertone of menace in it. The slave was not convinced and hesitated. The laws that this red-bearded giant of a robber spoke of had never been enforced unless someone wanted to bankrupt some Jew or to revenge himself on one. The kings themselves had been blind to it except sometimes to please the priests. Years of habit were hard to break. But his younger fellows had already begun to cut their donkeys out of the herd, squabbling over the better ones in muted tones and glancing nervously at the Goths.

Abruptly, he turned and joined them. There was nothing to be said. Within minutes they were gone up the path. No one spoke in the little group of Goths during this time. It was as had been agreed upon. The loss of the wealth which the slaves and their donkeys represented was considerable but they had no use for it. Worse, it had been the source of a near killing among them. With it in camp they had begun, vaguely, to feel like robbers. Now that it was gone they felt relieved, like warriors again.

Still, there was the Jew to be disposed of. He sat there like an old, fat statue. He was sweating a little in the sun and the mountain breeze lifted his wispy, gray beard. Otherwise, he made no motion.

"What about him?"

It was the boy Teudemiro again. The wine made him want to talk. He was already looking forward to the boasting they would do when this business was finished. He was impatient for the chance to strut and brag in his newfound manhood. Pelayo responded although he was beginning to weary of the need and the boy's hurry grated on him. Anyway, he knew that the old man's death had already been decided. He had done it with his need to invoke the law. They would not spare a Jew. They could not.

"Think a minute. The slaves are gone and with four animals apiece to seal their lips. The guard is dead. None of them were of too much account. They won't be missed for long. But this one is different. He has to be rich to judge from the size of the caravan. He will have relatives in the south to look for him. To cause a stir we don't want. It might be better just to put him on an animal and let him go. He can't go very fast and he doesn't know where we're going."

"And let the old blowhard warn every trader he meets," snorted Fruela.

"Either way, there's a chance. The caravan drivers will find out about us soon enough. What we need to consider is how badly will they want to get rid of us. At this point we are only four—five with the boy. If it's a matter of blood with the merchants they could hire a war party to hunt us. It's not likely that the Africans will have time to spare to bother with us but there are a lot of warriors around with little enough to do. If we kill the merchant that may just stir up the rest of them enough to finance a war party. Even if they can't find us they could make it hard for us to operate. You can't plan an ambush while you're worrying about being ambushed yourself—about your own back.

"On the other hand, if we let him go it may not be worth the trouble to them. He may warn a caravan or two but they have to come past or through these mountains to get north anyway. We can take a caravan, even one whose guard has been warned, easier than we could a band set on nothing but fighting."

Pelayo could tell that he was losing them. Fruela's face was set stonily and the others were just not following his words. They had been puzzled at the freeing of the slaves and the conflict it had provoked. Now they were just waiting for him to finish because he was their leader. It was a courtesy but they weren't paying any attention to what he said. Fruela knew that too.

"Christ's body, Pelayo, that's a lot of thinking. But it doesn't come to any sense. We already stole his goods. We freed his slaves. We have ourselves a fine enemy for life already. Letting him keep his life won't change that. These Jews value their goods as much as they do their skins.

"Like you say, they have to send their caravans up here. They may hire a war band or they may not. But whether we kill one old Jew or not won't have much to do with it."

The merchant screamed hoarsely. Then the sound trailed off into bubbling noises as the blood rose in his throat and spilled out of his mouth. He sagged and fell sideways as the young warrior, Teudemiro, stood over him, weaving a little with the wine and staring blankly at the old man. Carefully and unsteadily, Teudemiro positioned the point of his new sword over the man's heart. Then throwing his weight on the hilt with both hands, he pressed it through. A convulsive jerk and the body was still.

Fruela watched Pelayo with a thin smile on his lips. The kid had followed his lead, not Pelayo's. The Jew is dead. Let him find a way to talk around that. But Pelayo's face remained impassive. His eyes flicked briefly over Teudemiro's face but the young warrior was too drunk even to notice. He was smiling. Clearly he expected to be rewarded.

Over the next days, their good fortune continued. First they came on a group of four Goths working their way north. A show of force was hardly needed. It was a nondescript group—warriors but without a leader, purposeless except to find one. They were ready to be impressed by Pelayo. They eyed Sunna and his rich clothing, not yet ruined. They measured the breadth of Fruela's chest. The size of the war band almost doubled.

Then they trapped a small caravan just as they were breaking camp in the morning. A quick flight of arrows and two of its guard lay squirming on the ground. Fruela's javelin took another of them in the chest and pushed him back across the dying charcoals. The last of them knelt, palms up in a pleading gesture. The twigs and leaves of his bed still clung to his hair. Teudemiro drove his sword into the man.

The four new members of the band had been taken by surprise by the swiftness and sureness of the ambush. They had been told that no mercy was to be shown to Africans but, all the same, they were a little surprised at the automatic way in which Teudemiro had dispatched the last of the guard and the small heed that anyone else had paid. They were enthusiastic now about their new enterprise.

The boy, Sunna, had played no part in it either, except that with Euric he had blocked any escape for the drovers. The three of those were a mixed bag. Two of them were Goths who had been reduced to slavery in the past year. Freed, they joined their captors on the spot. The third was a native, a Roman, who was acting as agent for his merchant master. This Felix, who was clever and knowledgeable, gave them much information before his release.

There was no knowledge of their existence or activities in Córdoba, he said. The caravans were setting out about their summer trading as normally as the times permitted. Felix told them of four whose routes would pass within their reach. He described the likely strength of the guards of each and the habits of their leader. He gave them an idea of the goods they carried, so far as he had learned them from his master, or from some judicious drinking, and from a little petty bribery.

He also said that he had heard of a new landing on the coast being planned in Africa. The talk was that it was a great army, more than ten thousand men, almost all Arabs and not Africans like the others. Their leader would be the African governor Musa and it seemed that Tarik was only a general of his. Everyone expected another summer of war between them and the remaining supporters of King Rodrigo, who had been gathering at Mérida. Everyone who could was selling off his merchandise and hiding the gold he got for it. For that reason the caravans were on the move early and aimed to do as much business as they could as soon as they could.

When finally they let Felix ride out of the camp with four donkeys, they had a much better idea of their prospects for the next month. They also felt a new urgency for carrying out their plan. A new army of Arabs in the south would not find much difficulty in completing the conquest there. The move towards the north assumed new importance in their minds. It was becoming less of a grandiose dream and more of a real necessity. Unless they were wrong though, the renewed fighting in the south would produce more fugitive Goths and so more recruits.

They chose the next two caravans largely because Felix had

told them of the foodstuffs that they would be carrying. Now that there were eleven of them, hunting ceased to be a casual affair. There were some quarrels over food and Pelayo knew that it was becoming as important a prize as weapons.

Still, they had no real trouble. Their very size now made them easy masters of the small guards of the unwary caravans. That, plus the element of surprise and the selection of the ground with unfailing perfection by Pelayo, kept them from even a single death. They had a few wounds important enough for notice but nothing more. At small cost they gained a moderate store of food, the weapons of seven dead Africans, two more freed Goths to swell their numbers and enough wine to celebrate their unbroken string of successes properly.

Chapter VII

Three days after the taking of the last caravan Pelayo lay atop a large boulder in the morning sun watching the progress of the figures on the trail below him. Above in the cloudless, bright blue sky a hawk circled easily. Probably it was regarding him, much as he was the men below him. The pines stirred softly in the breeze which still carried a hint of the morning's dew. Just before his face a small lizard stared over the edge of the rock at him, surprised and immobilized by his unexpected presence. He was not easy about this particular decision but it was done. Ahead of the men below, an ambuscade was in the making. Fruela had urged the decision upon him in council and would lead the blocking force. Fruela was impatient of the rate at which their band was growing and had seen an opportunity in this prize which excited him. It was Pelayo who saw the problems.

The men below were slavers. Goths from the look of them and well armed with warrior's swords and shields. Five in all, they had come down from the north with a little supply train of donkeys behind. Before them, except for the one who went ahead, they drove another fourteen men. The hands of these were bound behind them and they were all connected by a long rope which looped from one of their necks to the other. There were two drovers with the six donkeys of the supply train and an old lady who limped alongside one of the beasts, holding on to the lashing of its pack.

The slaves were obviously Goths. They were what had aroused Fruela. They seemed to be warriors taken in some fight to the north. Some still wore rough bandages. Liberating them would more than double the size of their war band.

Pelayo watched them wind along the trail. Fourteen men, but without weapons. He could manage bows for most of them and spears for a few but there were no swords or shields to spare. Arms would become an immediate problem. In a band so large the difference in weapons made differences in rank. Could he entrust Euric with the direction of a force of archers? The old veteran was quiet but he was always in the right place at a fight. He had a sense for the main chance. But would he command? Could he control such a group and would they accept his leadership?

Pelayo was not ready to give Fruela a command. A quarrelsome bull, he was always a possible threat to the purposes Pelayo conceived. He would resent Euric's promotion even to the leadership of such a lightly armed force. Teudemiro would be his fellow malcontent. The young warrior was too stupid to lead anything but a pack train. He fought bravely enough but was going to get himself killed one day by his own heedless enthusiasms. He spent most of his time alternately posturing for and bullying the boy, Sunna. The newer members of the group contained no very strong individuals. Perhaps the different strengths of himself and Fruela did not allow for one.

Food would become an immediate problem too. Already they were living from one caravan to another. The stores that they captured and the game that they could kill hardly lasted the interval. But in the four weeks that had passed, word, or at least forebodings, had to have circulated among the traders and rulers of the plains. Either the caravans would cease to come, or they would be heavily protected, or a party would be sent to hunt them down. The food problem was going to get worse and even in summer there seemed to be no easy solution for it. So much for the life of a general thought Pelayo sourly.

Below him the last of the donkeys rounded the bend in the trail. Beyond the turn, the trail turned down into a ravine which was thickly wooded at the bottom along the sides of a swift-flowing mountain stream. Fruela, Teudemiro and four others waited just within the wood, ready for the descent of the slave train. Pelayo rolled and slid off the boulder. The other six rose silently from the shade where they had been squatting and followed him down the slope.

The timing was perfect. The slaves were halfway down the trail. At the top of the descent Pelayo advanced, shield to shield, with four other warriors. As they moved, they began to beat rhythmically and rapidly on the metal of their shields with the flat of their swords. Behind and above them, clear for fire, were Euric and the boy Sunna with bows at the ready. At the same time, Fruela and his men broke from the woods, javelins ready above their shields, they raced up towards the head of the line.

On the path between them, the leader of the slavers began to bark orders rapidly. Even with the thrill of battle playing along his shoulder blades Pelayo was impressed. Before Fruela or the others were within javelin-throw, the slaves, drovers and the old woman had been herded into a compact if unwilling mass of bodies between them and the slave traders. On Pelayo's side the bridles of the six donkeys had been hurriedly lashed together and they moved confusedly on the trail, a jumble of hind-quarters and packs, disposed to kick. The slavers had fortified their position and stood ready for the attack. Even if exposed and confined, they stood well armed and determined. Only in numbers and by the advantageous position of Euric and Sunna with their bows, did the ambushers retain their advantage.

Pelayo raised his sword to halt Fruela short of that press of bodies. A bird's song filled the long silence. Pebbles rolled from Euric's feet as he braced himself and pulled his bow for a shot.

"Give it up, slavers! Throw down your arms!"

No answer.

"If you fight, you're dead men, carcasses for the wolves. Give it up!"

"What you get won't be worth much, bandits! And most of you won't live to get it anyway."

Pelayo could see their leader clearly. A large, big-boned man with one milky-white eye that stared fixedly, he carried a broad scar across the left biceps. He had seen fights before—probably a soldier. The rest of them seemed to be warriors too.

"No bandits here. Just African-killers."

"You'll have enough work elsewhere."

"We don't kill Goths unless we have to."

"Then we should talk."

It was the step back that Pelayo had to have—that he had been hoping for as the germ of a plan grew at the edge of his consciousness.

"We can talk. Fruela, you and I will meet him on the downhill side of the trail. No weapons."

"No weapons and no knives."

The stances they took on the uneven ground added to the tension. Any one of them might slip, or pretend to slip, and the blood-letting would start instantly above them on the trail. The caravan leader folded his arms over his chest. It was a gesture of good faith, of defenselessness, but an easy one since he was unlikely to live the next hour anyway. Fruela was scrutinizing the man very closely. Pelayo judged that the fellow had decided to live by his wits for the moment. It was hopeful.

"You are soldiers, you and your men."

"We are."

"Slave trading is a funny business for soldiers."

"The times are funny."

"So you do what you can because you don't have a chief. All my warriors were like that before I recruited them. It's a poor way for a warrior to live."

"Not so poor if I'd gotten this string to Córdoba. They're stout fellows, strong backs."

"But you've lost that. There's no money in them now. I'm taking them for warriors, which I judge them to have been. They'll more than make up my losses. They won't help you."

"You'll free these slaves and arm them?"

"Since they're Goths, yes."

"And if we don't fight, you'll let us go on—with our weapons?"

"No. Since you're Goths too, you either join us or die here. If you were Romans, we'd let you go, but not with weapons. If you were Africans, you'd be dead now. We don't talk with them, or Arabs either. Those are our rules."

"You want us to join you—and the slaves too? What do you want an army for?"

"For now, to kill Africans. In the fall we march north. I have estates in Galicia."

The slaver looked at Pelayo. No doubt that he's a noble. Plenty of muscle on the big frame but lean and hard. A redbeard, but smart. It had been a neat trap, neatly sprung. His men moved to his commands. He could talk but there was a steely single-mindedness back there somewhere, a trace of madness. A real king of the mountain who would kill us quickly enough but who has lost touch with the real world.

"I know this man now, Pelayo," broke in Fruela. "His name is Masona. He was one of Witiza's men. He fought against King Rodrigo, I heard, but the last time I saw him he had two good eyes. Likely he got to be a slaver by helping his African friends out."

Masona's arms tightened across his chest.

"So you finally know me, Fruela, You're still slow with everything but the javelin. I knew you when you jumped out of the trees down there, roaring."

Pelayo was sure that he wanted Masona. He would be a balance to Fruela. He could fight just as well and was probably brighter.

"In our war band we have no friends of Arabs, Masona. Nor do we have Witiza's men and Rodrigo's men. They're both dead. There is no king of the Goths. Here everyone is Pelayo's man. I lead every Goth here but the dead ones. Do I have your hand on it?"

"You have my hand on it for me and my men."

"I'll have the hand of each of your men for themselves. They're my men now."

"First my slaves—now my men. A bad bargain, Pelayo."

"For a life? For a hope? For a chance to play the man's part again against these Africans? It'll cost you more than that. The slaves will be free, not freedmen, but just as good as you, Masona."

"I gave you my hand. But a man's is good as he makes himself. By the saints, I may be master again some day. And they may be slaves again. You judge who is as good as who, watch and judge."

Above them on the path the tension had relaxed a little, insensibly, as the talk went on. Now, as the three of them clambered back up, it dissolved on all sides leaving only a sense of strangeness and apprehension. Masona took the lead, moving among the slaves to cut their bonds, while Pelayo offered his hand to one after the other, first Masona's followers and then the slaves as they were cut free. Everyone had heard the exchange on the slope but no one quite understood that it would happen. It was too strange. They couldn't be allowed the time to make objections, raise questions.

"The donkey drivers go free," Pelayo ordered, "Euric, give them a day's food and set them on their way. Tell them that we don't need them anymore and that they'll keep their freedom and their hides if they duck the Arabs and head north. Get them out of here!"

He turned to Masona. "How about the old woman?"

"She's a cook and a nurse. Not a bad nurse either. She kept a couple of these alive and got them ready to march when I thought we'd have to leave them. She can keep up."

To Pelayo she looked like the oldest woman he'd ever seen. All these Roman women aged fast after girlhood but this one's skin was almost the color of the black olive. Only her eyes were darker. The lines of her face and limbs lost themselves in folds of wizened flesh. He saw, as she spat, that most of her teeth were sound and yellow. Well, God knows, she wouldn't tempt anyone to fight over her. She would be the first woman in camp.

"Alright, back to camp. Lead off, Teudemiro!"

They followed his lead, walking in groups still, looking sidelong at their new comrades, not sure what to make of it. It was a long march and the sun was at its height. He drove them hard, setting the example, stepping out fast and snapping at those who knew him best to have them do the same. He wanted them tired, dog-tired and thirsty. He wanted them lost and bewildered. He wanted them helpless and isolated and in need of a leader. It was easier for his own men. They knew the route, could pace themselves. Without being quite sure why he was doing it, they caught what he was doing and entered into the spirit of it.

"Let's go, Goddamit, move your asses!"

"Come on, come on."

"Put that old bag of bones on the jackass."

"Watch the rocks, stupid. You'll roll the whole damn mountain down the side!"

It was late afternoon before they reached the camp that he wanted. They were tired, even the veterans, and ready to be impressed. They could see immediately the advantages of the high valley with no easy approach. The brush shelters and their shade was inviting. There was wine and food and Pelayo urged it on them unsparingly. The old lady, Anna, rolled up in a ball and went to sleep but the others gradually softened their fears in the wine. They began to talk—it was garrulous, pointless, obscene—but talk. And not just to their own little groups.

After a time, a long time, Pelayo began to draw them out. He wanted information and they had great stocks of it. The former slaves had been part of a war band under the Count of Astorga. Most of that party had been cut off and killed or captured by Africans operating out of Salamanca. The Count himself escaped but wouldn't be disposed to come south again in a hurry.

Yes, they knew of Count Bodo in Palencia. Who knows what he's doing. The same as everyone else. Playing a double game, or anyway, a waiting game. All the chiefs of the north were waiting and talking. Messengers had gone round all winter to call them south to Mérida where King Rodrigo's partisans were to have gathered in the spring. But no one much went. Messages had come from Witiza's son, Agila, also promising pardon to all of Rodrigo's supporters and demanding recognition. Yet other messengers had come from Queen Egilona, Witiza's widow, counseling peace and submission to her son and herself. No one knew what was happening or going to happen. Now, it was said, Mérida was under siege.

"Just like always," said Masona. "The chiefs are always fighting, always wondering what to do, drinking too much and thinking too little. Like the apostle said, they don't have any God but their bellies."

"A soldier who runs slaves and quotes gospel," said Fruela, "Christ!"

Masona ignored him and continued, "Tarik spent precious little time in Toledo last winter. His men hardly had a chance to shrink their blisters before he was pursuing more of Rodrigo's men north towards the Ebro. When they turned due north, instead of crossing it, and finally holed up at the rock of Amaya, he followed them there and set up siege lines around it. He's still there maybe. Before he lost Toledo though, he threw out garrisons, two hundred men at

Siguenza, another two hundred at Segovia, maybe a hundred and fifty at Salamanca and another fifty in between at Ávila. Tarik has covered every pass back over the Guadarramas. He might as well have sent the chiefs a map of his campaign but they're too dumb or frightened to be able to see it.

"How far can he go?" asked Pelayo. "What's he after—loot, women, what? Look, he's an Arab with an army of Africans. In the south there's another army of Arabs led by another Arab, this Musa. Then there's Agila fishing for the crown and the old queen, Egilona, is pushing the whelp. Tarik's a bear on the end of a long limb."

"Not so long as you think, Pelayo" answered Masona "Egilona will come over from Africa with Musa's army this summer. From what I hear, she sleeps in Musa's bed. The boy Aquila is nothing but bait. If the chiefs jump for him, they still land in the Arab's camp. If they don't, they're rebels. And there's an Arab governor named Musa and a general of his named Tarik who are taking the country without a Goth to say no to them meanwhile."

"With a lot of Goths to help them," broke in Fruela. "You run slaves back and forth for them. You jumped in bed with them as fast as that bitch, Egilona."

At that the talk died away suddenly. The skin across Masona's jaws tightened, but he answered evenly.

"What does a soldier do, Fruela? What did you do, desert? What else could anyone do? The Archbishop of Toledo ran all the way to Rome. The great chiefs and the nobles sit around pretending they can't see the Africans. What do you want an old soldier to do?"

"Fight!"

It was Pelayo, speaking just loudly enough to be heard but with an intensity which drew every eye to him. The old crone curled up in the firelight reminded him of Elena in her death sleep. Masona and Fruela made him think of himself and his brother, dead in Toledo. What could anyone do? He was answering himself, but they heard. At first quietly, then a rising chant. He was on his feet. His sword was out.

"Kill them! Fight and kill them all!"

He swung the steel battle-blade from side to side in the fire's light, in great, whistling strokes.

"No mercy! No peace! Kill the Africans!"

He threw it from hand to hand and over his head. He struck with it, downwards at the nearest pine, carving away a great gout of wood and bark.

"No talk! No business! Kill them everyone!"

A tip of the arc touched the fire's embers, showering sparks and ash across them. He bounded among them, punctuating each cry with a stroke. Only half-drunk, he felt the wildness of disgust and frustration creep up to the edge of his self-control. He enjoyed the feeling. He would split a skull—one of these wide-eyed dolts!

"No whoring with them! No praying with them!"

They understood nothing! They cared for nothing! Like foxes, they ran from meal to meal, spoiling everything, leaving nothing untouched. He could do it. They would not lift a finger.

"Just death! Death for all of them!"

With an effort, he restrained himself. Abruptly, he stopped. With one hand, he thrust the sword point through the embers into the ground below. It stood there, the fire glinting from it.

"For that," he told them, "I brought you here, It is enough. We shall do what we are strong enough to do. I, Pelayo, will tell you what that is."

He turned and left them. Fruela and Masona had watched the frenzied dance impassively, if not without fear. Their eyes met, now, in brief agreement. What showed on the faces of the others was true. He had a devil. He might die madly, might kill them all, but no one there could stand openly against him. He had the cunning of the wolf and the careful reason of a great chief. He had the terrible fury of the spirits and the infuriating, easy superiority of the great noble. They were afraid to follow him but they had no choice. He was chief. In that conviction, one by one, they slept. No one touched the sword, which stood there amidst the dying embers till morning.

Chapter VIII

With the morning, Pelayo set about the organization of their fighting force. A dozen men under Euric's command, mostly the slaves of yesterday, became a skirmishing and covering force armed with bows but carrying spears as well. Euric understood what he wanted almost at once. They were to be not isolated archers but a single unit, firing in unison and upon command, striking predetermined objectives and attacking or withdrawing upon order as one man. The veteran set about training his command immediately, examining himself the bow and arrow store of each one, setting some of them to work at making new shafts and others to hunting for proper game birds for the feathering. Each he tested personally as a marksman against his own skill and set to practice those who could not match it. For the boy Sunna, who was assigned to him also, he was careful to pose the same set of tasks and performance.

The remaining men divided fairly naturally into two divisions: the one under Fruela and the other led by Masona. Fruela's group included those with them the longest, over whom he enjoyed an already established preeminence. Masona kept his own men as a nucleus and added three of the newer recruits. Both groups were heavily armed with iron shields and swords in addition to javelins. They were intended to be the shock troops in future fights who would operate independently but in coordination. Only a few of them had helmets and Masona alone boasted a breastplate but for mountain fighting they were probably adequately armed. Certainly they were well led.

The competition between those divisions, and more subtly between their leaders, began at once. It pushed each to the routine tasks of maintaining weapons and gear. More importantly, it gave each of the Goths a new identity and society and detached them from some of their old quarrels.

Pelayo welcomed every diversion, for the problem of food alone was becoming very serious. The stocks, that would have taken Masona's band out of the hills to the markets of the plain, would last them now for only two days or three at most. The old woman, Anna, had slaughtered and skinned one of their donkeys and was now at work dressing it. It was meat for a day. The men whom he had sent out for game bird would supply some fowl as well as feathers but the spring game was thinning and growing smarter. They could move east or west in the range but he doubted that it would improve the hunting by much. Later in the day he took counsel with Fruela, Masona and Euric about the problem of provisions.

"There are too many of us for the hills to feed and too few of us to operate on the plains," observed Euric, posing the problem.

"Just so. With all of us on foot we might manage to raid a few villages for food but they'd cut us off before long and then cut us up. Just as they did to the Count of Astorga's band. They have four times as many men and enough horses to move some of them around. Out on the plain we'd be helpless pretty quick."

Masona's observations almost required Fruela to speak.

"Unless we kept moving north. If we moved fast and hit hard, we might get away with it. The Africans are spread pretty thin up there from what you say."

"I don't know," replied Masona, frowning. "They move pretty fast too. And its early enough in the season so they'd have no good reason to give up a pursuit. We could have our tongues hanging out to our knees before we stopped running."

"That is, if there's no help up north. But what do they hold beyond Salamanca? There are other Goths up there who'll side with us quicker than with them."

"But then we join them as refugees, not as a war band," put in Euric.

Involuntarily, they all glanced at Pelayo at the remark. It was obvious that he agreed with the import of Euric's observation. They would go nowhere as fugitives or on the terms of another.

"Well, if we're not strong enough to move north yet, then we have to find new ways to feed ourselves here. Berries and rabbits and donkeys won't do it. But the Romans have their sheep out in the hills and enough of them do a little farming to make the difference. They'll have grain stored by now for the fall and the beans will be coming in. They'll have to feed us for the next two months, that's all," said Fruela, looking directly at Pelayo.

"So far, Fruela," responded Pelayo, "we have no quarrel with the Romans nor do they with us. They know we're here, where we are, how many of us there are. My guess is that some of those we've freed have joined them—or visited with some of them anyway. They leave us alone because we leave them alone.

"By now the Africans may be looking for us. We don't need to supply them with guides. Some of those shepherds and farmers know the hills as well as I do. It's best to leave them out of it."

"So long as we can, Pelayo, so long as we can," It was Masona. "Then we have to eat. How long will anyone follow us on short rations with food to be had for the taking?"

"You know how the Romans live, Masona," said Pelayo in answer. "Any grain we took would be seed or his own food. It would have to be both to be worth our bothering actually. For a shepherd, the sheep are his life. We'd be killing them.

We'd have to kill them to keep the alarm from spreading. We'd really be what you called us yesterday, bandits.

"And the word would still be spread, if a little slower. In two weeks time we'd be the enemy to every Roman in the mountains. They'd warn every herdsman and every caravan too. They might even go down into the plains to get help. Then we'd have to move before we're ready."

Masona looked at him long and steadily. "True. True enough. But logic doesn't fill bellies. There are ways to handle this kind of thing and you know it. We can make a wide enough sweep the first time to get us provisions for a month. At the same time, we're careful so that no one escapes and no one survives. It would give us at least a month. You're a soldier. You've campaigned. That's the way its done and you know it.

"With a month's time, with good food, we'll have a trained war party here. A couple of wide sweeps might even give us twenty or thirty more men. By the end of August we could be readier to march north than we are now and then who will need the natives?

"I've no fight with these Romans either, but they're there and there are other methods than the ones you've been using. We don't touch their flocks. We avoid their crops. We free them when we take them as slaves. Why, Pelayo? I see the wisdom of it, maybe, when we don't need them. But when we do? Would you sacrifice us to them? What are they to you? They're not of your blood."

Pelayo knew that the argument was lost, or close to it. More, they were asking him to explain himself, to justify himself. He could not do that. As chief, he could give explanations only on his own terms, as a favor, not on theirs. Moreover he knew that he would not let them pillage Elena's people. Before that, he would kill these three himself and lead the others out on the plains to die. But for now, an answer was needed.

"You talk like a Goth, Masona. Like the Goths have always

talked—and acted. Like a rebel. And the Goths were such great rebels that now we have the Africans on us. Rebels live off the population, Masona, rebels and bandits. Since the times of King Reccesvinth the Romans have been subject to the same law as we Goths. They are our countrymen and we cannot afford to drive them into the hands of the Africans."

Masona was surprised at this turn but Fruela had seen him take it before and spoke to their old quarrel.

"There is no country left, Pelayo. The Africans have it—or will have it if someone doesn't act. There is no king, no law. You have no king. You're a chief. You follow your own law not a book."

"So we're to be conquerors, Fruela, mighty conquerors or dead heroes. But successful conquerors let the peasants follow their own law. It's easier that way. For a hundred and fifty years our grandfathers let them follow the law of Rome while we Goths kept our own law. Now, for those people, Reccesvinth's law is theirs and ours. We have to act or we are bandits and rebels in their eyes. Just now we don't look like conquerors."

They knew that he was wrong, that he was mouthing words, but they could not argue with him. He would discover, or make up, another law or another king. It was a game he would always win, this game of words. Still, they were not quite ready yet for an open break, for a clear contest of will. They sensed that they would have to kill him. Who would take his place?

Fruela cast about for an alternative. "What about a trade for provisions then? The Africans wanted the boy, Sunna. Likely they still want him. We can give him to them. It would be no favor to them; he's not worth much to us. The little fox eats but he won't fight like his father, I'll bet."

Pelayo regarded Euric who was troubled by Fruela's words. A shadow crossed the old veteran's face.

"Won't fight, Euric?"

"He's not blooded, Pelayo, that's true. But there hasn't

been all that much chance. I haven't seen him send an arrow home. Still, he's only a boy."

"Christ's blood, Euric," retorted Fruela, "the little fart has hair on his chin. He's old enough. But he hangs back in a fight. You know it. You've seen men like that. They end up behind you in every battle and when you turn around in need of them they're running away like a goddam Syrian."

Pelayo watched Euric. He knew that Fruel's words were true. So did Euric. But obviously the veteran liked the boy and tried still to defend him.

"It's true, Pelayo. He does hang back but he's hardly a man. Just fifteen years. Who of us has forgotten the first man he killed? It comes harder to some than others. With the other archers now, he could make his first kill easier. I can see to him."

"He can get a couple of good men killed, Euric. You think he can't bear to wing a man? I say he's afraid they'll shoot back—puncture that skinny, white hide of his." It was easier for Fruela to argue with Euric and he was faintly relieved at the chance. "He might do for you, till you find a real whore, but he'll never make a soldier. Old Anna has more guts. I say that if we can't use him as a warrior, we use him as a hostage. Better he gets us grain than that he eats ours."

Pelayo watched a frown slide across Masona's face, at the implication of Fruela's words, and then disappear. Euric just gazed stubbornly back at the latter without replying.

"We agreed from the beginning, you and I, Fruela," said Pelayo, "that we make no agreements with the Africans. Everyone else has agreed to that too. And every time we fight them, we beat them. That's what keeps us together up here in the mountains. Would you change your mind now because you think you may be hungry next week?"

"Not think, Pelayo, not think! You called this council over the food problem. Now you tell us there aren't any answers. Next you'll tell us we're not hungry. Or do you have a way to solve things?"

Masona broke in on Fruela's question. "The boy is useless to us, Pelayo, if he won't fight. If we don't trade him to the Africans, can we trade him to his father?"

"Sunna is a member of the war band. He accepted that from the beginning. If he won't fight, then I'll kill him myself. The only way we'll use him is to force his father to join us. But for now the Count of Palencia is too far away. There's not time enough for such a swap even if he could help us."

They looked at Pelayo in astonishment. For the first time really it occurred to the three of them that, so far as this strange noble was concerned, they were bound to him for life, from Sunna to Fruela, from least to greatest. He didn't think of it as a common enterprise, a desperate adventure. He saw it as a permanent allegiance and the beginning of—what? Now he talked casually of enlisting a count in the band. They might have jested about it, or even laughed, had they not been so afraid of him. Even in his lucid moments, he was possessed.

Pelayo understood at once that he had regained the initiative although what it was that had overawed them now he could not think. They could be dumb brutes as well as sullen ones. What moved them sometimes was a mystery. He knew though that the issue was far from settled but that, for the present, he had some more time.

"We need to think more about this. See to what your hunters brought in, Euric, and we'll estimate the cereal again."

"You'll find it easier to figure tonight after we eat," Fruela called after him as he walked away. "There'll be precious little left by then."

But it wasn't until their night meal had been concluded that the last of Euric's hunters came in. He was a short, slight man of dark hair and skin named Wala. Pelayo suspected from the first, as he did of Fruela also, that there was Roman blood somewhere in the man. But Wala was tireless on the trail and passed through brush like a wraith. He had ranged farther than any of the others that day and at the end of it had come upon an African.

From the first he recognized the activities of the other so that he had not even tried to kill him. It would have been simple enough for Wala because the other was hunting, intent on some track which Wala could not make out. He slipped along behind the long-limbed, brown-skinned Berber, puzzling over what kind of quarry a man alone in the mountains would seek so close to dusk. Abruptly the other gave up his careful casting back and forth over the ground and set off into the gathering gloom at an angle to the trail. At first Wala thought that the man had detected him and so he almost lost him. Waiting for an arrow, he followed on what he took to be a parallel path and recovered sight of his quarry in a brief span.

The African was clearly now a hunter on his way to camp. Intrigued, Wala followed him into the growing dark. Finally they reached it; Wala sucked in his breath despite his habitual caution. There must be fourteen or fifteen Goths there, he couldn't be sure in the firelight with their moving about. But they were all heavily armed. Breastplates and helmets, shields and swords lay around in easy profusion. And the pack animals, hobbled for the night, must have numbered close to forty. There was a guard posted too. Wala's quarry had called out as he had approached the camp and another Berber had joined him from the shadows. Now a third African had joined the two as they moved to the center of the camp and the one he had followed was engaged by a tall blond Goth in eager conversation.

Pelayo guessed, before Wala's tale was quite finished, who they were. These were their executioners. They were hunting the bandits who had made the mountain trails unsafe for caravans. Someone had sent them into the hills.

But he had to be sure so he left that same night with Wala to observe the encampment. Before leaving he instructed Fruela and Masona that all the warriors were to be kept in camp and that no fires were to be lit. The archer-hunters of Euric's command were to take up station at the best points of observation surrounding the area of the strangers' camp, as described by Wala. They were to watch the African hunters from a distance only and to avoid all contact with them. Only if they discovered the camp were they to attack them and then they must be sure to kill them. For the next day he and Wala would be within the enemy's search area but would rejoin them after the strangers had posted guard for the night.

Well before dawn he and Wala had positioned themselves and, when the damp dark dissolved, followed after the guard as they drew back into camp. They witnessed the conference between the three Berbers and the strongly-muscled, blond Goth which probably dealt with the outlines of the search for the day. Then the two settled down to watch the camp after the departure of the Africans. Or rather, Pelayo watched the camp while Wala guarded against a sudden return of the scouts.

There was no doubt that these were old soldiers that Pelayo was watching. Secure in their own strength, they hardly armed themselves at all. Still, the way they tended their weapons, the way they diced and the way that they drank all marked them for what they were. Probably they thought that they were out after bandits and caravan-robbers, something that involved a long hunt and a lot of marching but wouldn't come to much as a fight. In the daylight, Pelayo counted seventeen of them, all with full armor as near as he could judge. They would in truth be formidable but there was no alternative to destroying them or most of them. He could not operate in the mountains at all in the presence of a force such as this. And the armor excited his envy.

He was puzzled at the lack of activity on the part of the main body of the enemy. He guessed that perhaps they had only just come up from the plains yesterday and were waiting on the results of some preliminary scouting. The donkeys were tied closer into the camp than would be likely if they

had had much time to foul the area. The men relieved themselves just on the edge of the camp too. They couldn't have
been doing that for very long for there seemed to be relatively
few flies. It indicated too that they would be abandoning the
campsite in a day or two at most. They hadn't bothered to
throw up shelters either.

If it was a long day for the watchers, who were grateful for
the clatter of the cicadas and the shrilling of an occasional
bird, it was a long day in the camp too. The dice game finally
broke up in a quarrel in which the blond leader had to
intervene. As he observed, Pelayo thought that the man blus-
tered too much, that he was not entirely sure of his control
and that the fact showed. When he walked away one of the
men whom he had rebuked gestured obscenely behind his
back. Some of the others in the group smiled quietly at the
by-play.

From then on, Pelayo watched the leader more closely. He
looked to be about twenty-seven or so, big-boned and heavily
fleshed. There seemed to be no scars on him and he was light
of skin. Most of those he led were older than him, tanned from
campaigning and liberally marked with its mementos. Two
had fresh scars. Their leader's armor was very good, almost
too fine for field use, and he alone wore it in the camp. The
others had stacked theirs. Except for the four who were
obviously on guard duty, no one in the camp wore even a
sword belt.

Pelayo decided that the blond was new to the group. The
relations between them were too formal and not entirely
good. Something of the old soldier's contempt for those who
are less experienced was evident even from this distance.
Gradually Pelayo discerned, among the former's gear, a
smallish leather chest. His attention was drawn to it finally
by the kind of elaborately casual interest everyone in the
camp paid to it as they passed it. That, he guessed, would be
the pay chest. It held the money, or perhaps half of it, paid
for this hunting trip into the mountains. And obviously it had

not yet been distributed. The small mountain of provisions that had been unloaded from the pack animals would feed a force like this for three or four weeks if filled out with a little casual hunting. The animals themselves were young and healthy ones. Obviously someone had paid handsomely to recruit and outfit this band, handsomely enough to interest a young peacock of good birth but not a great deal of soldiering time. It wouldn't have been the Africans then who would have been able to buy cheap, as conquerors always can. Likely the relatives of the Jew that Teudemiro stabbed, he thought. Vengeance is expensive but it could be good business too if it opened the mountain passes.

The shadows stretched themselves out from the wood towards the camp. The hush of dark hung in the motionless air. The green of the shrubs became momentarily more brilliant in the gathering dark. Wala's foot touched his as one of the Berbers reentered camp. They waited, very alert, for the other two. In the camp two small fires had been lighted after some argument. At last the other two scouts came in. Whatever they had found, it had not been critical. Pelayo and Wala withdrew slowly. The stiffness of their muscles gradually disappeared and was forgotten in their growing excitement.

Before dawn, Pelayo had his forces in position. The camp lay on a slight rise which was itself backed by a very steep slope, difficult or impossible for men in armor to climb except very slowly. In front of the rise was a mountain stream, across whose bed the trail passed, which ran on down towards the plain and led, in the other direction, higher into the valley. The divisions of Masona and Fruela had been posted in the scrub, one on either side of the camp, forward of the stream. Pelayo himself was with Euric's men who were aligned along the edge of the wood behind the stream. They would open the engagement. If the enemy moved forward to attack them, archery and the stream would have to delay them long enough for Fruela and Masona to take them on either flank. On the other hand, if they moved to one flank or the other, the division threatened was to withdraw slowly while Euric's men kept up a harassing fire. If they pursued far enough the other division was to try to run off as many of their pack animals as possible.

It was a good plan but everyone recognized how little advantage they had. Surprise and the fact that the enemy expected only bandits were with them. Euric's men were likely to be taken as the whole force. But even if they were drawn forward into that trap their heavy armor would go far towards making up the disadvantage. It would be a bloody fight with heavy losses inevitable if they really made a fight of it. If they moved off to either side, Pelayo's men there would have to pull back slowly enough to lead them on but fast enough to avoid contact or they would simply be overwhelmed and slaughtered. Everyone in the little force recognized the situation as a turning point. Should they not either quickly cripple the enemy with casualties to force the remainder to surrender, or so discourage them as to force them out of the mountains, their own numbers would be so reduced as to make their later escape to the north a flight of fugitives, not the march of a war band.

Tension rose as the morning dawned and grew. In the camp the loading of the pack animals was being completed by Goths and Berbers alike. Some decision had been reached to move the camp. Somebody cursed ferociously at an animal that had stepped on his foot. The leader personally supervised the loading of the pay chest and his other equipment. Then he stalked back and forth, not sure whether to try to hasten the loading by abuse or not. Fretting, he was joined at last by the three Berber scouts and by another blackbearded Goth, perhaps his second in command for the march.

Euric's men were becoming more and more anxious at Pelayo's delay. The pack train was loaded now and in the camp the men were donning their armor slowly. Every passing second made a crippling or killing bowshot more difficult. Out on the flanks, Masona and Fruela and their troops knew that too. Pelayo could feel it in his own stomach. It was the hardest time, just before it started. He looked at Sunna, posted ostentatiously in front of Euric. The boy was white to the lips. Pelayo glared at him and the tip of the boy's bow trembled briefly. In the interval the conference in camp had ended. The Berbers were moving out away from the two Goths who still discussed something.

"Now," Pelayo said.

In the following flight of arrows, Wala's shaft dispatched the tall Berber he had first followed instantaneously. A second took three arrows, one in the stomach, and fell doubled on the dirt. Almost at once he began to scream continuously. The third, with a flesh wound in the shoulder and another arrow through the muscle of his right thigh, fell heavily on that side and then began to push himself desperately over the little interval to where the force was forming-up even now. The big blond Goth stood transfixed by surprise but his second-in-command bounded quickly towards the scout who was half-crawling towards them.

Just then the second volley of arrows struck. The screaming figure on the ground stiffened under the hail and then relaxed, a scream trailing off into silence. The last of the scouts pitched forward dead as three arrows entered his chest and lungs almost at once while another arrow rattled on the breastplate of his would-be rescuer and yet another pierced the latter's forearm. With an oath the soldier raced back to the now formed ranks of his comrades. One of them covered him with his shield while another broke the arrow shaft close to the feathers and drew it through by the protruding, bloody head.

There was silence. A beetle droned towards the dung of the past night. A bird called—very far away. Suddenly the smell of pine was very fresh in everyone's nostrils. There was something there, just beyond the edge of perception, which the smell suggested but no one dared the distraction. Out there the blood of two of the Berbers ran together into a common puddle. In the forest, Euric's archers were poised for another shot. In front of them the intruders had formed two ranks, each drifting back slightly from their center. Within them, each man crouched enough almost to shrink within his shield's rim. To the flanks, the bands of Fruela and Masona pressed their bodies hard against the earth.

Without exposing himself Pelayo cupped his hands and shouted, "Welcome to the mountains, Goths and soldiers."

As prompted, a line of catcalls and whistles ran across the edge of the forest from archer to archer and then died away.

"You came in search of bandits with Africans for guides. But you come too late. You find a Gothic war band instead and Pelayo is its chief."

Pelayo watched their leader narrowly. Their line was ready to move. It waited only on an order. He estimated that, the word of command once given, his men might get off two or perhaps three shots at the charging ranks. Maybe three or four more casualties. Then better than a dozen heavily-armed men would break over the forest's edge with Fruela's and Masona's men falling on them from behind. Any of Euric's skirmishers who had not picked their line of retreat carefully would die swiftly. The moment lengthened. Still, their leader hesitated, unsure of his course of action while the loaded donkeys jostled against one another and a couple of them bolted towards where Masona's men lay hidden. The man's face was red and flushed against his golden beard.

"You have no chance if you fight. Give it up and join us against the Africans. We march north to freedom."

Out on their right flank a donkey skidded, puzzled, to a stop just in front of Masona's men. Now they knew, any half-trained soldier would understand what that meant. Their leader, facing the forest, responded now.

"We have given our word. We have taken pay."

Pelayo understood that he wanted an excuse to surrender, that he could form no plan to extricate himself. He had no stomach for this fight.

Pelayo decided. Deliberately he drew his bow full. The loosed arrow struck the blond in the eye. His sword slid from his hand and his body fell backwards against the first rank, sliding down along their shields, pressing against their legs, the war helmet rolling sideways from the head. In that moment, Pelayo stepped alone from the forest.

His appearance checked those ranks which had half-moved as if to charge. Calmly he stepped into the little stream and crossed it. His strung bow he still carried in his hand. He walked towards them, a tall brown warrior with a red beard in plaits and an undrawn sword. He had not stopped to retrieve his shield. Timing was everything and the timing had not permitted it. Any javelin from those ranks could bring him down. Would his own men understand? Any movement on their part now would be his death. Would they accept his gamble? Would their nerve hold?

Just beyond spear point he stopped, meeting their eyes as his own swept along their front.

"I am Pelayo—chief among the Goths. Welcome to the mountains, soldiers."

For a moment, there was no response. Then the black-bearded one stepped forward. He drove his sword into the earth at Pelayo's feet and extended his bloody right arm.

"And I am Huneric, your man by Christ and his saints."

Surprise and relief made the man want to laugh. He did not but a broad smile spread across his face as he stood there with his arm out. Pelayo took the arm and then drew him forward, dropping the bow, to embrace him in a great bear-hug. One by one, the men in the ranks behind them drove their swords into the ground and lowered their shields. From the forest and the scrub, shouts and whoops filled the air in a crazy crescendo as the unbearable tension was broken. Pelayo's men raced into the clearing to hug and pound on the backs those whom they had just been prepared to kill.

Chapter IX

For almost two weeks after what came to be called by everyone "the battle of the chiefs" Pelayo was intent on preparing his force. A war band now it was, if not an army, and its size acted to reinforce the confidence of every member of it. No longer did they need to make a real effort of the will to see themselves as something more than fugitives or brigands. Clearly they were a fighting force and the bearing of each of them reflected their enhanced sense of importance.

The newest and best-armed group, that of the "battle of the chiefs," Pelayo kept for his own division. He had conquered them singlehanded and all appreciated the justice of that arrangement. At the same time it increased his distance from, and his bargaining power with, Fruela and Masona. He kept Huneric too as a second in command of his division and treated him casually as their near equal so as to emphasize his own general command. Euric, increasingly distant from his old subordination to Fruela and conscious of his independent command, was devoted to Pelayo and that too reinforced his authority.

During those weeks nine more Goths were gathered up on the trails and recruited. Three of them even found their own way into the camp. These last three told Pelayo that they had been directed to the camp by shepherds whom they had chanced upon. Pelayo did not press the point but he knew that Fruela and Masona understood then something of the utility of his argument that the hill people must not be plundered of their subsistence. He was able then to increase the size of their divisions to a dozen men apiece enlarging, at the same time, their importance and the effectiveness of the whole band.

The provisions which Huneric's men had brought with them for their punitive expedition filled out their own supplies so that the problem of food was put off for a time. Still, everyone knew that the respite was temporary. No caravan was likely now to carry foodstuffs in sufficient quantity to feed a war band of almost sixty men for more than a few days. In addition, the sending of such a party as Huneric's into the hills argued a growing consciousness of, and trepidation about, their presence. There might be precious few more caravans even attempting the passage.

Pelayo was aware of this unsolved problem and others besides. The pay chest, which he had claimed as his own, proved to contain a hundred gold bezants. It was treasure enough to arouse the cupidity of any of them even though it was presently useless to their way of life. The boy, Sunna, too continued to be not quite a hostage and not yet a warrior. He avoided Pelayo and the others with the exception of Euric and the old woman, Anna, both of whom treated him more as a child than as a man. Finally, there was the spirit of the entire band. Now that they had begun to think of themselves as great warriors, some object had to be found that they would regard as worthy of their attention. Otherwise that fine glow would fade and they would again question their purpose and his leadership, and would become a quarrelsome mob of Goths. In mid-July it was still too early in the campaigning season to strike out north. Besides, there was no word on Tarik's whereabouts and if his force had continued west it would be ahead of them out there, an army which could roll over them without effort. It was better to wait but he needed some plan of action which would hold them together till late August seemed closer.

As always he tried out his plan first on the little council before taking it to a general council of all the warriors. He called together Fruela and Masona, Euric and Huneric by night over the dwindling stock of wine. After the usual talk about the abilities and peculiarities of certain men and about the general state of their weapons and especially the remaining stores of arrows, Pelayo broached the subject.

"The food is getting as short as the wine and it's still a long way from the end of August."

They looked at him curiously but no one ventured a comment. All but Huneric had argued over this ground before and were reluctant to repeat the quarrel. Huneric would not take the initiative.

"We don't know where Tarik is, Masona. Was there any talk of his swinging west?"

"No talk that I heard in the wine shops, Pelayo. But I think he will. I think he'll have to. Even with an army the size of his he can't go too far towards Frankland when the chiefs of the northern plain are still unbeaten. He has a few garrisons in the strategic spots but they can't hold down the whole of the Goths. My estimate is that he'll swing around to the west while they're still debating and, at some point or other, sweep from there south. He'll bag most of them and leave some more garrisons before coming back through Segovia or Ávila to Toledo for the winter."

"So we wait him out," stuck in Fruela. "We stay out of his way and figure on picking up the pieces, however it turns out."

"You're turning into a regular general, Fruela," said Pelayo smiling. "Do you think that we're capable of anything that big?"

"Two weeks ago I'd have laughed at the idea," said the swarthy warrior. "But now, with all the gods on our side, we might do it. Anyway, won't the bastards be surprised to see us try it?"

Pelayo returned to Masona. "You say that Tarik will come

back through the mountains by Segovia or Ávila. Which is the most likely?"

"That depends on how big a bite he wants to take—or maybe can take. He can't have a lot of supplies and he has a big army to feed off the land. He may meet a good bit of resistance or the chiefs may all cave in. There's no way to estimate it and we don't have any news. If it goes the same as last summer, he could march across the whole north and march back through Ávila without even working up a sweat. My guess is that it will go just that way."

"What if Musa marches north from Mérida and joins him at Salamanca?" asked Euric in his quiet fashion.

"Then, my old campaigning friend, you'd better find a priest before fall and confess all the time you've spent on that white-skinned boy of yours," laughed Fruela slapping his thigh, "because we'll, the rest of us, all be in hell before the rains come." He took a long drink of wine and coughed over it, shaking with amusement.

"Musa can't come north. He plans to camp around Mérida and could be there all summer from what I hear. There's a real fight in the making there and he may face a long siege even if he wins in the field." Huneric made his first contribution to the council.

"So some of the Goths got their manhood back," Fruela said, turning sarcastic.

"Some of the others, Fruela," Pelayo broke in. "In any event, Masona, Tarik would hardly get to Ávila for a month yet, even if he chose that route?"

"Probably not."

"And Ávila had a garrison of only about fifty men you said?"

"About that, although there were a dozen or so more who didn't live through the winter. They may have gotten reinforcements though since I left Salamanca."

"Not very likely," mused Pelayo, "if there is to be major fighting in the south and Tarik wants to break the back of the northern chiefs. Why strengthen a garrison that nobody has threatened if you have better things to do? I think we'll march on Ávila."

Fruela brightened at the words, "All hell will break loose at that." He obviously enjoyed the prospect. "What do we want with Ávila though? We can't hold the town."

"We wipe out the garrison. It will give our warriors a taste of a real victory and some practice for the fall," responded Pelayo. "We'll pick a market day for the attack so that we can carry off enough provisions to feed us for three or four weeks until we're ready to march north. Besides, the garrison will have a store of weapons, and arrows especially, which we will need badly. And if there are slaves at the market we can recruit some more fighters," he finished, smiling over this last at Masona.

The one-eyed warrior was thoughtful. He spoke with a slight frown as he mechanically whetted his knife against a small oilstone. "Ávila is fortified in the Roman style. It could be a costly victory."

"If we don't take them off-guard, yes. But they won't be expecting an attack from us or anyone else. There haven't been any so far. The Africans will be fat and soft after eight months of town life. They know that Tarik is out to the north on the plains keeping everyone occupied. They think of us, if they think of us at all, as mere hill bandits, caravan robbers. And we'll take them on the morning of a market day when the south gate, at least, will be open. That's where the live-stock market is held, on the slope between the bridge and the gate. I've passed through the place on my way to Toledo."

"Fruela and I know it too," put in Euric. "We could make a drawing of the streets and gates so that all of us will know the problems."

"What about the Romans?" asked Masona. "You haven't wanted to involve them up till now but you can't charge through a market without splitting skulls."

"The peasants understand that all right, Masona," Pelayo

returned. "But it's different from systematic plundering and they know that too. Even if they don't like it, they'll know that the town was our target. They don't waste any love on the town dwellers and they'll have some pickings before we withdraw, you can be sure. As far as the merchants and townsmen go, they're already our enemies. They have to be as long as they do business with the Africans."

"How soon do we march?" asked Masona, and Fruela, who had been frowning at him, broke into a happy grin.

"Tomorrow night. We'll march at night only. We can't take any chances on the Africans being warned. Two nights should get us there and we can leave a third night to get into position. Every man has his equipment checked tomorrow and Fruela and Euric will make a dirt-drawing of the town and the country outside it so that everyone knows what they're doing and what everyone else is doing too. We leave the sick here with old Anna. There are saplings enough around Ávila so that we can make the scaling ladders there the night before. Now let's decide on our best tactics before we have to convince the warriors."

Long after the council had ended Pelayo sat before the dying embers of the little fire. Its coals swelled into red, died into a blue glow, and sank to a gray ash, before bursting softly into red once more. The man watched the play of its advance and retreat, half occupied by it, half distracted by it.

Fruela had been right. All hell would break loose. Their attack on Ávila would change everything. No longer could it be a matter of mere killing. An attempt on even such a sleepy little backcountry town would mean a declaration of war. The Arabs would read it so in a minute. To that kind of a direct challenge to their shaky hold on the land they would respond, sooner or later, with all the force they could muster.

And what could he do after Ávila—if the attack carried home? Break for Galicia with all his men as soon as the Africans began to pull back to winter quarters in the fall? The estates of his father there might still not have gone all to seed.

The valleys of the northwest, almost islands among the forest and mountain, were prime campaigning country for a smaller force. But would his father's old retainers rally to him? Would the magnates of the valleys accept his lead or would they cut his throat and sell his head to Tarik?

My blood is noble. That's an advantage. If it was not royal—well, by this time Rodrigo must be dead. No one had had news of him and a king is not easy to hide. Witiza's sons had good claim but they had tainted it by throwing in with the Arabs. If there was to be any resistance, if the running was to stop somewhere, sometime, who could say this is the place. This is the time.

Shuffling out the last of the embers, Pelayo thought grimly "I can say it, dammit. I can say it once, dammit, and they can kill me for it if they can."

Three nights later, the leaders lay at the edge of a hill. Below them the ground sloped down gently to a small river and then rose just as gradually to the south gate of Ávila. On the slope across the river cookfires glowed in the night and the moonlight that shone on the small, deserted Roman temple behind them was bright enough for them to make out tents and occasional figures. The breeze carried the lowing of cattle and the bleating of sheep up to them. The size of the market to be held in the morning promised well for their plans.

"There's your target, Euric," Pelayo whispered to the grizzled veteran beside him. "Take your men down the river to the south to cross and then bring them back to the cover of that copse before morning. Stay in it deep enough so that the animals can't get your scent. Remember in the morning to make it appear that you are intent only on a cattle raid. Strike only after the gate is opened if possible. We want the whole garrison awake and ready to come out. There will be three or four of them down by the bridge by then inspecting carts. Don't try to kill them all but get a couple and then keep up a covering fire on the wall and gate. Begin to cut out the cattle and drive them into the woods. If the gate commander sends out men after you, fight from the edge of the wood and then fall back slowly. Don't lose contact if you can help it but keep your division together and don't let them catch or surround you.

"Masona, keep your division in the valley behind this hill. Be careful not to let the country folk coming in to the market see you. And you'll be up here yourself in beggar's rags. Remember to wait out Euric's attack and don't send in your men unless the garrison is out in numbers double to Euric's command and is driving into the woods. Ignore the gate and try to cut them off and finish them before they can get back to the gate. If they're too quick or they commit more men to your rear, retreat slowly towards the river and try to connect your flank to Euric's. Make them come to you and try to form a line on the other side of the river but don't let them get behind you.

"If they don't take Euric's bait at all but just close the gate, give them a little time and then march your men down the road and across the bridge. Act like a covering force while Euric's men drive off cattle, sheep, slaves—anything that's loose. Make it hard for the Africans to sit still and watch but don't be so aggressive that you give them pause. Don't attempt an assault on the walls unless Fruela and I are so close on the inside that you can hear us shouting for you."

The five of them took a final look at the town of Ávila, illuminated by the bright moonlight and an occasional fire or lamp from the houses. The houses themselves were packed closely within the small, square circuit of the walls. Along the eastern and western walls they regularly backed up against the wall itself with their roofs not much more than a man's height below the inner parapet. The two streets of the town ran north and south in rough parallel. The main one entered a central square where a small church squatted close by a large building that they guessed would be the headquarters and arsenal of the garrison. A cross street, hardly more than a path, led out east and west from the square to old Roman gates on those sides, long-since blocked up to make defense easier and now chiefly distinguished from the rest of the walls only by the low towers just over them. It was too large a town, small as it was, for fifty men or so to defend against a determined enemy but an active commander would have hired locals, Goths probably, as mercenaries for guard and wall duty. They would know in the morning.

The five of them scrabbled back from the brow of the rise and rejoined the war band. While they ate, the other four rehearsed again the plan of battle with their own divisions. Pelayo himself sought out the boy, Sunna, and drew him off to a little distance. There was time for talk before the moon set and they could start the business of cautiously taking up their positions for the morning.

"Euric is going to need your help tomorrow, boy. Your division is the goat, the lion-bait. Every man in it will have to be tough and nimble if anyone is going to live out the first hour."

The boy didn't respond and Pelayo could feel his anger rising quickly. He could, he reflected, take Sunna with his force and despatch him quietly during the night march with a sudden knife thrust. To do it here would set everyone on edge and might make Euric worthless for tomorrow. Christ, the kid was toughened enough from the past month to be able to handle himself! What was in his head that made him flinch when the battle-yell went up?

Sunna watched his chief tensely. He could see his anger. "You promised to kill me yourself if I didn't fight?"

Pelayo ignored the question. "Were you blooded in the last fight?"

The boy answered slowly and very quietly. "I hit the scout who was wounded and screaming. I think that I helped to kill him."

Pelayo paused, relaxing a little, and finally sat on a large stone, "That was different, huh? You didn't like to hear all that screaming?"

Sunna had remained standing and now he shifted uneasily. "I've heard it before. The Berber was as good as dead anyway." And after a long pause, he continued with a kind of dogged desperation, "I don't want to kill anyone."

"Sit down, boy!"

Sunna obeyed and Pelayo fixed him with his eyes, holding his gaze. The boy looked back steadily, frightened but without flinching. It seemed to Pelayo that the youth was probably not simply a coward. It was exasperating.

"Do you think that anyone is going to give you a choice? We won't. Do you think that the Africans will? If you ever get back to your father, the Count, will he give you that choice? You were born a Goth, a noble. You were born to fight."

Again Sunna declined to answer. He stared at the bow across his knees.

"Look, boy, before the Africans came your father might have protected you, humored you. You might have been a priest." There was a flicker of movement in the boy's face. "You might have liked that? Maybe you would have been a monk, a scholar? Well, there's no room in the world for that now. The Africans don't need Christian priests or monks, or scholars either. They have a different god.

"By Christ, boy, do you know what your choices are? Even if I'd let you go, your father will only need you to fight with him or to help him toady to the Africans. If you won't do the one, would you like to do the other? Or you may be dead, or a slave. Or would you like to run away to the hills and become a farmer?"

The last came out sardonically and the boy, despite himself, half-smiled momentarily at the incongruity of the idea. Pelayo saw it and was encouraged.

"I don't want to kill anybody, that's all," said Sunna, "You do. You like it. For some reason, I don't know what, you hate the Africans. You want to kill them all. But I don't hate them."

Pelayo was impressed by the boy's courage. He set himself up in opposition to his own chief even though he sensed his own life was in danger.

"Yes, Sunna, by God, I hate them. I don't just enjoy killing them either, killing them is the whole reason to my life. You couldn't understand that. But nobody has another choice but the peasants. You kill them or they kill you, these Africans. Or you become their slaves, or their servants, or you try to run away. I tried to run away once, Sunna, it didn't work. They came after me. They....I had to fight. I have to hate. So will you."

He hadn't meant to say that last about running away. The boy had caught it and looked at him curiously. Damn! Now he would have to kill him. No one else must hear that. A hint of that would weaken their obedience. Masona, Fruela, they would wonder. Euric might understand. Wala, maybe. Who else? This boy?

Pelayo continued to talk to Sunna but he knew what he was doing. In reality his words were now addressed more to himself. He was justifying the thing he had to do, would do soon now.

"It's not so much, boy, this killing a man. Everyone dies anyway. The longer you live, the older you get. The older you get, the sicker you get. Your wind goes, your stomach goes, your eyes go, even. You drag around. You can't fight, you can't make love, you can't eat, you can't even see. Women treat you with contempt, priests fight for your inheritance, and in the end, the worms get your carcass.

"It's better if the end is quick. If the Africans kill me, then they deserve to win. But they've taken my home, my king, my people. So long as I can, I'll kill them for it, and I like doing it. I want to see them tremble, I want to see their stupid, stupefied faces at the sight of their own blood running out on the ground.

"Can't you understand that, boy? Have you ever felt the battle anger?"

He had touched the boy, somewhere, somehow. He did not quite understand what it was that he had said that had touched a chord. But the boy was not with him, he was appraising him in some quiet fashion, appraising him with some sympathy but not without a reserve that kept its own counsel. Wearily he thought to himself that Sunna was dangerous. He knew too much, or guessed it. He wouldn't fight. He might make a useful hostage except that now his knowledge made him dangerous to his captor.

Pelayo had resolved to kill him when he became aware of Euric's presence. How long the veteran had listened he couldn't know. He did know, from the look on the old warrior's face, that he could not take the boy with him tonight. He would have to chance everyone's being too busy this night for talk. Perhaps the boy would be killed tomorrow. Perhaps he himself would be killed tomorrow and it would no longer matter. Or, if the boy didn't fight, he would certainly have Fruela execute him promptly after the battle as a coward.

"Keep Sunna with you, Euric. He's your responsibility. See to it."

Pelayo rose abruptly and moved away, leaving the veteran and the boy wondering and troubled behind him in the growing dark.

Chapter X

Among the grapevines, the damp of night had begun to burn off. The morning sun played on the large, soft leaves and the slowly ripening fruit. Pelayo watched a ground spider move his long, delicate legs along the glossy surface of those globes in a hunt for mites too small for anyone but the quiet predator himself to see. Fruela lay, facing him, a few feet away. Their men were scattered similarly, parallel to the vines, along the gently terraced vineyard with the four rough scaling ladders which they had lashed together in the night beside them.

The sun had been up for three hours, or a little better. There was only intermittent movement on the walls towards which the ground rose irregularly. The infrequent arrival of country folk at the north gate, around the corner of the wall to their right, was far enough away to make any danger of their detection slight. The owner of the small vineyard and his slave worked among the vines, tying and pinching off sickly shoots, sweating more from fear than from the faint heat. They had been shortly warned on their arrival, not long after sun-up, that they would be spared so long as they raised no alarm but they were confused and terrified by their novel predicament and the strain had increased by leaps and bounds over the past two hours.

Now they started, looking up, as suddenly a drum began to beat rapidly from within the walls. The sound grew in volume and tempo and Pelayo warned the nearest of them in a curt whisper. They stood fast but open-mouthed, forgetting even the pretense of work, looking towards the wall, where a bustle of activity was suddenly noticeable. Fruela saw two half-torsos appear above the parapet, one man dark and clearly an African, the other a Goth, fair and running to fat. They stood, likely, on a firing step and surveyed the countryside in slow sweeps. Perceiving nothing after long minutes, they fell into animated conversation. The African motioned along the walls to the left and right with his arms, and the Goth nodded continuously. The import of the pantomine was obvious to the watchers among the grapes. Then both men abruptly disappeared. For long minutes, the men in the vineyard lay silent and still. Within the town the drumbeat continued its rapid stacatto and periodically heads appeared above the wall hastily glancing over the farmlands below. They saw nothing but the slow, regular movement of oxen in the distance and a scattering of farmers in their fields, confused by the unfamiliar sound of the drums.

Pelayo nodded to Fruela. The garrison commander had had enough time to decide that the attack was from the south only and perhaps to draw off some of the men from this wall. In any event, he would have dispatched some of his slender reserve to that area by now. Fruela's command rose at his signal and raced towards the wall with two of the scaling ladders. When they had covered a third of the distance, Pelayo and five of his men followed them, bows at the ready. The leading men were halfway there when a head appeared, started, and raised a hasty shout on the ramparts. Pelayo and his group pounded on for yet a little distance and then stopped. There was no cover but they trained their bows, searching for a target along that section of the wall, close to the north corner, which had been selected for Fruela's assault. Arrows now began to fall among the latter's men but already they were close enough in to make it necessary for the defenders to expose themselves to get a clear shot. In a moment they were there, straining to find a steady purchase for the upper ends of their ladders against the stones.

Pelayo turned and raised his shield. The remainder of his division broke from the vines, heading with the other two ladders for a point two-thirds of the distance down the wall between the north corner and the old, filled-in eastern gate. Directly above Fruela, whose massive body obscured the ladder up which he was now climbing with furious rapidity, a defender appeared with a stone three times the size of a man's head. Pelayo, waiting, put an arrow into the man's neck just where it joined his chest. The stone and man toppled backwards. Around Pelayo his men fired rapidly now as the defenders showed themselves in their desperation to get a shot at the climbers on the two ladders.

For an instant, Fruela was poised at the top of the ladder, fending off a spear from his left with his shield, while his sword arm beat steadily against the sword and shield of another opponent. Then, by main force, he was over and driving against the man on his right who tripped under that enormous force and went down while his other enemy dropped his javelin, cursing from the sudden appearance of an arrow in his biceps. One of Fruela's men came over the top while another jostled close behind. Fruela's great bull-voice raised the cry.

"Victory and King Rodrigo!"

The little clump of defenders around the head of the second ladder stumbled backwards as two of Fruela's men lunged towards them. Pelayo turned just as the top of a ladder further down the wall passed the vertical and the uppermost man on it plummeted heavily to the ground, the others sliding down it in awkward haste. At the head of another ladder, Huneric was fending off, with his sword, the pole of a defender who sought a purchase against the ladder on which he stood.

"To our own ladders," shouted Pelayo. The six rushed, at an angle, along the wall, fitting and firing arrows as they came. The other ladder was being raised again. Along the wall, Fruela and a companion were holding a small group of men at the north corner immobilized with their bellowing cries of "Victory! Victory!" His remaining seven men were trotting down the wall towards the assault point of Pelayo's command as their opponents leapt to the rooftops below to escape them.

"King Rodrigo! King Rodrigo!" they screamed.

"Rodrigo and victory! Rodrigo and victory!" came the rejoinder from Pelayo's men.

Uncertain and unnerved, the defenders broke. Huneric's men swarmed up the two ladders. Pelayo and his five reached the top only seconds after them.

"Clear the north wall, Fruela," he bawled. In minutes, Fruela and his force had turned the north corner, driving the confused defenders before them, and then scrambling down the gate stairs to overwhelm the little force of Africans who made a stand there.

Pelayo could see that the greater part of those who had held the walls had been Goths. The vigor and audacity of the attack and the raising of the battle cry in the king's name had broken their resistance. Those whom Fruela had pushed along the north wall before him had been the first to turn their swords against the Berbers at that gate, raising the cry "Rodrigo and victory" themselves. The momentum had to be kept, increased.

He led Huneric, and the other eleven men surviving to him, along the wall. The roofs were deserted. At the old east gate, they rushed down into the cross street. Fruela would be pushing from the north towards the square. As Pelayo entered the square unopposed, he swept the scene. The little church was crowded with refugees. In front of the arsenal perhaps as many as twenty Berbers were drawn up in fairly good order. Their leader, an Arab, was shouting at almost the same number of Goths who had fallen back from the walls and backed themselves sullenly and raggedly against the church portico. "Fire at the Africans," Pelayo instructed his five bowmen, while the other eight of them hastily formed a shield wall. "Rodrigo!" yelled Pelayo and crashed his sword across his shield. "Rodrigo!" the others took up the chant beating rhythmically on their shields as they slowly advanced towards the Africans.

"Rodrigo! Rodrigo!" A few voices among the Goths by the church portico hesitantly took up the cry. "Victory! Victory!" bawled Fruela bursting into the square from the north at the head of fifteen men.

The Arab cried a string of commands rapidly to his Berbers and they retreated into the head of the main street leading towards the south gate, some of them falling to the arrows as they went. Ignoring the Goths by the church, Pelayo led his men along its other side into the parallel street to the south. Fruela pushed across the square in pursuit of the Africans, his numbers swelling again as some of the Gothic mercenaries broke to join him.

At the south gate Pelayo's and Fruela's men met again. Ahead of them the garrison's commander led a dozen remaining men down the slope towards a line of battle almost at the river line. Pelayo could see the figure of Masona, sword flashing in the center of his line of veterans. "Rodrigo Rodrigo!" Pelayo took his men down the slope, bearing towards the stone bridge. Fruela and his command, if it could still be called that, angled down between the woodline and the gate. The defenders retreated now, where they could, from Euric and Masona's men. Good arrow shots were everywhere among their constricting numbers. Others cut off, surrounded, disappeared beneath lance thrusts and sword blows from two sides. Some threw down their weapons only to be butchered as they pleaded to surrender. A final group of nearly twenty under their commander retreated, trapped beside the bridge in the shallows of the stream. Outnumbered, outmaneuvered, they died to a man, there in the shallows, before the final attack of Pelayo's reunited war band.

Their blood colored the sandy pools and they fell amidst the green slime of the stagnant waters. It was over then.

Pelayo stepped up from the streambed to the low bank where Fruela sat panting and grinning. The warrior looked like an obscene Bacchus—the blood from a deep cut on the left side of his face matting his short beard and dripping from its ends. His sword arm was thoroughly covered with blood and splashes of gore dried slowly on his harness and chest. "Victory," he croaked between deep gasps that filled his chest cavern.

Just up the bank Masona was wearily thrusting his sword over and over in the spongy black earth of the river bank to cleanse it. Yet higher on the slope Pelayo could see Huneric seated, his back against the wall by the south gate of the town, and those whom Pelayo had left with him sprawled about him. Wala and one or two of the other archers had already begun, slowly, to gather up stray arrows.

Almost at the line of the woods, on the river bank where Masona and Euric's forces had just managed to link up a half-hour ago, Pelayo could see the boy, Sunna, standing motionless over a body. Mechanically, the chieftain sheathed his sword. Euric! As he walked woodenly towards the boy, his eyes surveyed the scene, the ground. The boy's quiver was empty. His face was absolutely desolate, empty and drawn, and tears flowed down it in silence. The old veteran lay facedownwards, his eyes staring. A little bald spot shone in the morning sun and his back was slightly humped over whatever weapon it was that had killed him.

Instinctively, Pelayo placed his arm across the boy's shoulder. Sunna bore the weight for a moment, almost yielded to it, then straightened and stiffened his back. He half-turned and walked down into the river. There he stepped into a pool that rose just past his knees and began to wash. Pelayo watched. Behind him a sheep bleated, A single, small puff of cloud hung in the light blue of the sky. God! In the town some of the women had begun a shrill, high wailing.

They stayed in the town that night. The day had been spent in seeing to the wounded. They had lost eighteen men in the assault, most of them in Euric and Masona's commands, and two of the badly wounded died in their sleep. They searched the town too, finding a considerable store of weapons and arrows to supplement what they took that was usable from the bodies of the dead. Some of the country folk, who returned timidly to see to their possessions, Pelayo had set to work to bury his dead and then encamped them on the same slope that they had occupied the night before.

At nightfall they closed the gates of the town and the victors fell upon the food stores of the garrison. They gorged themselves, delighting in the taste of the rich food as they proved to themselves over and over that they had indeed survived. With the ample stocks of wine which they discovered, they drank themselves into stupefaction, dropping off into exhaustion one by one. Strangely, few of them felt any appetite for the women of the town. Those who did simply took them and there was scarcely a murmur of protest. Even after the moon had set, the cowed population kept uneasily to their houses and managed some snatches of sleep while their conquerors snored or occasionally sat up to retch and then reclined again.

Pelayo had eaten and drunk with the rest but, as the wine-sickness had begun to come on him, he had felt a strange distance taking hold of him and he left the group. He inspected the quarters of the Arab commander with disinterest. He was vaguely uncomfortable within the thick walls. Finally he sat down on the portico of the little church and wrapped himself in his cloak. There he watched the sleeping figures in the little square and the play of the moonlight, after the fires had burned down. They're all dead men, he thought. The entire town was dead. Maybe the whole world. He felt that. He felt absolutely alone. It did not frighten him nor did he feel any loneliness or sorrow. He wished that his cloak were not so coarse so that he would feel nothing at all. Eventually, he slept too.

The council was held the next morning, shortly before noon, in the little square. The afternoon would be taken up with the preparations for departure. They would return to the mountains by night marches to make pursuit difficult. Each command would travel separately but, even so, the cattle and livestock which they would drive before them must leave a trail which nature would only slowly cover. Everyone had to be clear as to their duties, especially the new warriors. It would take time and the mood was foul. Those who were not stiff with wounds were still half-sick from the wine. Even those who felt neither of these suffered from the depression that followed on the excitement of battle.

The necessities of the situation had aroused Pelayo from the strangeness of the night and he knew their need for ceremony. He sat on a chair on the church portico with his captains standing behind him. They were all there. His war band, the Gothic mercenaries of the garrison, the townspeople, the peasants who had come back, they gathered, each to themselves.

The Gothic mercenaries were, some of them, at ease. They had fought with strangers, eaten and drunk with them. Others, who had simply left their weapons and stood aside in the events of yesterday, were not so sure. Pelayo could see their fat captain who had commanded on the walls shifting uneasily. One by one, on the advice or at the request of his captains, Pelayo assigned them to his various divisions. When it was over his troop was a dozen men stronger than it had been before the attack and only the fat Goth stood alone before Pelayo.

"You commanded under the Arab?" he asked the man.

"I did—for the money, lord. We all did. None of us liked it—liked them. But they were masters in the land."

"A Goth chooses his leader. Your men chose you, another Goth. You chose the Africans."

Pelayo turned to Wala whom he had made the captain of the archers, Euric's division. "Have him guarded, Wala." Pelayo watched the fat man shrivel—he seemed to wrinkle-up and age before his eyes. The man's face went gray but, to his credit, he did not speak or beg.

He now turned to the peasants. "We have no quarrel with you. You came to market, as farmers must. Some were killed. That is too bad but men die like the seasons come and go. But if a farmer loses his money for seed, or tools or wine, that is worse. We need the animals that we have taken but if any of you can show that they are yours. We will pay you for them."

There was a stir in the square and townsmen and peasants alike looked at him, disbelieving what they had heard.

"We will pay you from the fines that we will collect from the people of this town who have deserted their king and served the Africans. Those among you who have lost property will speak to my Captain Masona here who is both wise and just. He will see that you are satisfied—if you speak the truth."

A couple of the peasants smiled now. They understood this kind of generosity better. Pelayo had earlier told Masona what he intended and what was to be done. The property of the little church was not to be touched unless it were in the hands of a layman. The poorer of the townspeople should be ignored. The peasants should be repaid, when they seemed to have a real claim, out of the property of the wealthier.

"This town," Pelayo now addressed the townsmen, "has deserted its king and his law in time of war. It has received a garrison of Africans. You all know the law of the land. What you have done is treason under it. For this reason, and under the law, the town will be punished.

"But we will be merciful, too. As warriors of the king, we have no time for your money or your women. We are fining you in food and wine to the extent that we require them. Remember that the Africans would have eaten more! We fine you for the losses that these poor farmers have suffered because you sheltered the enemy. That is just.

"Above and beyond this, as rebels, we declare that your slaves are freed. Those of your slaves who are Romans are free to leave and they may take with them their clothes, tools, a single animal and the food they can carry. Those of them as may be Goths will join our war band."

Actually this latter had already been largely done. During the morning Masona had questioned those of the town who were Goths and were of an age to be militarily useful. Some nine men had been summarily liberated and incorporated into the various commands, most of them going to fill up the depleted ranks of the archers who had suffered the most on the previous day. Nevertheless, the announcement caused a stir and a townsman of about fifty years stepped forward. He was lean and graying, with a certain self-importance about him.

"With your permission, lord?"

Pelayo eyed him. "What do you want?"

"What you have said is true—but you have not said it all, lord. We received the African garrison but we could not do otherwise. We are not warriors here and there were too many. Resistance was impossible."

"Resistance can begin with a single man."

"That is so, lord, but the Africans were everywhere. No one else was fighting. King Rodrigo was dead, killed in battle."

"Some of you saw his body?"

"No, lord, but we have had word. All the towns have. The Arab showed us the letter of the queen when it was brought through the town. It supported his authority as military governor and ordered our obedience to him. We acted within the law, lord. Humble townsfolk do not dispute with the queen."

The man thought that he had made a point and scarcely repressed a smirk. He was stubborn, if frightened, and obviously of some intelligence and learning. Pelayo was beginning to take some savage enjoyment in his opposition.

"You speak of Queen Egilona?"

"Yes, lord."

"King Witiza's widow, now claiming to be queen mother for Agila, Witiza's son?"

"Yes, lord."

"But the Goths chose Rodrigo king, not Agila. No one but the Africans and Egilona chose Agila as their king."

The man was silent. Pelayo shouted at him now. "The queen sleeps with the African Leader, Musa. And when he's worn out he says that Agila may be king—to please her and amuse himself. Is that how the king of the Goths is chosen? At the begging of an old whore?"

The other gestured helplessly, "Can simple people dispute such things, lord?"

"What of you then?" said Pelayo. "You have some importance here. Have you been a judge?"

"Yes, lord." The reply was just audible.

"You have been a judge! You know the law. You have caused these poor people to desert their king. You led them into treason, persuaded them."

The man read Pelayo's narrowed eyes, saw a hatred in them that he had not noted before. He knew that he was lost. This great, red-haired, bloody barbarian was going to kill him. Soldiers, he thought, that's all they know. Aloud he said slowly, "I did then only what I do now, lord. I try to guide the people."

"And if you misguide them, yours is the responsibility then? You, then, advised them to give their allegiance to Egilona and Agila?"

No answer. Pelayo motioned to Wala. "Put him with the other." Wala drew the man over towards the fat captain of the mercenaries. They made a funny couple there under guard. The fat man looked more like the merchant and the tall, lean one the soldier. Pelayo knew it was the best time.

"Ávila will keep its leaders," he said to the people, "and will get back its garrison too, every one of them. Before we leave tonight, the head of every African will be on your walls, at their posts—on a stake. And so will be the heads of these two traitors. You will leave them there until they rot and the birds strip them dry. Anyone who removes even one of them will forfeit their life. This too is just. The council is ended."

Pelayo rose and left the portico. Fruela would see to the orders. The townspeople were crushed and his own men wondered about the grisly business—but it would be done. And his band would know who they were, would know that they had defied the conquerors. Rodrigo lived so long as Pelayo said he did and the Goths were still a people thereby. It had to be that way.

Chapter XI

August was long and blazing hot, even in the mountains, and the men's appetites fell off. That stretched provisions. Fortunately there were no fires but the ground was baked and hard where the sun touched it and the shrubs and vines hung limp and faded for the lack of moisture. Only the lizards were at home in the land, full of unwonted activity, as the heat prompted their slow, cold bodies into peculiar, darting haste. Other game was scarce and thin and stringy in the pot.

But if no one was fat, no one was sick either. Everyone in the force was hard and brown as the Africans themselves and might have been taken for them except for their hair colors and the character of their armor and weapons. Their tempers were bad, thoroughly foul from the unending round of day upon day of unrelenting, uninterrupted heat.

They were, all of them, hungry and bored. They were ready to move. It was no longer possible to drill them for they were as near perfect as warriors get and they knew it. They would not be practiced. It was too damn hot for games. Pelayo and the captains were grateful for that angry mood for the enterprise was desperate.

There had been no pursuit from Ávila. The land was asleep under the unbroken heatwave, unparalleled in memory. The mountains had received them back, swallowed them up. Only shepherds moved among the hills, their gray-brown flocks raising the dust as the fat animals stripped the dry shrubs of the hillsides and stirred the clear, rocky streams into sudden mud.

They took but one small, poor caravan trying to sneak north and rounded up some fifteen more Goths, tired, lean and hard like themselves, drifting north in little, dispirited bunches. Each of the three divisions of swordsmen now numbered twenty men, all of them steel-capped and breastplated. The remaining thirty-odd men of the archer's division had swords and shields too, as well as two full arrow-quivers apiece. They would need them all thought Pelayo grimly as he turned the plan in his mind once more.

On the road to Salamanca, Teudemiro thought twenty times a day of the cool mountain pines they had left behind them. He was barefoot for his sandal strap had broken and it was worn too thin for repair. He had carried the other one, tied to his belt, a full days march before it came to annoy him with its flapping and he threw it away. He would get a couple of pairs off dead Africans at Salamanca.

His feet ground over the rough road where the wind had swept dust and pebbles across its Roman stone surface. It had been better when they marched at night the first two days on leaving camp. But then no one had been able to sleep very well in the inferno that was the day. We lay around gasping like fish on the beach, he thought. This marching by morning and evening is better. We make better time and at least a man can sleep at night.

It may be that the Africans will be warned of our coming but I haven't seen any scouts. The peasants don't even seem curious about us, it's so hot. Pelayo gave orders that we should seize any horses or donkeys so that nobody would be able to ride ahead and warn them. Jesus, these people are so poor that they haven't any horses. Pelayo paid them for the few mangy donkeys that we took. Crazy son of a bitch!

No, that's not it. He's smart enough. Smart and hard. Terrible even. He scares me. He liked seeing all those chopped-off heads at Ávila. But he loves the Romans though.

No Roman blood in him for sure. Maybe he likes their women. Likes brown skin better than white.

Teudemiro lost himself in fantasies about the women at Salamanca. He'd gotten drunk too fast in Ávila—and in the morning there had been no time. Well, Salamanca was bigger. There would be full-breasted, soft-bellied women enough there. It was more exciting just taking it than paying for it. As many as a conqueror wanted and nobody daring to refuse.

Christ! He shifted his shield irritably away from the spot it had been chafing. He liked the weight of it though. Why haven't I gotten a command? Everybody else who was in at the beginning had. Even that old fart, Euric, before he'd caught it. I killed three of them at Ávila even before it turned into a hog-sticking. And I'm still just one of Fruela's swordsmen. Old big-chest will last forever.

Wala has a command, even if it is just over the archers. And he's part Roman. Probably some Goth's bastard but he leads men and a fullblooded Goth like me still takes orders. I'll show them dammit, I'll show them at Salamanca. They'll see what I can do in a real fight. Somebody's going to get killed there. Maybe old one-eye, Masona. I'll ask for his men. They better not refuse me then.

Lost in his reflections, Teudemiro walked right into the man in front of him. The soldier glared at him wearily and a couple of others laughed. They laughed at him a lot—but wait till Salamanca. The whole band had stopped and ahead Pelayo was talking with the captains.

"You understand, Wala, that it has to look like a peasant rising. Get as many of them together as you can, two hundred wouldn't be too many. Be sure that they understand that they really won't have to fight and it won't be too hard. Give them a coin apiece and it'll be easy. Burn a couple of fields to make it look good. There's sure to be somebody they hate. And have one of your men carry the warning to the African governor if you don't find a peasant that you're positive you can trust.

"You should have enough men. In any case, I can't spare you more than the dozen and I think they're the ones that look most like Romans anyway. Make sure their weapons are well hidden when you begin the march on the town. Maybe in a couple of carts, under the scaling ladders. Just don't look too formidable in case they have spies out. We want them to come out and to come out expecting a romp.

"If you start tomorrow morning, you should be able to get a big enough mob together by dark. The following morning remember to start late and march slowly. I want them to see your dust a long way off. Burn some huts along the way. Make it look good. Once they do come out, I'll send one of your men back to warn you. Tell the peasants to go home and bring up your men as fast as you can. If anyone gets by us, try to pick them off. God knows where Tarik is by now and we don't want any survivors to tell him where we are."

Wala had listened to all of this impassively. Now, at its finish, he broke into a broad smile which ended in a little laugh.

"I can do it, Pelayo. These people will trust me. They can see my grandmother's blood in my face." His dark eyes glinted and he swung his little troop off towards the river. They moved at a half-trot and soon far outdistanced the main body whom Pelayo had directed off the road behind them. He wanted to be far enough behind them when they crossed the river so that any chance observer on the other shore would report the movement of only a handful of men. They themselves would cross after dark.

Two mornings later they sat among the trees gnawing at the pieces of smoked meat that old Anna had distributed. "We'll have better than this leather to eat tonight, old woman," said Fruela.

She looked at the swarthy Goth and bowed a little. The excitement and a little rest had refreshed her after the long march. "You may be so much meat yourself by noontime, braggart!"

"Even if they do come out, Pelayo," Masona continued his interrupted worrying, "there are a lot of things they can do. A smart leader could draw his forces back off that bridge quicker than we could cross the river to stop it. There's room to fight on the slope between it and the wall on the other side. We'd be downhill and he'd have cover from archers on the wall and gate."

"Yes, we'll have to trap them on the bridge. If they have a chance to pull back, there's no sense in trying to go after them. We've been over this before. In that case, we'll just have to march north hoping they'll worry enough about the peasants to let us get clear. That's why everyone's first target is their horses."

"Maybe the Goths in the city will rise," added Fruela. "Remember Ávila. Old King Rodrigo was worth fifty men to us there."

"We'll try it again," responded Pelayo, the memory bringing a faint smile. "But if they know about that, and they probably do, they'll have been more careful. At best, it would give us more time. Then too, they can't follow us too far from the city. They're the garrison."

"They would track us with a scouting force," said Huneric. "They could hang on like dogs to a bull and wait for us to run into Tarik's army up north. It's a big plain and no cover."

"But if we do it, we eat in Salamanca tonight." It was Fruela. His battle-blood was up. "Think of the wine. Think of the women. Never think about losing, it's bad luck. I'll wager that you were worrying when you lost that eye, Masona. You just get behind them and drive them into my arms. I'll see that they don't get off the bridge at my end."

"You had better start, Masona." It was Pelayo. "Keep your men behind the ridge and try not to raise any dust. You're sure that you can cross the river quickly?"

"I'm sure, Pelayo. I waded the spot myself last night with a stick. Damn near drowned a couple of times but it will be easier in daylight. The summer's been so hot that the water level is almost down to spit."

"Well, make sure while you're crossing that the men keep their arms well covered. If they spot you from the bridge and guess your purpose, the game is over before it's well begun. Move out now. With luck we'll meet in the middle of the bridge."

Pelayo listened as Masona's men disappeared back among the trees. They were good. No clinking of armor, nothing.

Hours they waited. While they watched the breakfast fires in the city sent up wisps of smoke into the pale, blue sky. It would be a hot day for fighting. Almost hot enough to dry up the thin, cold mist that gathered along one's spine in the last minutes before the joining. Funny how fighting was like making love. All anticipation and then it was over before you knew it. No, he thought. Not with a wife. With a woman you loved there was time for play before the surge of heat. A time to talk, a time to laugh, a time to be tender first—and afterwards. Memory came of her. It was always there, behind his thoughts. Now it came up hard and sudden. He stiffened himself against the unexpected onslaught. As always, the fighting-back produced in him a cold, calculating rage. He liked that better because he could direct it. It served him well.

Fruela nudged him. "There's been smoke in the sky behind us for an hour now, Pelayo. Wala must have set half the houses in the province to burning. They'll have to come out soon if they don't smell a trick."

"Any time now, Fruela, any time now. Their commander will want lots of daylight to slaughter the peasants. Time to burn the rest of their huts. Time to kill the captives slowly. Time to play games with their women."

Fruela could hear the deep hatred in his voice. He was startled as it always startled him. As always, Fruela was angry at himself. The current of fear that Pelayo's rages started in him! The bastard was so unpredictable! And, once again, he was right. Across the river, the gate was opening.

Well, now Pelayo would have a target for his madness. Someone else. As a warrior, the thought pleased the massively built captain. The blood began to sing in his head and the tendons of his legs drew taut. He flexed unconsciously and rhythmically as he watched.

It was a big column. There must be two hundred or two hundred fifty of them as they issued from the gate. He counted forty horsemen. They expected nothing, for Christ's sake! No scouts. At least not yet. They swung onto the bridge with the horsemen in front like it was a goddamned parade. They'd deploy on this side, of course, but the bastards were never going to make it. We have a little surprise for you. It was good. With the mounted men in front, even if they saw Masona's men crossing upstream and smelled a trap, their impulse would be to come on. Otherwise they'd have to ride down their own men on that narrow bridge.

Pelayo watched the leisurely advance with satisfaction. The shock of surprise produced half the victory. He could see Masona's men drifting across the river in the distance but they didn't seem to notice on the bridge. The leader was past the halfway mark now. A proud man who sat his horse with studied grace. A little closer now...they saw something. The horsemen reined in and looked upstream towards Masona's men who had gained the far bank. It was time.

"Huneric! Masona! At them!"

His two captains broke from the trees at the words. Their divisions followed them, running silently, but feeling the pressure to shout build with the pumping of their hearts. On the bridge, it was the footmen who noticed them first. The horsemen's attention was still drawn by Masona but the column behind them had been waiting with the distracted boredom of all soldiers. Now their shouts alerted the African leader. He reacted like a wounded cat. The sword came out, his arm went up. Leaning parallel to his horse's neck he raced for the end of the bridge towards the two armored columns converging now towards its mouth.

The swiftness and decisiveness of the African captain's actions took even his own men by surprise. Five of the mounted men, those closest to him, had acted almost in concert with him and galloped hard upon his rear. But the rest of the mounted men only now set themselves in motion and the footsoldiers were still at a halt.

Pelayo sprang from the tree-line. "Rodrigo!" The remainder of the archer's division loped into the open after him, a long, curving thin line, the ends of it arching towards the river at each end. "Rodrigo! Rodrigo!" Ahead of them, Huneric's and Fruela's columns roared the battle cry, finding in it sudden release.

The African commander and his five rode clear of the bridge. Their momentum carried them beyond the divisions of Huneric and Fruela, who reached the bridge-mouth almost simultaneously with their passage. Clearly, they would have wheeled-up behind them but the further appearance of Pelayo's archers now caused them to slacken their pace in uncertainty.

"The bridge! The bridge!" shouted Pelayo. The rest of the mounted Africans were bearing down on the steel wall across its mouth. A flight of arrows followed his command and two of the lead horses went down followed by others which had no room to avoid them, slipping and sliding on the stones as they tried to jump them. Their speed reduced, they crashed into the double rank of spearmen at the bridge's end. It bent and swayed. It broke momentarily. Three of them fought through and clear. But it reformed and closed.

"The riders! The riders!" commanded Pelayo. Disconcerted, the African commander chose wrongly. If he had wheeled his men against the rear of the tiny force holding the bridge he might have crushed it against the confused mass of tangled horsemen now confronting it. But he chose to go after the archers.

Pelayo made for him. The center of the archer's line fired with cool desperation. Two horses were down! Three? Kneeling, Pelayo drew his bow full and released the string. The arrow struck clean at the base of the horse's neck. Its forefeet failed suddenly. The African pitched over its head, landing on his sword arm. Pelayo could hear the crack of it as he sprang up. The man had no shield. Pelayo killed him with a backhand stroke as the African was rising, unsteadily, from the dirt.

Ignoring the screaming horse, Pelayo surveyed the scene. Four of the Africans had ridden clear of the archers. The rest were dead or dying. As he watched, one of his men tried a long shot at the four who had paused, looking for their commander. The arrow caught a horse in the shoulder and the beast pitched. Its rider slipped off it and climbed up behind one of his fellows. That decided them. Four men on three horses, they galloped for the ridgeline and disappeared.

"Shoot the bridge!" yelled Pelayo. "Shoot the bridge!" Back there a weaving mass of men and beasts contended: the riders urging their snorting animals forward against the thin line of Fruela and Huneric, the horsemen themselves pressed forward by the footsoldiers massed at their rear, and the armored men weaving back and forth under the advance as they thrust savagely back with spears at the horsemen's legs and loins, at the unprotected chests and necks of the horses. The dozen or so archers left to Pelayo now began a systematic advance on that straining plug, first firing over the heads of their own into the easy bunch of targets, then running forward some paces while fitting another arrow and firing again.

Suddenly the battle turned. The rearmost of the mounted Africans turned their mounts. Bowling over, slashing the footmen behind them, they tried to fight clear of that packed humanity. The leading horsemen, slipping and sliding on the bloody stones fell one by one to Pelayo's warriors who now could move freely as the sheer weight of numbers on them eased. The African foot divided too. Some, mostly towards the rear and not yet even blooded except for the rough passage of their own horse and an occasional arrow, broke and ran after their own retreating leaders. The other footmen, most of them, tried to join the fight with the quickly perishing horses. The remainder of those horses and riders hampered their efforts until the last of them had fallen. Even after that, their lighter weapons and largely unprotected bodies made equal struggle difficult. They, despite their still superior numbers, could bring no more weapons to bear than Pelayo's two divisions who still stretched from side to side of the stone causeway. The sheer weight of numbers might have told if it had not been for Pelayo's archers who continued to find largely helpless targets. Most of the enemy foot had bows too but there was little chance in those confined quarters to use them. They were leaderless. They were stopped. They wanted to break free and near panic caused a heedless, hapless advance against their nearest foes. And the rain of arrows continued.

Then they broke. Advance was impossible. The bridge stretched out endlessly towards the far shore behind them. Panic gripped those who were not yet themselves face-to-face with the enemy. Turning, they ran back from the bridge's end with long, loping strides. They ran without even looking back as warriors will who know death is at their very heels. They kept just ahead of the knives that their minds could feel at their backs.

Pelayo found Fruela. The swarthy warrior's great barrel-chest was heaving to long-searing breaths. Wondrously, there was not a cut on the man but he was half-dead from exertion and drenched in gore.

"After them! Keep after them, Fruela! Huneric! Get your men down the bridge. It's working. Don't let them get their wits. Don't let them get range with their bows. Close up on them. When they start trying to surrender, take some of them. Save me maybe thirty. I have an idea."

Unable to speak, his breath coming in long sobs, Fruela made a gesture obscene enough to match the glint in his dark eyes. Huneric had already started half-trotting and half-shuf-fling forward. Fruela stumbled after him and what was left of their divisions followed him, panting and cursing, as breath became available.

Pelayo's archers were fresh and almost unhurt. He led them forward now alongside the stone bridge piers in the warm water of late August. It was shallow and stinking. The algae clung to the stones in ropes of green slime. On either side of the bridge, they advanced. Despite the slippery stones, they easily outdistanced their tired fellows above. Only in a few places was there enough water for a man to flounder for a moment. As they reached the farther quarter of the bridge, men were already beginning to drop from its sides.

"Rodrigo! Rodrigo!" The archers had breath enough to raise the cry again. Swiftly they moved with spear or bow against the dazed Africans dropping from the bridge sides. Before they could find their footing they were met first by a mortal enemy. Then, as they came in quicker numbers, deadly little fights developed everywhere and the shallow pools pinked with the dead.

Pelayo killed four as they stood to jump, or as they hung from the stone parapet, or as they tried to rise from the drop, before he had anything like hand-to-hand combat. Even the fifth, a skinny Berber, could not find sure footing and wound up scuttling desperately backwards in the shallows, like an overturned turtle, till Pelayo's short javelin found him. Then no one else jumped. Around the bridge piers, some thirty-six men lay dead or dying. Six of them were Pelayo's.

Masona and his division had stopped the other end. Though they were only a single division of twenty men and without the support of archers, the foe they fought was already once defeated. Moreover, the remaining horsemen, in their flight across the bridge had so distanced one another that when they reached Masona's men they did so almost singly. Grasping the situation immediately Masona had placed his men in a loose V so that the first riders had a

narrowing gauntlet to run. By the time the last of the horsemen had reached the trap four horses were down kicking and
screaming in the center of it. Seven riders lay among or near
them. Three horses had passed the bridge mouth but no rider
had—or would. They were all dead before the first of the foot,
in near total disorder, could arrive. Masona moved his men
out on the bridge beyond the carnage. Then he began a slow,
steady advance onto the bridge so as to limit the impetus of
the advancing enemy and to shorten the interlude in which
they could use their bows—those who retained so much
presence of mind. The pressure against his troop gradually
built up and forced them to a halt. The place where they
halted quickly became a butcher shop of thrusting, straining
men still upright and gasping, and moaning men inert under-
foot—a scramble of tendon and intestine, blood and bone, all
speedily dead.

Still a third shock had to be withstood as the last of the
footsoldiers, repulsed by Fruela and Masona's men, streamed
up to enter the fray. They were desperate to escape and at
first Masona's men were forced back, pace by pace. It lasted
a few minutes more until Fruela and Huneric came limping
up at their rear followed by their bloody veterans. Then, the
jumping from the bridge began in earnest. Hardly seconds
later the remaining Africans began to beg for quarter, throwing down their arms. A score more died, defenseless, before
Huneric could stop Fruela's men or his own in obedience to
Pelayo's orders. Scarcely three dozen of the Africans survived but their numbers were almost equal to those of
Pelayo's band who had fought at the bridge.

"Get them up to the wall. Next to the gate." Pelayo and his
remaining handful of archers had scrambled up the river
bank to the bridge-mouth. Roughly, the prisoners were
forced up the gradual slope at swordpoint. Next to the massive Roman gate they were herded together against the wall.
There was no sign from within. Not an arrow had been fired

or a shout raised. In silence, the gate sat closed in the afternoon sun.

"Rodrigo! Rodri-go! Rodri-go! Rodri-go!" they set up the steady, even, menacing chant. No sound indicated that they were heard within. But still no arrows, no stones. "Rodrigo! Rodri-go! Rodrigo!"

"Rodrigo! Rodri-go!" The chant was picked up from the far shore. There Wala's men had broken over the ridgeline. He had done well. He had more than doubled his force somewhere and now it moved down to the opposite bank. Some of them guided a cart loaded with ladders. Systematically, as it trundled across the bridge, Wala's men began to dispatch the enemy wounded. "Rodri-go! Rodri-go!" The two chants met and mingled. The bands joined before the gate.

"Rodrigo! Rodrigo!" The shout was raised from the wall above. There were other shouts—and screams. Abruptly, a body fell from the wall above. It struck a few paces from the base of the wall. Pelayo looked at the writhing thing, its back broken. It was a Berber lad of about fifteen. Teudemiro cut his throat. In a minute the gates swung open. Three Goths stood there beckoning, lightly armed and bloody.

Chapter XII

Pelayo and Fruela made for the old forum where they knew that whatever government had been set up would be found. Pelayo had given the necessary orders during the march. No quarter was to be given to any Africans found within the town. Their women, whether Goth or Roman or Arab, were to be the spoils of the victors. Beyond that, the native population was not to be molested. He had confidence that, for now at least, his surviving veterans and their new Gothic allies of the garrison would have sufficient to occupy them. The Africans whose surrender had been accepted on the bridge had been slaughtered as soon as the town gate had been opened. Pelayo had spared them only long enough to give the impression to its defenders that quarter would be given.

As they suspected, the small provincial square showed them a tiny, rundown basilica built of the native, yellow stone. No one opposed their passage. Within, it seemed as empty as without. Then, as they hesitated, a tall Arab appeared in the doorway of a small chamber, converted to living quarters, on the right ahead of them. He was muscular, but not armed. His two arms he held stretched out before him, empty and palms up. After his first appearance, he made no further move. He was tensed, poised, but not visibly frightened. Still, his every action thus far had been designed to show them that he was defenseless.

"You will be Pelayo, chieftain of the Goths." The Arab

spoke, matter-of-factly, addressing himself to the tall, red-haired warrior. Fruela stopped almost in mid-pace, knife at the ready, but unsure now in his original purpose to dispatch the man without further ceremony. The blackbeard glanced towards his chief. Pelayo too was dumbfounded. Wondering how to reply to the astounding greeting, he found no words at all.

"I am Yusuf al Rahman," the Arab went on, "civil governor of the conquered district of Salamanca. Or, until this moment, I have so been."

The words roused Fruela and he started forward again. His intent was evident. "Fruela!" A tone of warning in Pelayo's voice halted the warrior.

"I will deal with this one myself—alone."

The burly black beard flushed with anger as he always did at that note. Still, he remained motionless while he protested. "The agreement still holds. No talk with the Africans. No treaties, no deals, just death."

"I know our rules. I made them. But I am chief and I will talk with this one. I said alone! Make sure the town is secure. Then bring the other chiefs here. Wala too. We'll need a council quickly now. Get them!"

Fruela hesitated a moment longer. Then with an oath he made not the slightest attempt to conceal, he turned and went out.

"Sit down on your hands and cross your legs." Pelayo addressed himself to the African.

The man did as he was told, silently, without protest. His eyes never left Pelayo. The latter glanced about the empty chamber. There was no sound but his own breathing and that of the man sitting motionless before him. On the hot air, shouts mingled with an occasional high scream filtered through the thick walls of the basilica. Somewhere, someone was ringing a bell, irregularly, by fits and starts. Somebody found some wine, he thought. Again, as at Ávila, he had this strange feeling of standing in the midst of a world that didn't touch him. An unreal world! The town was his. But he had no part of it. In the cool interior of the building, he was afraid. Afraid of this unarmed man who so unexpectedly had known his name.

"I am Pelayo, chieftain of the Goths. How is it that you know me, African?"

"I know a great deal about you, warrior. Until today you were one of my problems. Now it appears, I am one of yours."

"You are no problem to me, African. Except to decide how and when you die."

His own words sounded hollow and hoarse to Pelayo. He wondered if the man believed them. He, himself, did not.

"In the past few months you have killed many men. Most of them, unlike me, warriors and armed, expecting trouble. You have closed the passes of the mountains to the merchants and their goods."

"So you know that. You know then about Ávila and its garrison?"

Again Pelayo launched an implicit threat. Again it rang in his own ears false and uncertain.

"Yes, I do. You had a victory at Ávila, And again here today. I watched from the walls. It was a well-conceived plan, a surprise."

The man spoke softly, deprecatingly, though still without fear so far as Pelayo could detect. Gentle and humiliated as he was, the African knew somehow that he had the advantage. It was Pelayo who asked the questions. Bit by bit, he was supplying some answers. So far, not the ones Pelayo wanted—needed. The man, seated awkwardly there, was fighting for his life.

"But the day of surprises is almost over, captain. Surely you must know that. And your men are too few—even if you lead them very well. As you have." The last came softly—to ease the blow.

"There are two Goths in this land for every African, Arab

or Berber! And your Berber troops don't love you Arabs very much."

"It is true, warrior, that the Berbers do not love us much. But they are of the faith. They will fight the infidel before they will a fellow Muslim. As for your Goths, their leaders are dead or have made their peace with us. Most of them are satisfied that nothing can go back. Rodrigo's kingdom is dead."

"I can raise them. You saw today how long the Goths will support you. Out of your garrison here I will have as many men as I lost on the bridge. And the news will spread!"

"The news is spreading already. The horsemen who escaped today will carry it to Tarik in the north. He doesn't have to raise an army, captain. He has one. Five thousand men he has. With what will you fight him five days from now. Or ten days, even ?"

Pelayo was silent because he had no answer. He had only a hint of what he was going to do himself. He had only a desperate gamble and a hate that drove him. The cold hatred that possessed him gave him the battle plan and the battle lust. But he was tired now and despite himself his sword arm quivered. The weakness he felt was not so much the aftermath of combat as it was the result of this man's easy confidence that nothing much had happened.

Yusuf recognized the silence as his only chance for life. He took his advantage in haste, speaking to the giant Goth by name.

"Pelayo, the war is lost. The news you speak of, like the news before it, will travel to Córdoba, and across the straits to Africa, and along the sands to Alexandria of Egypt, across the Sinai to Allah's city, the sacred city of Mecca, over the smooth sea to Damascus of Syria—and from there men will hear of it in Babylon of the Persians. All of these lands are subject to my lord, Pelayo. Allah has given all of them to him as he has given him the kingdom of the Goths. There is no man who can resist the commander of the faithful, my lord.

"And this kingdom of God, this kingdom God has given to the Arabs is all of a piece, Pelayo. Everywhere faithful, everywhere obedient, everywhere one. That is why it is indestructible. The faithful are of one mind in the possession of what Allah has given them. To you, it is like a great web. You have seen the spiderweb. Touch the outermost part of it, and the movement runs unerringly to the center, vibrates in every part. Nothing that touches it escapes. The greater the struggle, the more sure the response."

"And that is how you knew of me?" Despite Pelayo, the words of his need escaped him.

The seated man softly nursed his gain. "That is how, Pelayo. You closed the mountains to the merchants for a summer. Your men are disciplined. The Roman shepherds did not betray you. We first could put a name to you when we questioned a Roman, a merchant he called himself, with too many donkeys and too few slaves."

Pelayo remembered the man, the wily Felix of their second ambuscade. Doubtless, he had made as good a bargain for this information as he had when he traded for his life in the hills.

"It was a great achievement with a beaten people, warrior. But you have seen it done before by people you would have called—bandits." He hesitated over the word. "But Tarik had much to do to secure this land. And the end of summer would have finished you. You needed this victory. Without it your war band would have broken up. Besides, you could not feed them through the winter in the mountains. And you would never have had the chance. Within the next month I was promised six hundred men to beat the mountains for you. Six hundred men, warrior!"

"There would have been some great fights!" The words were bravado and Pelayo knew it and hated the knowledge. The man was right. He was beginning to see himself as a bandit, a caravan robber and the thought was sour in his mind. The impassive, sitting man seemed taller. He felt dizzy, drained.

Yusuf appeared not to notice. He was careful not to rub the soldier's desperation. He spoke quietly, cajolingly. "The Caliph has need of great captains, Pelayo. Allah has work for them. What has been done in war, has been done in war. It can be closed as simply as that. There will be a place for great captains in this land whether they choose to rule or whether they choose to fight. You are such a captain. Men follow you. You have secured a place for yourself today. And for your men too."

"And I should become a Muslim?"

"It would be easier for you if you did. Some of your chiefs have, as you may know. Others have not, at least not yet. Some of them do not yet see that what has happened in our day is the work of God. But they will see it. They will come to believe. As you will, if you live. Allah has proved himself in the invincible might of his faithful. Surely you see that?"

Again Pelayo had no reply for the African.

"You and your people are not idolators. You follow the one God. It is only the Prophet you do not know. It is not so hard. Twice before your people have changed their belief. Each time for the better. Now this last will be the best."

The man's words were overpowering, fateful. For the first time in months, Pelayo came to feel as he had in Toledo. How long ago! The despair, the hopelessness, that had unmanned him then came flooding back. The Africans knew everything. His own identity, the history of his people, everything. They were everywhere and the land was theirs except for this desperate little island he and his men had won for the moment. It would sink as surely as a stone in water, in a pond, and the waters would close over and, as the ripples died, it would be as if he had never been. As if none of it had happened.

Instinctively, he drew a great breath—as if he were drowning. Stubbornly, assertively, he struck back in the only fashion that seemed open.

"I do not believe in God, yours or mine!"

"One is wise not to believe in the gods," Yusuf replied quietly. "Their time is done, finished. If they had been gods, instead of clay or stone idols, Allah would not have prevailed over them. To see their unreality is the beginning of wisdom, Pelayo. If you now feel abandoned, betrayed, it is only because your eyes are but partially opened. It is like the last of the night, when the moon sleeps and the stars are hidden, but the sun has not yet risen to give warmth to the world. Should a man wake then, he feels old. He fears that his seed is wasted and his life poured out on the sand like water, wasted, running to no end, lost in the desert. It is a bad time.

"But if we wait, Pelayo, if we wait and hold our souls in our two hands strongly, as a man should, the sun rises. And we see that there is purpose. We see that all creation lies in God's hands. That he has not forgotten us. And then we live again, Pelayo. Food has savor again—and the body of woman. And one's seed finds a place in the great chain of life and service that Allah has ordained. There is again a life to be lived, a land to be ruled in justice, and battles to be fought against those whose dreams have no issue and whose thoughts are far from God's."

Yusuf's words were such that Pelayo felt the movement of his own heart. The man knew the blackness that he felt, that he tasted. He could not speak so, now, unless he had. Perhaps, in some small measure he felt it now. Seated there, tense, at the edge of death, he was struggling himself toward a confidence he could portray, present, but not wholly possess. For the first moment in their encounter, Pelayo felt himself to be an equal to his foe, perhaps even superior, for his own sword was cold iron in his hand. Yusuf wielded only an idea, a dream which could end with his life itself. Pelayo liked him for their partnership in despair. It made the other human understandable.

"Every empire has had its day, African. Because yours has reached its noonday, perhaps, you think that your God, your life is different from the others. That's a child's dream! No child thinks that he will grow old. No boy ever lived but that thought he would avoid his father's mistakes. And everyone of us grows old. Every one of us stumbles. Bit by bit, piece by piece, we lose that fine conviction. Every morning we wake up a little stiffer, a little colder, less alive. Finally we are meat for the crones to dress. Your god will not change that!"

"I will die, Pelayo, here or elsewhere. But don't turn your face from God. Man's life is a little thing and a big thing still. I know that the Greeks had a word to speak, and they ruled until they forgot its meaning. The Romans had a word to speak, and so they ruled until they were so stuffed with food that they could no longer say it. But these were partial words. They were words mirrored in a mirror of a mirror. Reflections which are gone now! The final word of Allah has been spoken to the Arabs and the world will hear it! All the world will hear it, and will be better for the hearing, and will learn from the word. What you see, Pelayo, is not a new beginning. It is an end, a flower to a thousand beginnings. A single end to so many beginnings and their pain! Think on it!"

Like a solid blow to the chest, the words thrust Pelayo back. His sympathy vanished. Once again he was afraid of this captive unarmed man. By Christ, there must be no blood left in his fingers by now! And he speaks like a deacon! He really believes what he says! How do I fight that—him...them? A profound sadness settled on him. He felt as he had when they made him a warrior. The loss, the farewell to all the joy he had known, was there. But this time without the pride of a new estate. Everything was backwards. He had been a warrior, sure of his place, but now he was becoming a child again! To grow up in a new world! What would they teach him? What would they expect him to learn?

"Tell me," he said dully, "what we might expect."

"No great change, Pelayo."

Yusuf had reasoned on this path before. Great warriors were all cowards in the face of little changes. Kingdoms might vanish and cities burn—but a change of diet utterly unnerved them. A change of clothing style made them anxious as girls that someone would laugh at them. Like getting a frightened idiot over a mountain pass, it was a weary business and dangerous if one was not alert. But he had done it a dozen times in the months just past. So it was that justice and order replaced the sword in a land. However unprofitable it seemed, it was Allah's work. Still, before, the sword was usually his to command.

"This city is yours by right of conquest, Pelayo. There is no garrison now but your command. As civil governor, I could continue as before. The merchant caravans will come and go as they did before you stopped them. The country people will bring their produce to the old market. Their taxes will support us both, as before. The churches will remain open as they have till now. We have taken one for our reading of the Koran and prayers, but no more.

"In our lifetimes, no more than that. A few new taxes will be imposed. Some villas in the country will change hands—to feed you and I. There will be little else but that. Musa, who will govern now in Spain, understands that it must be so and I have his ear. You will find me a powerful friend. I can ease all this and it is my duty to do so. You may even find that you have other friends already in the government. But, by myself, I could arrange it all."

The last was said with just a tinge of pride as well as calm assurance. Pelayo was not sure he could believe all of it. Yet what he knew, what captives in the hills had told him, bore much of this talk out. He was tempted—weary and uncertain—if stubborn in the embers of his hatred for them. Perhaps there was no other way. Still, out of that hatred, he threw up more defenses.

"What of my men? They are sworn to the death against your kind, African. They may not follow me in this."

"If they are your men, Pelayo, they will follow you. Have they not till now—in all your plans—even though they never understood your dreams? If they are like most men, they will follow their bellies. Even warriors like a show of arms more than the use of them. A soft post, sure pay, and a leader they respect—this is what you would offer them. They will follow."

Again, Pelayo found himself agreeing though he fought to hide it. Fruela might object. And Teudemiro would follow Fruela's lead, stupidly, as he always did. But Masona, Huneric, Wala—they all would support his decision. Even if old Euric were still alive, he would have seen the point of it. No one fights forever. The boy, Sunna, would rejoice at the end of war. Pelayo wondered, momentarily, that he should even consider the kid.

It would be manageable alright. None of them had ever believed him fully. They all thought, when they dared, that he was crazy, mad even. Early in the mornings, before battle, he half agreed himself. And he was their chief. Once over the immediate change, they would follow him because it was the grain of their life to do so. If they had never ventured into a world more than a few months—years—distant, he could then pledge them to a whole new world that they would never see—and unseeing, would accept. Such they were and he despised them for it.

Fruela would object because the muscle-bound fool lived to make trouble. He resented Pelayo's leadership as he had doubtless resented every leader he had ever had. But he was not a thinker. He could be killed. Teudemiro too. Who would care? Pelayo was weary of them both—of coping with their petty ambitions.

"Would it be so easy then?" he heard himself asking of his captive.

"Easy? Yes—by comparison with what you have done today. And today's achievements are the foundation for it! Easy? Yes—by comparison with what you have done the past few months in the hills. And today's chance is the merest recognition of what you have done. Of what, perhaps, you alone could have done. Your people and ours both appreciate greatness, Pelayo."

Yusuf praised him freely now. He knows that he has me, Pelayo thought bitterly. He reads me for vain—or maybe a little stupid. He has ambitions to manage me, this African does. But these thoughts were quickly wiped from his mind as he began to thrill with wave after wave of horror as the African continued.

"There is only one thing difficult—so you must do it quickly. If I know the greatness of your spirit, even that will not be difficult. Wealth is the prize of mean spirits and no purpose of yours. But you must give up the treasure. Musa will demand that. He has to."

"Treasure?"

The word was a croak, a whisper. Pelayo seemed to have said it by swallowing his breath. Yusuf knew that he had lost. The madman was going to kill him. But why? Why? Not for gold and stones!

The man's sword arm was trembling, moving. Yusuf rocked to one side and slid his legs out from under himself in a single motion. His numbed hands sought frantically to give him leverage to roll away from the arching blade. Hopeless! He could not prevent himself from raising his left arm against the descending steel. He was as much an animal as this Goth. His paralyzed hand hung strangely at the end of it. He felt nothing but the force of the blade as it bit angularly across bicep and shoulder, blocked by the length of bone it found.

He knows! The thought exploded in Pelayo's brain. He knows it all! My brother! The church! He knows me for a coward too! They all know it!

Pain—and shame—and horror—they all rolled over him in a suffocating, choking wave. He did not decide to kill Yusuf. He just killed him. The anger, the fury, the loathing that gripped him made decision unnecessary. He saw the African move, thrust away. He saw the sword bite skin and tendon. The bluish bare bone glinted briefly, as in a butcher shop. Then the blood came in a flood. The arm dropped and he struck again at the back, severing three ribs from backbone. As if to see the carnage, the head began to turn. He struck directly at it. The skull gave and bits of bone and brain mixed before his eyes. The body dropped—twitching. Again and again he struck at it. Each blow the product of a new urgency.

Gash upon gash he opened up. Blood spattered everywhere. So long as the twitching remained—and after—he struck and struck again. Awkwardly, without science, without purpose, it went on.

Finally, exhausted, he was done. The thing upon the stones—a mangled, broken bag of guts and bones. The face, marked in its own crimson, comprehended nothing, felt nothing. No African now! No questions! No thoughts! Just wreckage.

Pelayo gasped at breath. He stood stupidly still, holding the bloody sword, and fought for air. Quietly the rage drained from him leaving—nothing—nothing except a despair so intense that he was sure he was dying. A great emptiness rattled about his head and a huge weight constricted his heart. He would die now! The thought came dully and unresisted. Something between a sob and a groan escaped him. They knew! And he? He remembered! Oh God!

Chapter XIII

"**I** knew that you must kill him."

The words came throatily in the silence. Pelayo's head jerked up. There in the entranceway to the small side-chamber stood a blond woman nearly as tall as himself.

"Pelayo!"

He forced himself to concentrate—remember the voice. His vacant eyes squinted in the effort to focus.

"Pelayo!"

His sister! His sister Amalsuntha. Looking regally beautiful in a soft white tunic. The way our father used to love.

All the time she had been here. She heard everything. Saw everything. What did she know? How much could she have understood?

"He had me brought up from Córdoba. I was a hostage to be used in dealing with you. He was anxious to know as much about you as he could."

The words tumbled out of the tall woman who was having difficulty keeping her composure. She could not bring herself to name Yusuf. That mangled cadaver lapped in its own blood—that was no longer Yusuf. Would he kill her too? Jesus, he looked like a madman. What did he suspect her of? He had never been very bright. Nor had he ever liked her very much. What could he suspect her of?

"Pelayo! Don't you know me?"

Motionless until now, she struck a pose from her girlhood,

half-turning the upper part of her body, fluffing out her long hair.

"Am I a stranger in only two years? Have you rescued a strange woman?"

Pelayo caught the brittle falsity in her voice. She was frightened of him! She was afraid he might kill her! As always, the bitch was acting, playing a little part for the men. How much did she know? What had she heard? Seen?

As across a void, he surveyed her. Trapped and terrified, still she managed an appearance of arrogance unconsciously and assumed a role out of carefully schooled habit. But her voice vibrated too widely in its husky way and her pale blue eyes were not averted now. They moved nervously over him and away.

"Pelayo!"

The others had arrived. Fruela and Masona walked with Huneric between them, supporting him loosely. Huneric's left arm ended shortly before it should have boasted a wrist. The stump was wrapped in bloody, browning rags bound with a blackened leather thong. The captain's eyes were bright and the pallor beneath his tanned face made him look yellow and old. The bones of his face seemed to stand out roughly, like old Anna's who padded behind the three, mumbling cautions. Wala was almost beside her and, as Pelayo looked, Teudemiro entered uncertainly.

"Christ's blood, Pelayo, you really did for him! It looks like a rabbit a bobcat's been at!"

All of the newcomers had stopped short. The carnage of war they were used to but the shredded carcass on the floor—there was not one of them but knew the cause. Again, as always, the strange, unsummoned rages of their chief disturbed them, left them awed and shaken. And as always too, Fruela was the first to react against it. He had spoken to deny its spell on him and to throw it off.

Pelayo ignored him. He would never explain the body on the floor. He spoke heavily, with an effort.

"This is my sister, Amalsuntha. The Africans took her as a hostage. They wanted information about me—about us."

Even as he said it, Pelayo wondered which of them would believe it. Not one of them likely. He didn't believe it himself. But they might not know that she had gone south, to Africa with Witiza's court. She had chosen the winning side the same calculating way she chose the winner's bed. The bitch had hardly waited until their father was buried before making her peace with his murderers. How did she like the Africans? By now she knew them well enough, he'd bet. Hostage? Whore!

Fruela's eyes were on her. A well set up bitch. Taller than him. But that always made it fun. Small breasts—but pointed and high. Long legs on hips like a girl. Blond too. She'd make a night camp lively if he didn't have to fight half the war band for her. She wouldn't make much of a fuss about it he guessed. But Pelayo would. His sister! The redhead's eyes were on him, he discovered. Despite himself, he felt a touch of cold. He grinned defiantly and shook his great head.

"My sister will go with us. Anna, find a house for her and stay with her. She is not to go out for anything—nor are you."

The old woman cackled a little excitedly. It was like the old days. To be a great lady's maid—the prospect warmed her like wine. She had quite forgotten Huneric and his missing hand.

Amalsuntha stiffened. She had not been afraid since the others had come in. Poor brother! He was much too confused to kill her now. Probably without meaning to, he had already associated her with his leadership. But he had not spoken even a single word to her. Now he consigned her like an ass's parcel. Well, a little at a time with men. With a small inclination of her head to Pelayo, she walked after Anna without appearing to notice the gory body, while walking around it. Save for Pelayo, the entire group watched her leave. A great victory first, then a bloody murder, and now a blond princess.

None of them understood in the least what was happening to them. They were suddenly afraid to be jubilant.

"What do you want, Teudemiro?"

Pelayo's question was savage in its intonation. His numbness was wearing off, leaving an immense, bitter hopelessness in its wake. The stupid youth was an easy target.

Teudemiro gaped. Why did he never know what to say? What could he say?

"I told him to come along, Pelayo."

It was Fruela. So the warrior wanted to lead again. Pelayo looked at the brawny captain with hatred clear, for the first time, upon his face.

"Why?"

The word stung like a whip. Fruela would not answer it but rather his eyes moved to Huneric. Pelayo's eyes followed but everyone kept their gaze upon their terrible chief.

"Are you going to die, Huneric?"

The question was brutal. The warrior's answer came in a whisper.

"Not while the wine lasts, Pelayo."

"Then we have our captains all here! Get out, Teudemiro."

The last came as an afterthought, crushing in its simplicity. The bewildered youth almost ran from the building.

"So now we will have our council. In there."

Pelayo preceded them into the small chamber from which Yusuf, and Amalsuntha in turn, had earlier emerged. The others followed. It was furnished simply enough. Two leather chests, a single chair, a table with some document rolls on them. The script was Arabic. A low couch against one wall. Hostage hell, thought Pelayo.

Huneric seated himself heavily on the couch, cradling his left arm on his lap. His face was grayish-white. The pain ran in irregular waves up and down.

"Can any one of you read those?" Pelayo indicated the document rolls with a finger.

They looked at one another briefly. Fruela answered.

"My guess is that by now there's not a person in Salamanca who can. Those who could are all dead. Unless your sister can!"

The last was put maliciously. Fruela looked evenly at his chief for a moment before dropping his eyes.

"She was never a student, Fruela. Maybe we can find someone later. For now, what is our strength?"

"Our own men, less than forty, and some of those will die. Then there are about a dozen half-breed farmers that Wala found somewhere. The Goths of the garrison number close to seventy—more than us."

"Do they have a commander of their own?" asked Pelayo.

"They did. He was killed in the fighting in the town." Fruela grinned widely and thrust his right thumb towards the ground. "They'll follow us."

"You can get us another twenty or thirty Goths, can't you Masona?" Pelayo turned towards the one-eyed captain.

"That many. Maybe more. It's a big town and soldier's work is scarce for Goths. But Wala says that they didn't see those Africans who escaped at the bridge, Pelayo."

"No, Pelayo," said the dark little captain of the archers, "Unless the farmers got them they're on their way to Tarik. Four men on three horses, Masona tells me. They are half-way to Tarik by now. They could reach him by tomorrow night if he is still up in Galicia and if they ride the horses to death."

The chieftain remembered Yusuf's words. He could see the web. It stretched around them in every direction. They would be caught. It was hopeless. It had always been hopeless. He felt the emptiness opening inside him. Bandits—that's what they were. The land belonged to the Africans now and his men crept from place to place on it looking for an unwary victim.

"Any horses in the town?" He didn't expect a *yes* but it seemed the only question to ask.

"Two or three, no more, Pelayo." Wala studied his chief's face. The question made him uneasy.

"We leave here tomorrow night then," said Pelayo. The others looked at him in surprise. "We have no choice. We must strike for the northern mountains. Tarik has five thousand men with him yet. We can't hold this place against him—not for a day."

Masona was used to his chief's sudden decisions. But it worried him. The tone was wrong. After those strange rages of his, Pelayo was likely to be depressed for days. This was such a time—but just now it could cost them dear. "The men have just finished a hard march and fought a hard battle. They won't be quick. Not one of them but has some wound or other. We'll lose men."

"And most of them haven't had a woman since Ávila," put in Fruela. "God's blood, Pelayo, we'll need a team of oxen to pull them off the women by tomorrow."

"Any Goth who doesn't march with us tomorrow will be a dead Goth. The rules are the same as always except that any soldier can bring a Gothic woman with him if he wants to—and if she can hold the pace of march. Huneric and those wounded who are likely to recover will go by horse-litter or muleback as long as the animals last."

Pelayo knew that he had to make the last two concessions. If Masona challenged his decision, what would the men do when they heard of it? He needed the old soldier's firm hand among them. It would be a shambles if they panicked. More than half of them were new.

"What do we do about provisions? Nobody gets far in this heat on an empty belly. And no one is going to want to leave good pig meat in Salamanca after eating stringy goat meat in the mountains for a month. They won't go without wine either."

Masona was right. Pelayo knew it. Damn the problems! Damn the men! A week, a month from now they'd all be dead—them, their women—their precious wine, their pig meat, their wounded—dead and forgotten forever. It was like the fighting in the water under the bridge. So much trouble.

Every motion had to be calculated. Every effort was new, difficult.

And for what? The desire grew inside you to stop, to die.

To hell with it! What was it for anyway?

But he knew that he couldn't stop. Not one of these four captains would understand. They had never seen him surrender or run. Only his will, only his purpose held the war band together. Only his leadership made them captains. That they knew well enough. Wala, Masona, Huneric—any one of them would kill him if he gave up now. Fruela would enjoy it. No! The Africans would have to kill him themselves. They would go down to the last man with him—out on the plain!

Rage welled in him at the thought—but no hope. Somewhere out there was death. Rodrigo was waiting for them. After Ávila and Salamanca, Tarik would take no captives. Not even his sister or old Anna!

The silence was uncomfortably long. Masona and Fruela exchanged glances briefly. Huneric was lost in his pain but Wala was watching him intently. He was like a hunting dog whose master had not given the expected command, Pelayo thought. Tense, poised, he puzzled and watched. If I order it, he'll kill Fruela—or try to.

"Look in the chests, Fruela. There is money there."

Surprised, the hulking Goth turned to the nearer of them. Clothing! It was his sister's. But the other larger one yielded, after more documents, the expected money bags.

"Some gold coins and a lot of smaller stuff, Pelayo," was Fruela's satisfied pronouncement.

"You can't be a governor without money, Fruela. Even an African needs money to rule," said Pelayo. "We'll use it to buy asses and what horses they have. No oxen. They're too slow. We'll use it to buy provisions too. The townspeople will give us a good price because they're too frightened to haggle.

"Buy as much as we can take along without slowing us down, whatever the donkeys can carry, those that aren't carrying the wounded. It's about a two weeks march to the northern mountains. What food or wine we can't carry, we can buy along the way. We'll need less the farther we travel even if Tarik doesn't intercept us."

"What about the boy, Sunna? Can't we get his father to join us? Didn't we talk of raising a revolt on the plains. Tarik doesn't have garrisons everywhere. Is our only chance to run?"

It was Huneric speaking slowly and with an obvious effort. His brain was still clear. Pelayo felt shamed in front of his chiefs. His own words rebuked him. The grandiose rhetoric of wine and campfire which he had used, and sometimes half-believed himself, to build the war band startled him in the mouth of his wounded captain. How had he forgotten? The others would recognize the question. He had to answer it.

To mark his confusion he asked, "Where is Sunna? Did he come through the battle?"

"Doesn't he always? He's careful enough about the place he chooses to fight from."

It was Fruela, speaking with scorn. He continued, "By now the ninny is drunk and probably crying too. His father is dead."

"Who told you that?" Pelayo demanded.

"The commander of the garrison here—while he was alive. The Count was assassinated by his own lieutenant. Knife in the dark. And now his lieutenant is commander in Palencia and has sent his submission to Tarik. So have all the rest of the northern nobles, all the great warriors. So that puny milksop is about as much use as a third tit."

Pelayo was pleased. Fruela's information had rescued him. His captains could not know whether or not he had had the same information from the dead Yusuf."

"He's just a bowman now, Fruela, but we'll need every one we have before we reach the mountains. Resistance here is useless. Tarik is too close. The other chiefs have made their arrangements with him. If we had more time we could negotiate, even at sword's edge, with them. Most would come over. But there is no time. Even if we could find someone to read those dispatches, even if we could find out who commands where and what terms he's given to keep command and who would like to replace him, Tarik would be on us before we could raise a thousand men. We have to reach the mountains to make a stand, to organize. Diplomacy is for later, now we run."

They agreed. He could see it. They weren't fully satisfied, his captains, but they would follow.

"It will be a very near thing, Pelayo. A real footrace," said Masona thoughtfully.

"Our real advantage is that the peasants will help us so long as we pay for what supplies we need. They can tell us things about the country that they won't tell the Africans." It was Wala speaking.

"That won't help us a damn bit if Tarik has enough horsemen—not with us moving as slow as the slowest big-assed woman in the band," growled Fruela.

"It won't be fast," agreed Pelayo. "We'll need to make the best time we can in the first three days. The farther we get from Salamanca the more problem they'll have to find us. And after we've started, you can tell everyone in the band that no one drops out alive. There will be no stragglers for scouts to question. Anyone who can't keep up we'll kill. That will urge them along.

"We leave tomorrow as soon as the afternoon sun has lost its full strength. We'll march till dark, camp till the sun's up, and then march again until it gets too hot. That's our routine for the first three days, or four if we can hold the pace that long."

"That pace will kill some of the wounded and lame some of the donkeys," observed Masona grimly.

"They are dead anyway if they stay here," said Huneric. "And a lame beast makes a full pot."

The others looked at the man. Both he and they knew that

his chances to be among the dead was very good, between the fever and the travel. No one said it. He looked like a ghost already.

"By march time tomorrow, I want the new men divided among your three divisions. Huneric, pick your man to lead if you can't. Masona, organize the provisions and the pack animals, manage the townspeople. And Fruela, don't get too drunk to walk.

"Wala, your archers will serve as scouts. Mix up the new men with the old ones. I want you out in front as scout with ten others. If you run into Africans, leave them to fight a delaying action and get back to me with the news. But it's better to hide than fight.

"On each flank, we need eight men. Pick a good, experienced man for each unit and give him the same instructions as I've given you. Three men should do for the rear. All they have to do if they see someone on our trail is run like hell.

"Something else. If any of your men see someone, anyone, from the band trying to desert, kill them. Don't bother bringing them back. We don't have any time to waste on them.

"And of course avoid all contact with the peasants if you can. The smaller the news we leave the better. Your scouts will carry their own provisions. They don't have armor to weigh them down. And I don't want them coming into camp at night or when we halt. We need a permanent perimeter. We'll have one out from the main body but two defenses are better than one."

He sounded almost like the old Pelayo but the captains still were not entirely sure. His voice was a little flatter. Occasionally the end of a sentence weakened. Something seemed wrong. They thought of the corpse on the floor in the main hall and wondered what had happened.

He may not make it himself, mused Fruela. His devil is troubling him. No great play for fancy tricks out here on the flats. And then there was the woman, his sister. No love lost between the two of them. Part of the trouble there? Had he known she'd be here? The bitch could be trouble as well as fun. Wonder if old Anna could get anything out of her? A great lady, she won't fancy a soldier like me—not yet anyway.

What if Pelayo didn't make it. Will Masona follow me? Huneric is likely through. Teudemiro is dumb but he'd back me if he led Huneric's men. Wala? Who knows what that half-breed might do? Follow Pelayo—but if the chief were dead? Who else would there be but he or Masona?

Wala watched Fruela obliquely, from the corners of his eyes. The big bull thinks he is to be chief soon, he thought. He won't be if I can put an arrow into him. He would have half the war band at the other half's throats in three days. Kill him and let Masona command. The one-eye was a thinker as well as a fighter.

"What do we do about the Gothic women who don't want to come, Pelayo?" It was Masona, looking after the loose ends. "What they want means nothing," responded Pelayo a little irritably now. "God, I'm tired.

"No woman goes unless a warrior wants to take her. There will be no whores in camp to stir up killings. And no man will lay hands on another's woman. If any one does, or tries to, he's to be killed outright. I'll do it myself if it's one of you.

"Those who aren't wanted get left here. They're nothing to us."

"I can get a doctor, I think, Pelayo. There used to be two to four of them in this town." It was Masona again.

"Get one who's young enough to walk. Bring him at knifepoint if you have to. But no slaves. Not with the doctor or anyone else."

Pelayo turned to Wala. "Are the gates shut, guarded?"

"Yes, Pelayo. My men are on the walls. I told them they would be relieved later."

"Good. We needn't expect an attack but the gates stay shut until we leave tomorrow. No one leaves the city. A light guard on the walls should see to that. Each of the other captains will find enough of his men for that before sundown, a side for each command and no new men on the walls. Just keep everyone in the town.

"I'll meet you all in the plaza tomorrow just after sunrise. Keep your men from raising the town against us. Let them get as drunk as they want but no fights. They can walk it off tomorrow if they are still alive. Share out the women as fairly as you can. If there is trouble, it will be over that. Keep them away from the townsmen's wives."

Pelayo turned to Huneric. "You can rest here. I want to see what is going on out there. When I'm satisfied, I'll sleep where I am. Wala will have old Anna send food and wine for you. She'll send a bitch too if you think you could handle one."

A trace of a smile showed on the wounded captain's face. "A man needs two hands to ride a new horse, Pelayo."

Huneric unbuckled his sword belt and put it carefully beside him on the couch. Head spinning, he eased himself backwards. I may die in my sleep he thought with sudden alarm. Before he could examine the idea further, the blackness closed on him. He fainted.

Pelayo and his three captains emerged from the tiny basilica and blinked at the sunlight of mid-afternoon. No living thing was in the small square but somewhere there was a drawn, thin scream. Some shouts sounded nearby. Behind them, in the little building, summer flies buzzed leisurely about the remains of Yusuf. The thin trickle of blood from Huneric's stump had no attraction compared to that feast.

Chapter XIV

The breeze blew, scorching and steady, across the flat, unending plain. Brown, brittle plants showed lifeless against the reddish, cracked earth. The wind drifted a powdery dust across the stones of the road and their feet puffed a little of it up and out at every step. If you watched it happen, you could pretend that you were splashing through a small stream.

Teudemiro watched the play of it about his new sandals. They fit well for there had been no short supply of dead Africans back there at Salamanca. Another pair flapped at his belt and they fit almost as well. He'd had enough of marching barefoot coming out of the mountains.

Jesus, maybe his sore feet had saved his life at Salamanca. It doesn't hurt to be a little slow in battle. Let the eager bastards take the first shock. No chance to choose a position or an enemy then. Come up behind them and pick your man and the moment. Four he had gotten himself. Another three he had shared the killing of. That didn't count the pig-sticking of the prisoners at the wall once the gates were opened.

Pretty damn good for any warrior—and not a scratch on him. Fruela had seen a couple of kills and appreciated them while Pelayo was off knocking broken legged Berbers on the head in the riverbed. Fruela had as much as promised him Huneric's command. But Pelayo, the stiff-necked son-of-a-bitch, was holding out on him. Ran me out of the war council like a goddamned boy! Not the first time either.

Well, Huneric had had it. Three of the wounded had died already. One around noon after the jolting of the litter on the stones of the morning's march had opened a big wound in his belly. A lot of screaming he did as the rags of the bandages rubbed the blue guts of him raw. He was glad to bleed to death in peace. Two more had gone, quieter, but pretty much the same since the march had resumed again. They were packing their bodies so as not to leave a trail for the Africans.

In a day, the damned wind would sweep out any trace of their passage in the dust of the road. Orders were strict not to leave the road or to throw anything away. Three men at the rear marched in the dust to see that nothing that dropped off was left behind unnoticed. Still, if one of the burros should die, there would be hell packing that.

It was going to be a march for the tough. Teudemiro glanced fondly at the smooth movement of his muscles under the tough skin of his legs. Son of a bitch, not a scratch. And Huneric is flushed already. Fever will probably kill him in a day or two more. Then there'll be a showdown!

Uneasily, his mind angled away from that idea. Much as he admired Fruela, he feared Pelayo more. There was a devil in that one. The big redhead knew what you were thinking before you were clear about it yourself. Crazy! In two days at most they'd have to bury some of them. Be a job to hide that! Some of the women too, from the looks of them! The heat and the pace would get them, them not being used to marching.

Hadn't brought one himself. Had three of them—big-assed bitches and young enough. Just rolled off one of them and went to have a couple of cups of wine and then found another. Didn't stay with any. What the hell for? They were good as dead any way—or farmer's meat. There were more ahead somewhere and a forced march was no place to drain your guts into some broad's belly. Save your water, save your food, check your gear, and don't do anything you don't have to. Remember that and you'll bury most of these dummies.

Teudemiro marched on in the same insulated isolation as

did his companions. The march was lonely as all marches are lonely. Except among the women, the silence was almost unbroken. Each man measured the firmness of his own tread. Each mentally calculated the contents of his waterbag twice an hour at least. Your legs and your water, they were the things that really mattered. Mind yourself. The others were there, vaguely comforting, but you made it on your own or you didn't. The internal reverie, soliloquy, was your company. Bullshit was for camp.

Over them the sun presided in a cloudless sky of blue. Like a great, fiery sponge, it drew every drop of moisture from the land, from them, from the animals. The wounded were especially vulnerable. The sweat dried into salt flakes as soon as it oozed to the surface. Dry harness chafed dry skin. Hiding yourself down deep, tucked away inside, alone, you could forget it all till nightfall. Pick 'em up, lay 'em down. No other way to do it.

Pelayo moved about the camp that night with deep unease. Everyone except his veterans was sore, even the recruits they had picked up in Salamanca. It had been a long time since those garrison soldiers had made a march like this. Still, they'd melt the fat off. The women were terrible. One of them had died walking. She had just fallen dead, parched by the heat.

Four dead in one day's march. And that with plenty of water! If the heat kept up, all the wounded would be dead in two more days. No animals lame yet. But fourteen bodies, even if all the other women made it. They'd have to bury them only three days out from Salamanca—a big, fat roadmark for the Africans.

But the animals couldn't pack them farther than that. Anyway, some of the superstitious among the warriors were already spooked. He'd heard some mention of ghosts, choked off as he came up. Warriors liked the dead buried, or left behind. It didn't do to think too much about your trade. Wine, women and distance laid the ghosts safely. Packing the dead along was bad luck and bad memories. It bodied out into a curse, bad luck, waiting for each man.

Teudemiro and Fruela were still watching Huneric too. The warrior was a little feverish. Anna had twice forced blood out of the stump. It was fiery, but not green anyway. He'd had plenty of wine as he rode and more wine in his water so that he had had to be supported. Even in his near stupor and pain, Huneric knew that he was fighting for his life and his command as well. He knew that not only Teudemiro but his men as well were watching him.

If he dies, Pelayo thought, there'll be no choice but to give his command to Teudemiro. Is that hulking boy as dumb as I think? A good warrior he is, and as tough as he is stupid but he has none of the battle sense of a commander. He'll get sucked out of position in the first fight and lose every warrior to the Africans.

Pelayo's depression deepened as he thought of them. At some point, the wrong point, in this march, they'd appear. First, out there, watching, calculating. Then, in superior force, alert to every mistake, they'd close. Wala's archers would screen well, making them pay. Masona would watch them coldly, meeting every disposition of their forces with some innovation, some strategem. Fruela would stand like a rock. But Teudemiro? Christ!

They'd chop him up at leisure and then come for the rest of them. Would they stand firm, fight? In the face of that sight? Or would they panic and run to be butchered? He could remember the taste of panic in his own mouth. It was familiar. Yusuf's words came back. "How many warriors will you have in a week, chieftain?"

"You are gloomy, brother."

It was Amalsuntha. Pelayo had ruminated his way back to his own campsite. Only his sister and old Anna were there for he had seen no need for a war council. He had nothing to say to his chiefs. He did not wish the effort of speaking to them.

There were no campfires by his orders but Amalsuntha was visible enough in the light of the newly risen moon. He looked at her and could detect no lines of fatigue. Her long legs were stretched out sideways as if the hard ground were couch to them. Her profile, highlighted by the darkness, showed an easy slightly cruel beauty.

She should be soft. She had graced one soft bed after another in her search. Goth and African had found her yielding enough of thigh. She should be soft and ripe and weak. But through the day she'd swung along in a long-limbed stride, oblivious apparently of the heat and thirst, silent and quite unlike the other women. Some inner force, strength, kept her composed, self-contained, regal.

"The march goes well enough."

Pelayo had not bothered to respond to her first comment but she pressed him—as always.

"Yes, the march goes well enough," Pelayo answered heavily.

"But you are not pleased. You think that we shall be caught."

"It is a broad plain and little cover. If we're caught, why then, we're caught."

"And if we are, you will not permit a surrender."

"For us, there is no choice," Pelayo emphasized the "us" heavily, purposely excluding his sister. She ignored the implied slur.

"I have not known you to be so determined, brother. Stubborn, yes, but not determined. You will accept no place in this new world?"

Pelayo looked steadily at her for the first time in their conversation. "I will accept no place not of my own making," he said flatly.

"Not of your making? How much power do you have to make a world, or to restore the old one?"

"One hundred and twenty swords."

Amalsuntha knew that Pelayo did not wish to continue the

conversation. He would not argue. He would not defend his decision. He had always been a sulky brute. A spoiled little boy as she had often told him and their parents, in the fashion of slightly older sisters. But she had never yielded to his moods, played his game. She did not now.

"The African, my jailer, offered you a fine post, you and your men too. But you refused it. You killed him for it."

Pelayo had suspected what she would say. He had wondered how much she had heard of that talk in the little basilica. "I had either to kill your Yusuf or do submission to him." Again Pelayo chose the personal terms of reference but his sister refused again to take notice of it.

"You have done submission before, to Rodrigo and to others. Your men submit to you. Brother, that is the way of life, only one rules and all the others submit in some fashion."

"In some fashion, yes, Amalsuntha, I in mine and you in yours. But Goth to Goth, kin to kin, not Goth to African." He almost spat out the last word. "There is no place in the world of the Africans for the Goths. There can only be death or slavery between us."

"And so you will be the champion of the Goths, my dear brother? Were you so fond of that worm-ridden, bloody, stupid world? Have you forgotten our father's death at the hands of his own king, his brains dashed out like mush? Your fine Rodrigo, his avenger, is dead. All the other chiefs are making their submission quickly enough. You are not even a chief except here in this dirty, little camp."

"The chieftains of the Goths will soon enough find out the real terms of their submission, sister. I have forgotten our father's death only as you have. That life is gone, murdered by the Africans. Rodrigo, as you say, is dead. But we choose our own paths, you and I, and mine is to fight. Now, by strange accident, I choose your path too. You will follow it with me."

Pelayo gazed hard at Amalsuntha. She looked away in the moonlight. She did not assent. That was not her way. Instead, she yawned lazily and stretched as if closing an interview with a tiresome courtier. Her body arched tauntingly, provocatively.

"What of our brother?" She said almost innocently.

Pelayo was taken off guard. His mind raced back. What does she know? What did the African tell her? How much had he known, to tell her?

"Our brother is dead—in Toledo. He died fighting the Africans."

Did it sound lame, defensive, to her? He felt sick, unclean again.

"But you escaped them?"

"I escaped them."

If he had said more, he would have betrayed himself somehow. She was peering at him closely now. How could he avoid her questions? She knew something. He bent his head and stared fixedly at the ground.

"There was talk of treasure."

It came lightly, almost coaxingly. She had heard! That was it! That is why she'd done nothing to oppose his decision to evacuate Salamanca! That is why she marches so contentedly. That fine, long, aristocratic nose of hers smells gold. She had joined with him for it and now she was claiming her share. As ever, the calculating hardness of her shook him. He looked at her again.

"For the mere mention of that treasure, your Yusuf died."

He would play her game. God knows where the treasure was now. Maybe found, maybe not. The grave keep it! But while she thinks I value it, can get it, she'll cause no trouble. The bitch! She'll tag along after me like a faithful, obedient sister.

"So that was why you killed him! You have plans, my brother. You have changed. But you'll not kill me, your beloved Amalsuntha."

Her words were edged with sarcasm. But she didn't know everything. She didn't know about Toledo! The tension in him melted away, leaving only a weariness at the prospect of the need for more pretense.

"You will yet be a great chieftain, Pelayo. If we escape! And I shall be a princess, your loving sister. As bride to another chief, I will be a second treasure for you, a prize for a good alliance—and more power yet.

"No, you will not kill me, brother, even though I know your secret. I can help you more with my body than can any of your captains with their swords. Besides, my death might cost you your leadership. Your men are not sure of you, you know. That strange and solitary slaying of Yusuf, after a secret talk, puzzles them more than it did me. They think you a little mad anyway, you know. Your rages, your silent retreats from their companionship, these things are the stuff of stories in the camp. Some think you possessed by demons. The men fear you, even Fruela, but they know how great a gamble this march is and they worry that you may have lost your genius. None of them want to die. Killing your own sister now—that would risk their loyalty too much.

"You cannot kill me."

Well as he knew her, Pelayo marveled at the courage of his sister. He was surely not the first man to do so, he reflected grimly. Her mind never relaxed. Most men he had known were fools by comparison. She used her woman's softness, her striking beauty, to fuddle them, draw them out, bend them to her purposes. Passionate she was, she sought the bed eagerly and especially the beds of the mighty. Men's lustful admiration was food to her, a tribute in energy and seed which she demanded just as she demanded the respect due her rank. But her mind she gave to no one, ever. He wondered what Yusuf had made of her. What had Allah to say of such a woman?

She is the most dangerous person in camp, he thought. The only sure way of dealing with her is to kill her. But she knows that I can't chance that now. In two days, she has learned much of this band and the tangled cords that hold it together.

Every man talks too openly to her—too hopefully. Every woman sees her as the promise of their own sorry life fulfilled. Even tough old Anna hangs on her every movement. The thought of serving such a great lady makes her old frame tingle like the body of a girl at puberty.

Pelayo had to smile acidly at the prospect. If they escaped the Africans, his own sister would be the most formidable challenge to his leadership. Unchecked, she would make of this little band a tiny mirror of the kingdom of the Goths, full of faction, resentment, plots, intrigue. Do I hate her or the Africans more? What they destroyed, I hate. Except for Elena—and my brother! What she would recreate, I loathe. A clean death and an end to it. A warrior's death. All of us going down to the grave as a man should—and her bright bird's mouth stopped too. Let Yusuf and his god try the world. Let them execute the traitors, and beat the cowards, grind taxes from the miserly, lie to the brave and overawe the stupid. Welcome to it! Christ!

"Such long silences, brother! You take me back to our childhood. You always hid from me somewhere when you had something that I wanted. But we are partners now, and more—princes. We must deal openly with one another. We need to begin to shape our state. It will help. You'll see. Even on this march, your men need a little glimpse of something grander. Men march better if the promise is solid, visible."

Pelayo knew she was directing him, leading him, but he did not resist. In a short while we shall be dead anyway. Let her play at rule.

"What is the price you will have for all this help, Amalsuntha?"

"Not price, brother," she went smoothly on. God, how he sulks, the great ninny! "Not a price, but a show. A little court for me. I need two more serving women. Let me pick two more from the best of those drabs that your soldiers brought away. After all, I am your sister—and a princess."

"You'd have two of them? Whores?"

"A man's name for them, brother. They were not wooed overtenderly. Yes, I'll have two of them to dress my hair and wash my body, to cook my food and sleep about my bed."

"You would have me take them away from my warriors?" He was astonished anew at her arrogance. "They are prize of conquest. It would make trouble. The men will hate me for it."

"They'll think you act like a prince. It is time you did. Anyway, they would soon tire of them on this march if they have not already. They have little time or energy for sport. And I'll not have my serving ladies describing my breasts, my loins, my words or ideas to their crude lovers. Nor would you want it so."

Pelayo could see the bright, superficial logic of her scheme. For all its attractiveness, it meant bitterness and injustice, more of it, in the band. Well, the rule against women in the camp had been broken for the men. Now I can order it anew. It is a chief's right, the choice of the spoils. And it will give the rest of the men some feeling of a familiar world. In a few days we'll all be dead anyway. "Pick your two tomorrow," he said slowly. "But pick them only from among the women of the men who joined us at Salamanca. No man who came with me from the mountains is to lose his reward."

Chapter XV

The sun was a deep red, fiery ball on the level horizon. It had lost its power to kill for another day. The wind flowed, searing from the residual heat of a million stones, across the plain, stirring garments of the little group without refreshing them. It pressed the heat more closely to them. It searched out every pore, rasped the parched, flaking skin with a living intimacy.

He's pushing the men too hard, Masona thought. They're in no condition to fight well. We should have camped an hour ago. No position is much better than another on these flats. It is going to be a long night. From now on we march under double pressure, now that they've found us.

Masona shaded his good eye with his palm. He could see nothing in the west for the low-hanging sun, but that's where they were—some of them anyway. That's where any sensible scouting force would be. The easiest place to observe us and the hardest place to observe them. Professionals, they'll come in tonight to see how much fight we have left, to see how good we are. Pelayo took the news stolidly enough. Hadn't surprised him, hadn't seemed to disappoint him. Almost acts like he's buried us already. Funny.

Six days marching at a forced pace—pushing too hard. Lost all the wounded but three—nine men. Only seven woman left. Old Anna, tough as shield leather, that one. The sister, cold steel, never complained, never even sweat. She and her two "ladies" on the only pack animals left. By God, she had to take them both from Fruela's men. More darts in the big boar! He's still smarting over the Teudemiro business. He's ready for some killing, that one. Damn bad timing.

Lucky that Huneric pulled through. A steady man, Huneric. His men think that he's immortal now, licked the fever, licked the heat, marching without sign of fatigue. One tough warrior. Had one of his men rivet a leather socket to his shield back—he'll handle it as well as before.

He'll keep his command and his men will follow him. Everyone knows that I'll support him. A one-eyed captain and a one-handed captain, natural friends. Hah! He spat dust.

Wala's with us too. No love between the dark little man and Fruela. But he's not likely to be in camp when the trouble starts nor his men either. We could still handle Fruela though. But Pelayo isn't giving a strong lead. Inviting trouble, he is. Always been desperation under the cool, hard surface. But desperate men can crack. Losing control now? Be a bloody business if he does. Could cost a dozen men besides Fruela and Teudemiro—half a command. Could cost even more in spirit with the Africans waiting out there.

Masona's calculations were interrupted as Pelayo signaled a halt. The campsite was as good as could be had. It lay just beyond a dried stream bed. The extraordinary heat of the last six weeks had left almost every stream dry. Still, they were not short of water, although food was becoming a problem. One of the remaining pack animals would be slaughtered for tonight. There would be hot meat, for the need to camp without fires was now clearly past. They had been discovered anyway. A little digging in the stream bed would give some water—enough.

On the other side of the campsite rose a bare hillock to perhaps the height of three tall Goths. Along the stream's side grew the deep-rooted poplar in a long even stand. Pelayo had chosen to camp between the poplars and the hillock.

Wala's men would be moving in now. Ever since they sighted the Africans, just as the afternoon march had begun, they had been pulled back closer to the main body. The contact had been accidental apparently. Wala's men had been saved from being overrun by their having sighted the enemy first. Footsoldiers make a lower profile on the plain. As the horsemen had gradually converged on the column's dust, it was clear that there were about thirty-five of them. Two anxious hours had passed before it became clear that they were not an advance guard but rather a scouting force. The march had continued at the same pace all the while.

With the enemy ahead, Pelayo had ordered the archers of the advance guard and flanks in close to the column, advancing the flank archers so that the three formed a rough triangle, an arrowhead, at the front of the column. They were close enough that way to be capable of supporting one another and far enough ahead to keep the column itself out of arrowshot from the mounted men. The archers themselves made a much smaller target than the mounted Africans and had the advantage of shooting from a steady platform. So they progressed, relatively unhindered, through the late afternoon, pushing the horsemen before them.

Still, it was an exhausting business. It could not fail to take its toll eventually. So far, the advantage had been all theirs. A scattered, long-range exchange of arrows had produced two dead horses, a wounded African, and no casualties to Wala's men. The methodically advancing archers had also recovered the African's arrows and most of their own.

After almost two hours of such desultory firing, the African horsemen had tentatively assayed to ride down the advance guard. In a short fight, the column had double-timed to their support while the flank archers had moved more swiftly forward to enfilade the horsemen. That little exploration had cost the enemy five horses and three dead riders. Since they had reined off, rather than press home the charge, Wala lost only one man.

Down to thirty-two men, one clearly wounded and four men riding double, the Africans had drawn off to the west at a good distance. Pelayo had then ordered the archer divisions to cover his front and left flank in roughly the same arrangement and the march went faster, almost unmolested. Probably there were still thirty men out there, since two would likely have been detailed back to report the discovery of the column. The aggressiveness of their command made it practically certain that they would attempt to come in, under cover of dark, to do whatever damage they could. That, and a continuing daily pressure, was as much as they could hope to accomplish until reinforced.

As the column began to break up to camp, the captains sought out Pelayo as a matter of course,

"Fruela, your men will take that end of the camp between the hill and the trees. Divide them up into two watches. Those who are off duty will sleep with everyone else in the center of this stand of timber. No one sleeps in the open. I want no easy targets for them when they come. Pick someone dependable to command while you sleep."

"Teudemiro can do it. He's the best of the lot," replied Fruela.

The captains exchanged glances as Fruela kept his eyes fixed on Pelayo's. The reply was too quick and the tone just short of truculent. Pelayo ignored the challenge.

"Huneric, your men take the other end. Same arrangement. Masona's will split up to take the last watch for both your men and Fruela's. Everyone gets more sleep that way."

"Wala, make three squads of your archers. I want one-third of them up on that hill, just below the summit all the time. Not much cover up there so spread them out.

"I don't think they'll come in that way. No cover for them either. But it gives us an observation post that they don't have. I'll want to know as soon as you see them and, after the fight starts, I want covering fire and a flanking action if you can manage it. They'll come in to hit us but I want the maximum casualties for them. The fewer men riding out there tomorrow, the easier the march. This may be the last time we have the advantage of numbers, or can surprise them, so we use it all we can."

He glanced around the small circle. They understood immediately and the idea appealed to them, surprising their tormentors. Their eyes fired at the thought. Only Fruela resisted the contagion. He stood there, fumbling for a complaint, not sure what point to pick. As always, Pelayo's mind and plans outran the burly warrior's prearranged objections. He could hit on only one thing.

"All that leaves the stream side uncovered. Where are we if they try there?"

Pelayo replied slowly, almost as if instructing a boy. "They won't come that way. They'd make too much noise in that dry bed. And they would have no cover either advancing or retreating. Remember, they're very weak in men and they can't even risk all of those. They have to keep enough men uncommitted to track and slow our march if they can.

"An attacking force of equal or superior numbers might try just that as a surprise. But it would be a disaster for the few they have. Their leader surely knows that much. We all saw today just how cautious he is. He'll try to infiltrate his men along the tree line, perhaps under cover of a feint somewhere else. There's nothing else he can do with a force that size and no other cover."

Throughout the brief instruction, Fruela's face behind his beard had become more inflamed. He could feel his own heat. The arrogant, noble bastard is lecturing me like a dumb recruit! Words! By Christ, he's full of them. Well, now it ends. He's made his mistakes too and now's the time he pays for them. Carefully, he strung the words out evenly—as he had been rehearsing them in his head for the last four days on the march—struggling to keep his voice even.

"Do we have a council tonight?"

If Pelayo was surprised at the question, his voice gave no indication of it. After a slight pause, the chieftain replied in a dull, matter of fact tone.

"Yes, after the men have eaten."

Here it comes, thought Masona, as the little knot dissolved in wordless tension. The boar is going to charge.

The turn of day towards evening seemed to quiet the wind. The heat still hung, stale and heavy, about them but it was no longer aggressive. The after-rays of the sun flamed against the few clouds of the western sky. A cicada shrilled insistently among the poplars. The camp itself was a subdued murmur.

Much too quiet, thought Pelayo. The men, some of them, are in too close to the council. He looked at his captains. Not one of them but knew that the only business of this council was Fruela's challenge to him. Still, they expected him to lead the council, deflect that challenge, anticipate and confuse the burly warrior by dominating the discussion. Maybe he should. Maybe that is what a chief always did. Some glory! Christ. He sat in continuing silence.

Fruela himself had expected that. Now he had to open the council. No understanding that redhead bastard.

"We're pushing the men too fast."

It was a lame start. There was no "we." They were all against him, the other captains. There was no other course.

"I have two men close to breaking. They don't know it but I can see it. Sometime tomorrow afternoon, at this rate, they'll go down in their tracks. Even if they're not dead when they hit the ground, we've no way left to carry them. Everyone else's command is in the same shape."

"Let's hope that they're dead when we leave them, Fruela. There is no way to cross this plain but fast. You know it. Tarik has found us now. But in two more days at this rate we'll be in the foothills of the mountains. If he can't spare too many men, we have the chance for a running action there. The deeper in we get, the less chance they can spare the time to come in after us.

"Those who can't march will die. If you think it is best, if your men will stand for it, you can kill them before we leave them. So can the rest of you."

He scanned their impassive faces. His answer had been curiously flat, restrained. Every member of the war band already knew its deathly logic. Confusedly, Fruela was grateful for Pelayo's restraint. He had expected sarcasm for he knew he had left himself open for it. The other captains were worried. Pelayo was inviting more argument.

Fruela plunged ahead, belligerently.

"But we still have three horses."

"Not enough. Not even if all the horses make it through tomorrow. They're in bad shape and they're bigger targets for arrows than we are. We'll have more men down tomorrow than they could carry."

"We could save some of them. I'd trade all three of those bitches riding for even one of my men."

It was out now—the line of attack. Fruela had intentionally lumped Amalsuntha with the women of Salamanca, at once an insult and a rebuke. Pelayo ignored it.

"Save some and leave others? How will you choose among them? Any way that you do it, your men will see you as playing favorites. It'll make bad discipline and maybe panic. Besides, we've no time now for doctoring."

"Discipline would be better if everyone was treated alike before now. I have two men who lost their women to your sister."

The reiterated insult would have carried beyond the council to some of the other warriors. In an hour everyone in camp would know of it. The captains did not stir, no one spoke, but suddenly each of them was very conscious of where and how he stood. They measured the distances between them with their eyes. Again, the voice of Pelayo came, even and emotionless.

"They are the stronger for it, Fruela."

In the tense circle, there was no chuckle at the jest. He had expected none.

"I have taken no spoils for myself. I march as you do—as

your men do. I claimed the two women for my sister. It is a chief's right."

"It was your right at the beginning, Pelayo." Fruela rushed on, his anger picking his words. "You should have done it at the beginning, not after the choices were made. Besides, we agreed at the start that Gothic women taken with the Arabs were sport for anyone."

"And I have held out my sister, is that it, Fruela? You don't believe that she was a hostage?"

Pelayo kept, and continued to keep, his voice soft. He began to speak now in an almost affectionate tone to the swarthy Goth.

"Fruela, you are a good captain, a very good captain, but you have two great faults. One of them is that you want to be chief.

"But that is impossible so long as I live for I am your superior. We both know that. I could kill you myself or have these other captains here kill you. But I will not do that any more than you will kill me. It would be utter madness to so divide the camp now. In a few hours the Arabs will try to infiltrate, to try our weaknesses. Tomorrow or the day after, he will have reinforcements. No, we will not fight to your death at this time."

Pelayo paused. He could stop here. He could see it in their faces. But nothing was settled. They needed a resolution of it more than he. As soon as he made the decision, the blood began to sing in his ears. He could feel the rushing in his head. The hair of his forearms stirred and stood upright.

"Your other fault is bad judgment, Fruela. You have judged the time badly. You judge me badly. You judge men badly.

"Because you have trained Teudemiro, you think that he is fit to be a captain. Because you have turned the boy into the warrior, you are lost in the pride of what you have done. You do not see that he will never be a captain. Teudemiro has the brain of a bull. His stupidity would kill us all."

The words hung in the quiet.

"Perhaps, you could be a chief, Fruela. Perhaps, I will allow you to become chief. And I? I will walk out into that gathering darkness to meet the Arabs—like a warrior. Perhaps I will do that."

Now the assembled captains moved, just perceptibly, uneasily. No one of them understood. No one of them believed that he understood. All of them feared the mood which had plainly taken their chief. They knew it. It was the demon. There would be terror now.

"First, Fruela, a test. Wala, give him your bow and quiver."

The small dark man hesitated for only a fraction of a second. From no other would he have accepted such a command. Even so, the anger showed in his eyes. But he extended the bow and quiver towards Fruela who took them dumbly. Pelayo's voice rose louder now, carrying well beyond his council.

"You remember, all of you, the shot with which I slew the noble Goth at the battle of the chiefs. A beautiful clean shot, fair in the eye! A shot that belongs to a chief, that marks a chief! You would be a chief, Fruela! Can you make such a shot? If you can now, you will be chief and I will leave all this war band to you, Amalsuntha too, even the horse she rides— the retinue of a mighty chief!

"A mark, man, a mark! There! See our noble Teudemiro! A brave man, a big man, wide-eyed! He is your mark, Fruela. But you must take him full in the eye. Only so does a chief shoot."

A vagrant breeze rattled the poplar leaves. A sound of laughter floated down from the outpost on the hillside. They were oblivious there of the sudden, deadly play in the camp. Here no one moved. Amalsuntha felt the hair start along her neck. Good Christ, he was mad!

The young warrior, Teudemiro, had stopped, frozen. Anticipating trouble, being forewarned of trouble, he had remained nearby. That made him an easy shot. He felt his bowels contract. He fixed his eyes on Fruela's belt buckle. It lay just between the two sinewy arms holding the bow. He could not think. His brain groaned with the effort but not a single idea could it summon. Its emptiness hurt him.

"Shoot then, Fruela! One good arrow and you are chief here. Make your shot, man!"

Fruela's mind raced while Pelayo's voice came as from across a canyon. Shoot the boy! They'd escaped the Arab together. He'd shown the boy every trick of his sword, shield-play, everything.

Whoreson! What if he missed? The bastard had said nothing of that. What then? What if he made the shot? Who would follow him? Or would that devil-possessed redhead have him chopped down, cut up for murder in the camp? It is an easy shot.

Run, stupid, run. Look at me, read my eyes, Teudemiro— like I taught you. Run, you great muscle-bound oaf, run!

He did not raise the bow. Slowly, Pelayo unclasped his swordbelt. Then the weapon clattered on the stones at Fruela's feet.

"Come, Fruela. Claim your rightful post. All of it is yours— what you've dreamed of through many a long night's vigil. You have it now. Only make the shot."

Head down, Fruela stretched the bow and quiver towards Wala.

"I cannot. Teudemiro is my friend."

"That too is why you will not be a chief, Fruela. A chief has no friends."

Leaving his sword belt where it lay, Pelayo turned and walked into the poplars. It lay there, untouched, as the captains moved singly, silently away. Council was over.

A little later, Amalsuntha carefully gathered up the sword and belt and took it to him.

Chapter XVI

"**W**hy is it, Masona, that the Arabs never came after us? They knew where we were."

The old captain regarded the boy sidelong as neither of them checked their pace. Four months in camp and Sunna still did not speak the soldiers' language. Probably, he never would. He had been trained at court, a noble's son, but it was more than that. Despite the bonds that he had formed with some of the band, the youth simply refused, somewhere inside him, to accept the warrior life.

"Who knows? You've heard the camp gossip. Everyone has a different idea."

The veteran reconsidered then. Gradually he had come to like the boy—to feel almost protective toward him. The kid was so out of place. He was just trying to make talk.

"Some," he picked up the thread of the conversation, "say it's our luck. Some say it's our God, although what this bunch ever did for God is a good question. My guess is that Tarik has lots to do that's more important."

"How do you mean that?" asked Sunna. "After Ávila and Salamanca doesn't he have to defeat us? Isn't his honor as a warrior bound to seek revenge?"

"Sure, sure. He won't forget us—ever. If he lives long enough, he'll come looking for us. God help us then. But right now, I think, he is a winning general first—a conqueror even—and a warrior second.

"Look at it this way. From what we know, or can guess, just about the whole country is in his hands. He seems to have paraded across the whole northern plains and crossed the mountains into Galicia. No serious fights even. But, in every town and every district he needs to leave some kind of a force, a token of his authority. The treaties that he is making with our brave counts and dukes are not worth much. The Goths have never been good at keeping their word. But these treaties are worthless if he shows himself too weak to even detach a few men to represent him. So he's stretched tight. There's just enough skin to cover the drumhead. None to spare.

"Now us, who are we? What are we up to now, a hundred fifty swords? —and we're running. We're running like hell and won't stop until we're so deep in these mountains that the hair on our backs lies down. We hold nothing, so we can wait, as far as he's concerned, until his own grip is stronger on those who aren't running—on those who hold the towns, and villages, and districts. That's where his campaign will pay off."

The two walked on in silence for a few moments. The low, rolling hill country which the war band had entered two days ago made placing one's feet a matter of more care. Shale alternated with granite outcroppings and thick, rich alluvial soil so that a regular pace was impossible for any great distance.

From the tops of the ridge lines, the shapes of the Cantabrians loomed formidable, forbidding, and close to the northeast.

"But then, what are we going to do? Where are we going? What is Pelayo's plan?"

Sunna did not know what question to ask, really, or what question made sense, but he wanted to draw the veteran out. It was the sense of things as they stood that he wanted from that warrior. He had come to respect Masona's cool appraisals and he knew that he could count on a certain tolerance of his awkwardness.

"We're going right off the end of the world, kid. That's where we're going. Right off the end of the world. You see those peaks?"

They had topped a small rise and the mountains of the northern coast lay yet closer.

"We're going back in there because we don't have a plan. We have a damn tough fighting band. It's well disciplined and well led but it's too small to do anything now. From what the strays and deserters told us, the Africans have chilled the guts of everyone for now. No one wants to risk war—except us and we're too puny to matter—because Tarik has won every battle till now and he has more help in the south.

"All the great chiefs will wait a bit. Everybody understands the need for that—-or has wound up dead like your father. The Africans have proved that they can fight. The question that remains is whether or not they can rule. The old chiefs have seen a lot of kings come and go. They'll bid for some time to test this new one. To see how well he can control his own men when the spoils are parceled out. To see how greedy he is. To see what kind of a bargain can be made.

"And Tarik wants to play the same game. He probably doesn't want a major battle himself if he can help it. He's had a great string of triumphs but nobody—no general—wins them all. Nobody knows that as well as a soldier. He'll talk now because he's strong. That's already started. In the south he, or Musa—or whoever is in charge—has already made arrangements. They fight at Mérida, because they have to, but in Murcia they bargain. They've brought back Agila and they may even make him king if the price is high enough. It's a time for horse traders, kid. The soldiers need a rest."

"And Pelayo doesn't understand that?" asked the youth.

Masona scrutinized the young man's face carefully. There was just the faintest shadow of a smile about the latter's mouth. He wants to draw me out, the captain thought. Well, he's not stupid. Besides, there's steel in him somewhere. He keeps his own thoughts. He'll not be running off to confide in Fruela or any of the others—even Pelayo. If he has to know what I think of our chances, I'll tell him.

"He understands it as well as we all do, son," the veteran said softly, "but he won't accept it. I don't think that he can. Sometime—before any of us knew him—it all ended for him. For him, the past is gone, finished. That's what the negotiations will be all about, you know. Everyone will be looking to patch the past together, to keep their old place and honors. Everyone wants to make sure that the old kingdom is still in place—even if it has a new king. That not that much has changed and they can go on living pretty much as they've always lived, that's what they want to make sure. Tarik knows that, if he understands men at all, and so that is what he'll tell—promise—them.

"Pelayo is outside of all that because for him the old world is dead. He hates the thought of it even. Maybe more than he hates the Africans. So he and Tarik are enemies to the death. The Muslim has no way to settle with him but by the sword. And that's how it will be settled. You can bet on that."

"But you will follow him—you and the rest of the warriors."

It was a statement rather than a question.

"Yes, I'll follow him, like the others for now. It's a risk. Good sense says that it's better to make terms. But soldiering doesn't make sense. Hell, the world doesn't make sense. He's our chief. He has our word. So we follow him until he loses and he hasn't been beaten yet."

Masona was silent for a long moment. Then he resumed. "There's more to it than that. You know it as well as I. Pelayo is something more than a damn good war chief. You feel it too. There's a strangeness about him. He's somehow—above us. In council, he listens but it is almost as if he's hearing another voice at the same time. One nobody else hears, his own private demon. Some of the men think that he's possessed—or mad. It makes him special. There's not a warrior in the camp who's not a little scared of him, even the toughest.

They never know what he's going to do. He makes the laws—the rules—and he breaks them. But, by God, he wins. He finds a way and we go on living for a few more days. Some of us do anyway."

Sunna nodded again. "I know. I feel the same thing. But where will he lead us now, do you think?"

"I told you—off the end of the world. Weeks ago, months ago, he said that we'd rouse the northern plains. He said that maybe we'd join with your father, for example, and other chiefs. But that's gone now. They're too frightened and Tarik is too strong. Or, he said, we'd move into Galicia. His family had estates there and followers too, I guess. But Tarik got there first so that's out for now.

"I think that we'll keep moving north, sticking to these hills just in case the Africans still decide that they can spare a little time for us. If we reach the sea, then he'll have to decide if it's west into Galicia or east into the high mountains. My hunch is that we're for the mountains, that its going to be a wet cold winter for us."

"But there's no way to live up there, is there?" protested the boy. "It's just mountain and forest and savages, isn't it?"

"Just about, kid. Real goat country. Nobody much has ever wanted it. The Romans put a road through once to Oviedo and parts of it, maybe most, can still be used. Still, they never really controlled the country. The tribes there—the Astures are maybe the biggest of them—still live the old way, follow the old gods in secret. We Goths never bothered them much. Some traders went up there for furs and salt. Lots of both to be had if you don't set too high a value on your life. Probably most of us who went up there went as slavers. It was just about the only real way to make money out of those rocks, but it sure didn't make the Astures very sweet-tempered."

This last reference bothered the youth. Still, it offered the chance to turn the conversation in a more personal direction. He had been hoping for that and decided, at the risk of angering the veteran captain, to try to turn the talk that way.

"You've been a slaver too, Masona, as well as a soldier."

"Once in a while. Once in a while. But only when I couldn't soldier. It's an ugly business, that. Never among the Astures though."

"But," the boy offered timidly, "you're a Christian. Most times I think that you're the only one in camp."

Masona was surprised at the daring of the observation. When the conversation turned to himself he had first thought of it as a chance remark. Now he saw something more of the loneliness of the young noble. Sunna was asking for friendship, even to the point of presuming it. He was pleased, even flattered, though uncomfortable as well. The captain was as alone as most good captains were. Maintaining control over the men of his command meant an inevitable distance between them and him. The knowledge that their lives were his to command, and that he would sacrifice one of them to the cause of discipline, or all of them for the sake of a victory, constrained them as well as him.

With the other captains his personal relations were closer, of course. Their similar professional position bred mutual respect as well as rivalry. Their isolation from the men of their respective commands pushed that respect toward camaraderie and a certain rough affection. Even so, they remained rivals, potential competitors always, and some sturdy reserve strongly marked their association.

Masona was closest to Huneric. That one's cool competence and long military career made them especially compatible. Huneric's loss of a hand at Salamanca presented him with special problems of leadership which Masona had long known by reason of his lost eye. Their natural solidarity fed on such circumstances.

Fruela was another matter. Not to admire the sheer brute energy and force of the raven-haired captain was impossible for any warrior. He was an able captain too even though his tactics were of the most direct and simple kind. His own extraordinary strength and courage lent the most formidable ferocity even to the plainest of frontal assaults. Not to sympathize with him when he was baffled and stung by the far superior and supercilious intelligence of Pelayo was difficult. He seemed fated to arouse the worst instincts in the brooding personality of the redhaired noble who led the war band. Still, Fruela was a born insubordinate. He could not abide the authority of another. Yet he himself would have made the most overbearing of chiefs. It was tacitly understood by the rest of the captains that, if Pelayo were to be killed, they would themselves have to kill Fruela. The latter would be simply too dangerous to the safety of the entire band unless constantly checked and disciplined by the cold ferocity of their present chief.

Then there was Wala. Both his mixed blood and the fact that he commanded merely the archers set the dark little captain off a bit from the other three. More than any of them he was absolutely and unquestioningly loyal to Pelayo. And for some dark reason his native blood seemed to make him especially acceptable to the Gothic nobleman. The rest of the captains rather found Wala's ties to the old population of the land slightly disturbing. They suspected that his sympathies were elsewhere and that he might even follow the old gods of the natives.

It was against Wala that Masona knew he was now going to offend. Sunna was one of the half-breed's command. Ties of friendship with Sunna would inevitably act to limit the authority of the captain of the archers over the young Goth. Maybe it was the fading of the danger which had dogged them for the past weeks. Maybe it was the gentle breeze which whispered of autumn and an end to the burden of grinding heat which they had endured passively for more than a month. Both would promote a festive mood which would make discipline hard to maintain in any event. Yet Masona knew that he was going to respond to the young noble's overtures.

"Yes, I'd like to be a Christian. I try to be when I can. But a man does what he has to do. Soldiering is my trade not farming. Soldiers run the world—one soldier or another. I'm not a chief and I wouldn't want to be one. Maybe, I wouldn't know how to be one. So I follow my chief—follow orders as best I can. Some of the chiefs are Christian, at least they reward the priests, and some are not. Pelayo is better than most. But I do what I'm told. That's my life. Who has a different one?

"Sometimes, when I've had no chief, I've run slaves. Somebody else would if I didn't and do it worse. It's an ugly business but the law says it's right. So do the priests. An occasional one may preach that it's good to free your slaves, but I don't see that they free their own. So you do what you can, boy. Take care of your men, honor your chief, help your friends and try to keep them and yourself alive and eating regular. That's what the world allows, boy. That's all it has ever allowed and if you can manage to do that much you're damn lucky. It's all the Christianity that I can practice anyway."

Sunna was encouraged. The veteran would listen to him. "But Christ said that we should love everyone, even our enemies," he responded softly.

"I know that, boy. I know that. But it doesn't work. You can't deal with people like that. They crucified Christ and that saved us—okay. But He couldn't lose. He was God. He went on being God whatever they did to him. Not us. We'd end up being slaves or dead men. Who'd that help? Not our friends, not my chief. They don't want me to love their enemies; they want me to help fight them.

"Do you think it would impress the Africans if we loved them? They'd sure as hell like it. It would make finishing up what they've started a lot easier. And they'd just take it as proof that their god is stronger than Christ. So they'd substitute him for Christ. Where would that get us? Do you think that they rule without swords, without chains? Do you think they'd even share our own property with us?

"Somebody has to rule, Sunna. Somebody has to give the law. There have to be rules for people to follow and some-body has to enforce them. That takes chains and whips and swords. What do you do if your wife decides she likes another man better? Or your slave likes another master better? There have to be rules. You can treat everybody as well as you can but there have to be rules."

The warrior's voice was a mixture of vehemence and pleading. He wanted this young man to understand him. Sunna recognized that he was being accepted as a friend. It touched him deeply and painfully. He wanted the veteran's approval but he desperately did not want to accept the sol-dier's world.

Perhaps it would be better to say nothing. What could he say? He recognized the rough wisdom of Masona's words. Who in the camp—who in the world would disagree with them? His own experience in the war band confirmed them as sound. But silence now would betray the friendship just begun. However inadequately, Sunna had to respond. His mind reached back to the times of his father's court and the lessons of his old tutor.

"Do you think that the rules are always the same rules though, Masona? Are there harsh rules, bad rules, for bad times and better ones for better times? The Greeks used to talk about a "Golden Age." And they said, as I remember it, that it was followed by "Ages" of Silver and Brass. My tutor always said that our own was an "Age of Iron." If he was right, then maybe the rules you speak of are only temporary emergency rules."

The grizzled veteran regarded the young man with a cer-tain fondness. He was bright, this kid. He was brave too. Not with the foolhardy valor of the soldier but with the kind of stubborn courage that it took to argue with a superior. Still, the boy was respectful too. He didn't argue his own views but pulled in the learning of the ancients. Almost despite himself, the warrior was moved further towards a certain intimacy. "Maybe, Sunna, maybe. But now is when we live."

And with an impish grin, which lent a fleeting youthfulness to his own scarred face, he continued.

"I'll bet though that your tutor was an old man. You've listened to the old men, to even the soldiers around the night's fire. You know that they all wish that the past would return. Back then—if you believe them—all the captains were great captains, all the wine was good wine, all the laws were good laws, all the women were generous. But all that that kind of talk means is that they were young then.

"Don't you think that perhaps your learned tutor was playing the same game? Old men can be awful fools. And even the ancients—couldn't all their theories of ages and times come down to the same stuff?"

The veteran was enjoying himself. You couldn't fence this way with the other captains. But the boy was impressed with the soldier's logic. He wondered if his tutor would have been discomfited by the rough analogy. Still, as he cast about for the shape of an adequate reply, he was chilled by the suspicion that the old soldier was right. Life had never been different. Life had always been cruel. He had been living in a dream of boyhood, refusing to grow up to a man's place to accept a man's responsibility. Yet he knew that he could not live Masona's kind of life—or Pelayo's. He had to resist.

"I don't know, Masona. What you say is true, of course. Everybody talks like that sometimes. And you know more of the world than I do. Anyway, the Arabs interrupted my education."

He grinned in turn.

"But surely times were better before the Arabs came—even if not much? And before that, weren't they better in the times of the Romans? You have seen the aqueduct they built in Segovia to bring water to the city. I remember my father's palace in Palencia. At Coruna they say that the lighthouse that guides the ships in is so high that its top is lost in clouds some days. We Goths have never built anything so grand. Certainly life must have been better, more peaceful, if money could be spared for such works as those."

Masona smiled thoughtfully and for some few minutes it seemed as though he would not answer at all. When he did, it was gently and with a certain sadness mixed with humor.

"You will be my tutor then, Sunna? Yes, there were better times—though not many now alive can recall them. There were times when the Goths were one people under one king. A strong king makes the peace and enforces the peace. During his rule mere soldiers need but follow him. There is no killing or plundering except at his orders and his judges decide whether one is slave or free, criminal or honest man.

"In such a time perhaps only the king is evil or good—as he wishes. All the rest are only obedient subjects. The priests say that just so the king brings Christ's justice to earth. Perhaps so, though I think that Christ would have wondered at the way in which King Rodrigo did his will—or even the great King Reccesvinth. But anyway, when there is one king, and he does not demand too much in taxes, or services, and even remembers his people sometimes, that is a happy age.

"But neither you nor I will live to see such a time come again, boy. These are times of war. Even before the Arabs came, the Goths had not been at real peace under a single king in almost thirty years. And now, even though Tarik has conquered, can he make a single people in this land? Not while Pelayo lives—and we are likely to live just about as long as that great redhead.

"So it's war for us, son. Much slaughter and little justice, and no mercy. If we want to be men and not just dumb savage beasts, only two things will serve us now. One is bravery and the other is loyalty. Forget the rest for these years will have no use for them."

The finality of the old soldier's words did not invite a reply this time. A silence fell between the two but one curiously unmarked by tension. They had not so much resolved their differences as they had reminded each other of the great, brooding, somber menace of their condition. In its face they could not quarrel without descending into childishness. In quiet they marched forward with the people and orange flecked mountain peaks to their right.

A burst of shouting at the head of the marching column brought Masona instinctively to a half-crouch. But no shower of arrows followed though the column slowed along its whole length. Wala's archers, out as flankers to the war band, raised no alarm. Group by group the marching files slouched to a halt and the worn men dropped to the grass, or to a rock or log alongside the track that entered a narrower defile between two low hills just ahead. Some of the warriors began to worry at their gear while others just simply dropped off to sleep. The small river valley that they had been ascending was too much like a dozen others to excite the interest of the freshest among them.

From the rear came Pelayo, striding easily through the scattering groups of soldiers. As ever, the alertness that the war chief wore like a second skin marked his every move. He flowed among them, scarcely seeming to notice their existence.

"Come forward with me, Masona" he said without checking his movement. In a minute the two had reached the point where a knot of the vanguard stood just inside the small pass. Wala himself, captain of the scouts, stood beside a sturdy pine to which a blond Goth was bound.

There was not more than a flicker of life left in the young man who must have been twenty-six or twenty-seven. Only a vine passed under his armpits and over a low limb held him upright. A small stream of blood had marked both corners of his mouth and his chin, the result of his efforts to scream against the dried branch that held the grass gag in his mouth and was lashed behind his head. His arms and his legs had been tied, well drawn back, almost behind the tree trunk. The victim's abdomen had been slashed repeatedly so that his intestines now hung down in bluish-black ribbons over his genitals. The flies were now thick upon them and the ants were beginning to take up their work as well.

"Kill him, Wala. Then have some men cut him down and bury him."

This from Pelayo who then turned to Masona and the other captains who had joined him automatically.

"He couldn't have been put there more than half an hour ago and still have been alive when we arrived. We're being closely scouted, probably for the past few days if they had time to find a suitable victim or to bring up a prisoner. Our route was easy to predict but they still went to considerable trouble to post this little warning for us."

Of the captains, none chose to reply except Masona.

"Welcome from the Astures."

Chapter XVII

Fruela drew his hand across his chest harness and looked automatically at the greenish slime with which the touch of the leather had marked his hand. He rubbed the mildew off against his black haired massive thigh and reached for the earthen jug in a simple motion.

"Christ, this shit! There won't be a decent piece of leather left in camp if the goddamn rain doesn't stop sometime."

He spat on the earthen floor of the wattle hut.

"And not even a decent drink of wine to warm your guts. This damn cider is like drinking rainwater itself. The only thing it makes is piss."

The group gathered about the tiny fire received the outburst of the hulking warrior without special interest. Fruela was not only bad-tempered but predictably so. He said nothing now that he had not said, almost in the same words, for the past seven months.

It was not a council of war exactly, although all of the captains were gathered there about Pelayo. Some of the more sardonic soldiers referred to these meetings as Pelayo's court. The chieftain himself had heard of the phrase's currency in the camp, and found it amusing and worrisome by turns. Part of the problem of their present situation was that the meanest soldier in the camp had very recent memories of a better life. Not one of them but could remember some chief's estate more grand than this, some warm city brothel, some fairground wine stall. But sardonic humor was the redhaired leader's own characteristic and he appreciated the neatness of the reference.

Amalsuntha, his sister, was there too. Her long blond hair curled at the ends almost violently in humid air. Her white wool tunic molded, in its damp but spotless folds, her magnificent body. The pungent animal smell that the wool gave off in response to the fire's heat might have been that of Amalsuntha. She was so visibly animal herself, so physically present, that she troubled everyone in the little huddle. She was a splendid, living remnant of the life that they had enjoyed. With characteristic acuteness and perversity, she herself knew that and enjoyed the power of her suggestibility. In turn, every member of her audience understood what she was doing and hated her for it.

All but one. The trader, Felix, was as amused by Pelayo's sister as he was by everyone and everything else. The Roman freeman was as much of a cheerful cynic as the conditions of his life and the times allowed. Of the men in the hut only he had revisited the world they had left. Four times during the long autumn and winter months he and his drover-slaves had fought through the weather and the mountains with fur and salt-laden burros to the flats of the northern plains and once even beyond the Guadarramas to Toledo. He alone had fleshly and recent knowledge of soft beds and soft women, of sweet wine and dry clothing. So for him alone Amalsuntha was not a symbol of things lost but merely a beautiful, idle bitch.

Felix had found his way into the camp that Pelayo had established in the small Cantabrian valley. He already had known the village of the Astures that occupied it until news of Pelayo's advance had sent the tribesmen scurrying off to refuge in other scattered villages of their kinsmen. Within three weeks he had come boldly into camp with his caravan for he remembered well the enigmatic chieftain whose ferocity and peculiarity had combined to turn him from merely a hired caravan master into an independent trader with animals and goods of his own.

The merchant himself could not be sure whether it was his nose for gain or his curiosity which drew him to the camp. He was, in any event, usually too busy studying the motives of those around him to spend much time reflecting on his own. He had known there would be some danger in approaching the refugee settlement. Indeed, some of the band had noisily advocated simply stealing his goods, eating his animals, and disposing of Felix himself in a variety of unpleasant ways. Still, the Roman had correctly estimated that Pelayo's discipline over the warriors would be, thus far, undiminished and that the taciturn chieftain himself would immediately appreciate the services that he had to offer.

So it was that he had entered into a loose and profitable contract with the Gothic chieftain. On his trips south, he took furs, salt, and small quantities of gold. The latter came from the chest Pelayo had won at Salamanca. Pelayo would allow him to take no slaves and—thus far—he had obeyed the prohibition. In Wala, Felix suspected, the Goth had access to information from the Astures almost as good as his own and news of his slave raiding would have found its way quickly to the chieftain's ears. For such a thing, he knew without understanding, he would not be forgiven.

Still, the profits were good and he had doubled his number of pack animals in six months. The gold coins with which he was entrusted were of such good quality that he fared better by melting them down and disposing of them in circles long known to him. The other goods had always brought a fair price and now fetched a good one since most trade was in a shambles. Bribery remained a regular cost of business, of course, but the bastard mixture of Arab, Berber, and Gothic administration now prevailing in the newly conquered lands offered a variety of channels which his acumen penetrated with facility and with a huge satisfaction at his own cleverness. For a man who lives by his wits, it was the best of times.

On his return from such expeditions he brought many things. The Astures could not be neglected entirely for he needed safe passage in their lands. But Pelayo's camp had become already his chief business interest. To it he brought news, weapons, wine, and refugees. The Goth valued them in that order.

Felix, on the other hand, saw things rather differently. News was free and wine was cheap. Refugees, however, turned him his greatest profit. The displaced, hunted, and the many luckless conspirators of the south paid him handsomely to ferret them away to the fancied refuge of the north which they had never seen and of which they had only heard bits and pieces. Even disgruntled soldiers were willing to part with hard coin for his services as guide to the camp of the chieftain of the north. Largely for that reason Pelayo's camp had swollen from a mere two hundred to something approaching five hundred in a mere seven months. Many of the newcomers were not of the sort that Pelayo wanted or liked but all of them had added appreciably to Felix's well-being. Once there, of course, Pelayo would permit none of them, however unwelcome, to return to the Africans under pain of death. It was a sentence cheerfully carried out by the Astures of the mountains who viewed with strong misgivings the growing number of Goths invading their native lands.

Weapons were most dangerous to procure. One had to come by them by bits and pieces or else seek out the very masters of the southern lands who held the keys to a score of Gothic armories. Some of the Africans could be bribed but the negotiations were intricate and often Felix had found that the most valuable item that he had in trade was information of Pelayo, the condition of the war band, and of its relationships with the tribes of the Astures. When he had to give such news to pry some weapons loose, he did. The merchant suspected that Pelayo understood that such exchanges were necessary but Felix regarded it as the better part of discretion never to mention that fact. As a result of them though, the Arabs were likely as well informed about Pelayo as he was of them.

Information is almost always the most valuable military weapon and its uses were probably the reason for the inclusion of Paternus in Pelayo's little court. As he sat now, crosslegged on the dirt, he seemed to be a small mountain of flesh. His round shaven head merged with scarcely perceptible neck into the gross corpulence of his body. His short legs, formed of layer upon layer of muscle, as is sometimes the case in very fat people who have nevertheless remained active, did the same. When Felix had agreed to allow the priest to join his pack train on their latest return from the south he had stipulated that Paternus must walk. The very bulk of him would have killed the sturdiest of his poor animals. The trader had expected the cleric to die or drop out but the latter had not only kept up on the rigorous trip but somehow contrived to remain as fat as ever. He seemed to be as enduring as the Cantabrian rocks themselves.

According to the priest, he was one of the few survivors of the siege of Mérida who had not been enslaved. Most of the camp believed that although few accepted his unlikely account of escaping at night just two days before the fall of the city. The most widely received story was that he had bought his freedom by revealing to Musa the hiding place of some of the treasures of a church there. At any rate, he was the best informed person in the camp on the most recent unhappy attempt of the Visigothic kingdom to offer some kind of general resistance to the Africans. He also possessed the most direct news of the state of affairs in the conquered lands of the far south. The former made him invaluable around the campfires. The latter made him of great use to the brooding mind of their chieftain.

Pelayo addressed him now.

"What do you say, little priest? Is the time coming soon when I can take this great, hairy beast back to the dry lands of the south or must we listen to his quiet complaints for a score of years yet?"

"That depends, my great chief, on what you wish to accomplish." Paternus habitually addressed Pelayo with an obsequiousness which was matched by his arrogance towards all others except Amalsuntha. He was generally viewed with contempt as a result.

"If you wish to restore the altars of the one true God, drive the heretics into the sea from which they came and to rouse the Gothic nation from its deplorable cowardice, the time may not be just yet. If you want, on the other hand, to make good terms as have so many other chiefs, now is the best moment perhaps."

The chief stared coldly at him. Pelayo could not understand how this mountain of flesh could fawn at one moment and insult by his tactlessness at the next.

"From our beginning, priestling, we have killed the Africans. Nothing has changed—or will change. We do not seek their terms. But if we should, tell us why this would be a good time."

"Because, as I have told you already, lord, the tension between Tarik and Musa will not be healed. The one has become very great with the Africans by a brilliant campaign of conquest at almost no cost in lives. The other is possessed of the jealously of a superior towards a too able—a too fortunate subordinate. And, I have heard, both have been denounced before the throne of their caliph in Damascus. It is even said that Tarik was summoned there and did not go but rather made excuses for his disobedience. Either could denounce the other for his own profit but I should think that Tarik has fatally lost the advantage in this by already defying the orders of Damascus.

"Now attend me further, great chief. If Tarik is recalled, or disgraced, or murdered, the hatred between the Berbers and the Arabs will find an outlet. The hill peoples of Africa here see a great conqueror in Tarik and they have shared liberally in the booty of his conquest. In Musa they see merely an Arab governor who demands a share in what they won and who makes treaties with the chiefs whom they have beaten.

"Add to this the fact that many of our own chieftains have not been beaten but have merely surrendered for the moment. They still possess war bands which have not been disarmed and whose real disarming they will view with misgiving. In such a world your four hundred swords could count for much. Musa would pay the most for your help but there would be no lack of bidders to drive up the price."

"Yet," broke in Huneric, "we would always be mercenaries. Whoever won, with our blood, would seek finally to disarm us in turn. Like others here, I have fought for pay. I know the lot of an unemployed soldier. Or would the fighting last our time?"

"None of us will live to see the end of the wars," rumbled Fruela. "But the Africans will be the winners. Our weak-livered counts and dukes wouldn't fight for King Rodrigo. They won't fight for each other."

"So if we don't fight for the Africans, we'll be on the losing side," said Masona, entering the discussion of the captains now begun. "I agree with Fruela. The leaders of the Goths are a sorry lot. Some have been bought. More will be. And any one of them would betray the others for a new title. The puppet Agila, old King Witiza's brat, has shown the way. He's still looking for Musa to make him king of some barnyard or other."

Fruela smiled and scratched contentedly.

"About time you agreed with me on something, you one-eyed bastard."

"About time you were right about something," the veteran responded equably.

"So," Pelayo mused, almost to himself, "all my captains agree that the Goths are beaten and that to join with them would be stupid. How then if we enlist them under our standard?"

"Your pardon, great lord," this from Paternus, "but it is beyond your means at present. You have a certain name, lord. Many have heard of your exploits at Ávila, at Salamanca, of the long march north. So it is that refugees to these northern mountains seek you out. These deeds, however, are the victories of a war chief, not of a general or a king. Many of the Goths respect your noble lineage as well but it is not the blood of royalty.

"All this being so, they will not follow you though they might accept you as an equal. Still, as Fruela and Masona say, what good are partners who will not fight. More yet, my lord, you lack the present means to compel them. Best to wait till you are stronger as more of their own warriors find their way to you among these hills."

His captains waited in silence to see how their chieftain would respond to this unasked impertinence. The silence drew itself out as Pelayo looked evenly at the priest. The latter dropped his small dead black eyes and half closed his lids. The rain became loud upon the thatch and a twig snapped softly in the little fire.

"Felix, what do you say to all this priestly wisdom? You have listened to the talk among the retainers, the warriors of the chiefs of the northern plain. Does he judge their strength correctly? Would they resist me? Or would their own followers join me instead?"

The trader was slow to respond. He wished to give the appearance of deliberation. But he already knew what he would say. What the chief had proposed was mad, foolish.

"I think, Pelayo," he said at last, "'that they would fight you and you would not win. They would surely have the help of the Africans in that. After all, you are a rebel in the eyes of both. Some of their warriors would surely join you but not enough.

"If you could raise three thousand men, Musa could muster twenty thousand. And they have been the victors almost everywhere in the past two years. Your own men would expect only defeat and death or slavery. Such do not make effective soldiers. Nor would I count overmuch on the hatred between the Arabs and the Berbers—at least not yet. That spirit needs time to ferment, to grow yet more bitter. For now, their god seems to be a jealous one, a fearful one. He will unite them against you more than Musa."

"Will you take counsel from cowards, brother? Listen to a priest who flees the martyr's crown and a low-born Roman pedlar?" Amalsuntha's throaty voice drew the eyes of the men to her as much as her provocative words. "We come of better blood than even your captains know, you and I. Our father was a count. The Goths have chosen their king from among such as us more than once before.

"Of course, they despise us so long as we hide here among the goats and foxes. But seize and plant your standard at León or Astorga, and those will not be wanting who would raise you on their shields as king. The wealth and palaces of the kingdom will be the prize of those who march to take them. Not to bandits who hide in the mountains and raid the flocks of swineherds."

Old Anna watched the intervention of her mistress impassively. She knew that she was, by Pelayo's orders, as much the captor of the fiery and petulant, golden-haired beauty as her servant. Still it was an honor and a pleasure to tend those milky limbs and body. There were better ways than rash speech to move men. Her mistress was a fool for all her cunning.

"Bandits, no," Pelayo interrupted. "So long as our first purpose is to kill Africans and not just to feed our own bellies, we're an army. An army that obeys one chief."

He slowly surveyed the occupants of the hut at this last. His gaze rested finally with his sister. After a slight hesitation there, it moved on to the Roman trader.

"Tell us, Felix, will they be ready for that down in the plains?"

"Not at first, Pelayo. They believe that you have fled here—

they think of you as refugees, as beaten men. Your first moves should be strong ones for they will be a complete surprise. After that—" he shrugged. "They will prepare a welcome for you, of course, and it will get harder."

"Preparations indeed. If you do not crush them, destroy them at the first blow and make yourself master there, they will make preparations. They will gather their forces, or their Arab masters will. They will find out where we are here in the mountains, and they will come to crush us. Only a fool stings a lion. Kill it or leave it alone." The words rushed out of Amalsuntha in a torrent.

"Lady," said the merchant levelly, "they already know where we are. They have a good idea of our numbers. Take my word, they will seek to destroy us anyway. The only difference is whether or not we let them prepare in peace and leisure while we get weaker."

"And who has told them where we are and who we are but you? Trust a Roman to betray a Goth!"

Amalsuntha was pallid with icy rage. This slave born swindler of slaves and peasants who pandered to her need for clothes and cosmetics would set himself up as counselor to her brother, a noble of the Goths. And that great fool would allow it. He had no dignity, no idea of his estate. His own captains pretended to be his equals and he took no notice of it. Well, this slimy trader could be destroyed at least.

Every man in the hut was uneasy. The chieftain's sister had said no more than what each one of them suspected in their hearts. Several of them had discussed the likelihood of it before but no one had ever spoken of it in council. Now treason had been cried and the expectancy of death hung in the air like the fire's smoke. The priest raised his lids and gazed speculatively at the trader. Then his look shifted to Pelayo though his head did not move. Everyone, indeed, was looking at the chieftain but the silence was broken elsewhere.

"Felix had no need to tell them or they to ask him. The

Astures keep them well informed about us." The speaker was Wala, the olive skinned captain of the archers.

"Your people then," grunted Fruela.

"Not my people, but like my people," agreed the archer captain, "who have small enough reason to love the Goths."

"True enough, Wala." Pelayo's voice had enough edge on it to easily reclaim control of the group. "No one loves the Goths. When have we asked them to? We have our swords as friends and, till now, that has been enough."

"Felix is right," he added abruptly, closing off his sister's deadly question. "Our first blows must be strong ones and the objectives carefully chosen. We need to pick, first of all, weak towns but rich ones. What we want are towns with Gothic garrisons as well as African ones. That way we gain recruits and bloody the enemy at the same time. We also want towns that have an armory as well. Weapons are needed for the refugees coming in now as well as those who will come as our fame spreads.

"And such towns will have gold. Not only the gold that we take from the bodies of our enemies but the pay chests of the African commander, the ornaments of churches if they have not already been stolen. They will be anyway. Our treasure from Salamanca is almost exhausted and we will need money to get through the next winter. If we do not buy food from the Astures, as we have been doing, we shall have to fight them as well. Every recruit is another mouth and we are not farmers but warriors. Anyway, the land is so poor and wet that this valley could never support us.

"For all of this we need our good friend, Felix. He is our best spy, our most intelligent spy. He will tell us about the commanders, the garrisons, the state of defenses, the size of the treasure within. He will even tell us of the best time to strike and perhaps prepare defectors to aid us. And when the winter comes again he will go and trade with the enemy again and see that our little priestling here has wine for his Masses."

The last of his words Pelayo accompanied with a broad

smile and a look fixed steadily on the merchant. Felix, in turn, answered with a mock sadness which was the best device he could contrive to cover his relief.

"You make my life difficult, Pelayo. My business almost impossible. All these things I can do, will do, until an African knife rips my poor guts. It is an honor to serve you."

Pelayo ignored him.

"All these early attacks will be against the towns. In midsummer we will leave a lull in which the enemy can convince himself that the war is over. Then, in the fall after the harvest but before the stock slaughtering, our raids will concentrate on food supplies for the winter. Cattle, sheep and wheat will be the main targets. These hills cannot feed as many as we are now and certainly not as many as we shall become in a year."

The chieftain now turned to the archer's captain.

"These raids for food and stock, Wala. The Astures will have had some experience of this kind of action. They could be helpful running the animals and carting the foodstocks while we provide a covering force. Do you think that they could be persuaded to join with us for a portion of the winnings?"

The dark skinned captain allowed himself a faint smile.

"They have lived in such a way before you or I were born, Pelayo. But they have never had a Gothic guard to do it. They will be quick to see the advantage. They even have some experience of harrying towns and might be of use there also. But there will be much bargaining over terms before we can secure their help. You yourself will have to meet with their chief."

"How much can we trust the Astures?" asked Masona.

"Right now," answered Pelayo, "they stand to gain something by betraying us to the Africans. How much of a price is on our heads we don't know but something for sure. The Africans, though, seem not to be ready to act yet. If before they choose that path we can persuade them to join us in a series of raids, then they become the enemies of the Arabs too—if they aren't already. Chances become less then that the Astures will someday guide our enemies here.

"What do we risk anyway? While we're on campaign they will be out on the plains with us. Either of us would risk self-destruction as the cost of betrayal then. If we can get them to join us for one successful raid, we may be able to turn them from hostiles into allies. If we lose, of course, they will cheerfully join in cutting our throats. But if we lose we are finished anyway and it won't matter whose hand holds the knife.

"Right now we have sources of information in Felix that they don't have. We have four hundred heavily armed warriors as a striking force which they lack. We have potential assistance from inside the towns that they would never have. They will see the chance for loot on a scale beyond their dreams and at very little cost to them. On these terms, I think that we may be able to enlist their help for at least one try. After that, we'll see, if we're alive to see."

The group in the hut was silent then. Surveying their faces Pelayo could read consent in the faces of his captains. They were not enthused with this unusual course but they saw some possibility of success. In any event they all had come to trust his luck, his instinct.

Amalsuntha was suddenly staring at her delicate feet. The priest would not lift his eyes. Felix alone was smiling and the chieftain could see in the merchant's attitude something of the excitement that his own words had begun to generate in himself.

"Try to locate, Wala, the paramount chief of the Astures in this region. Talk to him and try to get him to agree to a meeting. These are the dice the gods have handed us and these are the dice we will throw."

Chapter XVIII

The sack of León was a brilliant success.

At the beginning of June the troops left the mountain village where they had wintered and marched to a temporary camp just over the pass which led down towards their objective. Ten days of the hardest kind of marching at a single stretch burned off the fat which they had been accumulating over the long, inactive winter. Conducted under precautions against the real possibility of attack by the tribal groups through whose lands they were so rapidly passing, it also restored the taut discipline which had slackened under almost nine months of camp living. Best of all, the prospect of action raised the tone of the entire body and veterans as well as new recruits found the sense of purpose of their leaders infectious.

Reaching the rendezvous, which was merely a small, high plain set among the foothills of the Cantabrians, they began with enthusiasm to raise the rough summer shelters and to surround them with a four-sided, four-gated palisade which was then ditched all around. They had been at this work for five days and it was virtually complete by the time that the three hundred Asturian warriors, led by their bandy-legged chief, Bodo, appeared tardily on the scene. Their small, dark, largely fur-clad allies settled down on the plain outside the palisaded Gothic camp in an arrangement which minimized the chances for clashes between the two mutually suspicious groups.

In any event time for the latter was scant. During the time spent awaiting the arrival of the Astures, Pelayo had designated Masona as the base camp commander for the campaign. The man's strong protests netted him no satisfaction at all. He had also to see some of the warriors of his command transferred to those of Fruela, Huneric, and Wala. In return he gained from the companies of these only those who had sickened or been injured on the march. He was to be left with almost a hundred fifty men to hold the camp in the absence of the war party.

That body was ready to depart within two days of the arrival of Bodo's men. Even within that short space of time frictions between the two oddly matched bands resulted in two stabbings and one man beaten to death with a club near the spring at night.

At the outset of the eight day march, the little army settled into what was to be both its marching order and tactical disposition for the coming battle. The Asturians, separated into two groups roughly equal in numbers, were thrown out at about a mile distance initially to the east and to the west respectively of the main Gothic party and gradually increasing as they approached the plains. They were to serve both as screening and reconnaissance forces for it. The eighty odd men of the archer force under Wala moved at the same distance in the van. Behind them came three companies, of about the same number each, commanded by Fruela, Huneric, and Pelayo himself in a compact mass.

These dispositions worked perfectly. Before the proprietors of the peasant farms and the occasional small villages, which they increasingly encountered, could be more than marginally alarmed, Wala's archers had loped past them and were already between them and León to the south. By the time that the passage of ordered ranks of the main force arrived to thoroughly terrify them it was already too late to flee south. They watched in numb terror until its continuing movement gradually reassured them that they were not its target. Wala, of course, had orders that no one was to be allowed to pass south through his ranks.

At night, each of the four components of the force extended their camps laterally. Since they camped without fires, safe passage through their lines toward the endangered city was an almost impossible feat. Only five men were captured attempting it during the whole march. After they had been questioned and executed, Pelayo was sure that the real nature of his advance was unheralded.

Off to the flanks, there was indeed a scattering of alarms created by the passage of the Astures. But those who witnessed only that could form a little idea of the real nature of the enterprise afoot. If some word managed to reach the African commander at León, and some seemed to have, it told him only that a not terribly impressive war band from the mountains was abroad in the land. A brief conference with his Gothic auxiliaries quickly convinced him that such forays were entirely to be expected during the summer months.

Such was the speed with which Pelayo's forces marched, that they were upon him before Ahmed ibn Yusuf had time to complete his preparations for dealing with an entirely misunderstood threat. In his city headquarters he received the entirely perplexing news that a small band of warriors, mostly archers apparently, had taken up an absurd position on the south bank of the river and were turning back all traffic from the town to the south, although traffic into the town from that direction was being ignored. After questioning of the peasants and caravan drivers who had been turned back as well as some of those from the south who had been let pass, the Africans by noontime, had gathered that this audacious band seemed to have crossed the river during the early morning hours, probably upstream somewhere of León. They seemed to be an oddly mixed group of peasants, from the conflicting reports he got, with some sprinkling of Goths and

Asturians among them. Their numbers were impossible to estimate but might be as few as thirty or forty.

There seemed to be no discernable logic to their behavior but its consistent pattern disturbed Ahmed. Since he profoundly mistrusted his Gothic auxiliaries beyond the range of his own voice and eyes, he decided about mid-afternoon to send out a Berber reconnoitering force of fifty men to either disperse the enemy or get him more adequate estimates of the problem so abruptly created. He felt that, in the first instance, he could detach no more than a quarter of his African garrison safely and they might be sufficient to quell what might be unusually determined native rebels.

Within four hours the Berber force had returned somewhat bloodied. They had lost four dead and had another seven wounded. Their attempts to force both the bridge and the river itself at some of the easier points had been repulsed. The captain of the Berbers assured him that, whoever they were, the men across the river were certainly not ordinary peasants. They shot well but also with discipline from the tree line of the opposite bank. They already held all of the good crossings within the distance he had been able to explore under his instructions. They were certainly trained warriors, well-led, and in numbers he could only guess but certainly superior to his own. There were at least a hundred of them.

Ahmed received the news impassively but with mounting interior alarm. If this was the Asturian war party of which he'd heard they were behaving very differently than anyone had led him to suspect they would. The obvious explanation of their tactics was that they intended to attack the city itself—or at least threaten an attack to exact a ransom. Yet their numbers were so far entirely insufficient to such an undertaking.

Feeling puzzled and somewhat foolish he dispatched mounted messengers to his sister garrisons at Astorga and Carrión with word that he expected to be under attack on the morrow by Asturian bandits and that he would try to arrange a parley with their chief. In the meantime, he would appreciate it if they would send what forces they could spare to assist in cutting off and destroying the marauders. He also ordered the city gates closed to all further arrivals. No use in allowing them to infiltrate the city if that was what they were doing. In addition he set in motion a house to house search in the city to round up every person who had entered the city during the past two days. The wall guard was doubled. Finally, work parties were formed to begin a hasty reinforcing of the worst spots in the old Roman walls of the city. In a number of places neglect had allowed those ramparts to become little more than loose piles of stone topped by rough wooden palisades. Such palisades themselves had no walkways and must be awkwardly defended from the walls on either side.

Far out on the road to Astorga the African's messenger topped a small rise to find himself suddenly in the midst of a group of howling Astures. Throat-shot, his mount went down and he himself died quickly in a hail of axe blows. The western blocking force had moved into its positions as early as mid-day. So had the eastern bank of Asturians but the messenger riding for Carrión was more alert and his horse fresher. Reeling and plunging amid a shower of arrows, he whipped his mount towards a gap in the ranks of his would-be ambushers and plunged through without his horse stumbling. Barely conscious at first of the long spear gash in his right calf and along the rump of his steed, testifying how close the ring had come to closing on him, he quickly outdistanced his unmounted pursuers. Avoiding the road itself and every copse that might conceal other enemies, he arrived back to hammer at the León gates just after dark had fallen.

Now the city commander was positive that the Astures were preparing an attack on the city itself. Nor could he count on any aid from Astorga because his messenger dispatched in that direction might have been intercepted. The next day would probably see the barbarians concentrating on the city itself. He would try to negotiate and play for time while defenses were put in better order. The only consolation, he reflected bitterly, was that the Gothic auxiliaries would fight well since they were no friends to the hill tribes of the north. They could expect no more mercy at the hands of the barbarians than he would get himself if they lost.

With that in mind he decided against the execution of the strangers in the town who had already been arrested. Instead, under the eyes of the Gothic captain, he had them put to work clearing a space behind the weakest section of the walls. If the huts could be demolished in time, then an open space devoid of cover could be created to form a rough killing ground if the palisade were breached there. Barricades erected between the houses farther back and the roofs of some of the sturdier structures would furnish protection for the defenders while they concentrated their fire against such disorganized attackers as might overrun the wall palisade. The work went with agonizing slowness. The ground was stony, the workers sullenly unfamiliar with their task, and the light huts surprisingly resistant to their untutored efforts. Well past midnight, having left orders that they should be worked till they dropped, Ahmed decided that he should get a few hours sleep. The way it was going, he would surely have to parley for time tomorrow. He must make a good and confident appearance.

Just at first light, Fruela's men raced for the palisade. The nervous energy that had been building through a three hour night march flooded their veins now, making the four tree trunks they carried seem almost weightless. At the same time, Huneric's and Pelayo's columns broke for the adjoining sections of the wall carrying light scaling ladders. The alarm drums began to roll before they had covered more than a quarter of the distance to the walls but the tricky half-light made accurate shooting difficult and the defenders were unnerved by the unexpected concentration of heavily armed troops against one section of the walls. They were spread too thinly themselves even if their shooting had been more accurate.

Ahmed reached the walls just before Pelayo's warriors did. Even newly awake, his battle-tried eyes could see the beginnings of disaster at a glance. These were no light-armed, loosely-disciplined troops attacking. It was a small-scale Gothic army such as he'd seen with Tarik. They outnumbered his Berbers better than two to one and, on this section of the wall where they had concentrated their attack, more like eight-to one. Too late he remembered the stories he had heard of Ávila and Salamanca. Too late he understood the war cries going up from the enemy now at the base of the walls. "Rodrigo. Rodrigo."

His own captains were already directing the just wakened reserves towards the point of the attack but the enemy had scored the crucial surprise. They were in close before they could be bloodied, weakened. Fruela's makeshift battering rams were pounding at the palisade whose wood groaned and shuddered at each blow. On the adjoining walls his own men were more than occupied pushing-off scaling ladders of the other two columns and firing at the men working them into position. They could hardly spare a shot at those belaboring the palisade almost unhindered.

Expecting the attack of Asturians he had placed the defense of the half-finished inner breastworks in the hands of his Gothic auxiliaries. That way they would have taken most of the casualties while his own Berbers fought from the comparative safety of the walls. But they might not fight at all against fellow Goths. Already it seemed to him that those of the auxiliaries on the walls were slackening their fire or shooting high although the halflight made it hard to tell for sure.

Suddenly two of the drier posts of the palisade snapped not far from ground level and hung at an angle from the upper crosspieces. As Ahmed watched with a powerless detachment a burly, blackmaned Goth squeezed sideways through the opening, followed closely by three others. An arrow from the rampart took one of them but the other three locked shields while those outside shifted their battering against the upper parts. A few blows tore the crosspiece loose and now those remaining outside leaped one by one over the jagged stumps. Working a borrowed bow furiously himself, Ahmed saw them form up and begin to rush the makeshift second defense with the shouts of "Rodrigo" on their lips. He saw his auxiliaries draw back, some throwing down their shields and swords and others simply turning their backs and running. He saw no more because an arrow took him beneath the left shoulder blade.

Bereft of their commander, the wall breached, the African defense crumbled. Some died still at their posts. Some went over the wall to try to fight free in little groups and perished in the attempt. Others tried to retreat along the wall to one of the gates which offered exit from the doomed city. None of them got so far. The entire assault had taken less than an hour.

By late afternoon the Astures were admitted into León to gather such personal loot as pleased them. They had, most of them, taken no part in the fighting but some of them had accompanied Pelayo's force in order that they might witness the prowess of the Goths. Before their main forces arrived, Pelayo had gathered up the weapons and the precious metals. The forces of the Gothic garrison had already been impressed into those of his captains which were now swollen to almost six hundred even after the losses of the assault.

Since their combined forces now totaled almost a thousand men, the allies spent three days in the town. It seemed sure that not one of the Africans had survived the ambuscade. Even if a few had escaped, there was little likelihood that the scattered plain garrisons could mount a comparable force for weeks. The heads of the Berber garrison were impaled along the walls. On Pelayo's orders, no quarter had been given them. For three days the allies drank the wine of León, ate its food, and enjoyed its women. Then they formed up for the march north.

Each man was allowed to take what he could carry. No slaves were permitted. Pack animals were limited to those which carried gold, silver, extra weapons, wine, and food-stuffs. Pelayo would have preferred that no women be included but a strict rule here would have incited too much trouble. The Goths of the former garrison were to take along their wives if they had one and anyone at all was allowed to bring a woman—at the cost of marrying her. Whether or not they could keep the march pace was strictly their own concern. The few riding horses worth taking were distributed among the captains only and the two best were reserved for Pelayo and for Bodo, chief of the Astures.

The same order of march was observed on the return to the forward camp in the Cantabrian foothills. Except for the rapidity of the pace, it had more the character of a regular route march now. Although guard was strictly posted, and well out from the encampments, cooking fires were allowed. Inevitably, discipline had been less well enforced among the Asturians and, burdened with often useless plunder, they lagged behind the Gothic main body. Pelayo observed this with a grim satisfaction. If there should be a pursuit, they would bear the brunt of the casualties. Also, he wanted the superiority of tight order to be borne home to his allies. The exploits of his own men during the assault were being magnified daily by tale-telling among the hill people. If the march itself reinforced that lesson, it was even better.

But there was no pursuit. In a little over a week, they marched into the forward camp. There provisions were made to send on the most valuable spoils to their permanent camp in the mountains. The wounded who had not survived the march were buried. The sick and recuperating warriors were transferred to Huneric's command who now replaced Masona in charge of the camp. Time was allowed to negotiate with the chiefs of the neighboring tribes for more warriors.

The prestige that had resulted from the easy capture of León greatly eased that task.

At the end of the first week in July, Pelayo was ready to undertake his second great raid into the northern plains. When he left camp almost six hundred Gothic warriors formed the core of his army. This number included both those who had been abruptly recruited from the Leónese garrison and a strong spinkling of refugees who continued to drift into the Cantabrian mountains from the south and from Galicia to the west. In addition the new fame of his war band and stories of the generosity with which it behaved had raised the numbers of his Asturian allies to more than five hundred.

Such were the numbers of his war band that provisioning during the ten day march became a major problem. Each of the warriors was given a four-day supply of provisions from the stock captured at León and the remainder was loaded on pack animals whose train now must accompany the main body. Even so, there was precious little that would be left for the return march and a quick victory would be essential.

For three days they marched west through the rugged country and then they turned southwest. Now among the rolling hills of the Bierzo they struck for the old Roman road between Lugo and Astorga. Dispositions for the march were roughly the same as during the prior one but now the hilly country made both communication and dispersion difficult by turns. The same conditions made it likely that news of their approach would travel ahead of them to both the south and to the west. That being so, cooking fires were allowed at night for the first six days to soften somewhat the rigors of the grueling march.

It was only on the sixth day that new orders were issued that from now on there would be no fires. On the following morning the line of march turned sharply southeast angling toward the Roman road as it led down towards Astorga. Since serious attack was hardly to be expected in these foothills, Wala's archers, aided by an equal number of Astures, were ordered far forward in small bands of fifteen men scattered well across the countryside.

Their orders were simple. It could be presumed by this time that Berber scouts would be watching the progress of the war band. They were to find and kill them at whatever cost to themselves. While Pelayo knew that it was very unlikely that such a mission could be entirely successful, the deployment of the archers across a wide front, well in advance of the army itself, would at least force the surviving enemy scouts to make a wide detour before they could begin their return to Astorga. Delayed news was often as worthless as no news. The archers also had orders to kill any peasants found heading south as well as to attack and kill any one or any group traveling the Roman road itself—in either direction. Only if they ran into an enemy military force of fifty or more were they to avoid immediate battle and seek further orders.

As it turned out no such numerous enemy was encountered. A half dozen Berber scouts were killed and twice that number of peasants who might have been spies or had simply had the misfortune of being observed traveling in a dangerous direction. In addition two pack trains were seized on the road, forced off it, and all of their members slaughtered well within the forests along its borders. So were three dispatch riders on the same road. Since Wala's orders demanded success rather than caution, his own casualties were high. One Berber scout killed four of the men pursuing him before being slain himself. In all, the captain of the archers lost twenty-five men killed, or so seriously wounded that they had to be abandoned in just three days of frantic activity.

Ali ibn Muhmmad, the Arab commander of Astorga, would have liked to disarm his Gothic auxiliaries. Indeed he had orders to do so if Pelayo's forces were to approach the city. Interrogation of the frightened, sullen inhabitants of León, with its burned gates and palisades and looted armory, had revealed that the auxiliaries there had refused to fight against their brethren at the crucial moment. They had not actually revolted and joined the attack of the rebels but they had been useless against them. In the aftermath of that success, however, his superiors feared even worse behavior from their Gothic allies in another such situation. Ali quite concurred with those fears.

What those pompous asses did not consider, however, was that his auxiliaries in Astorga were roughly equal in number to his own two hundred fifty Berbers. The news of Ahmed's disaster at León had made his own Goths both suspicious and insolent. They might even now be plotting to seize the city except that they would have no clear idea of what to do if they should succeed. For the present, the bravest of them deserted by twos and threes whenever the opportunity offered. That was a development which Ali secretly welcomed and which he discretely facilitated to the extent possible.

If he judged their temper rightly, his auxiliaries would revolt outright if he attempted to disarm them. There would be a little civil war fought right inside the city itself. He knew that he could win such a fight, especially if he himself chose the moment to precipitate it. But when all was said and done he would surely come out of it with less than two hundred effectives to hold the entire city. What he'd asked for was another two hundred Africans. With them he could have disarmed the Goths without any danger of their resisting. After that he could have sent the reinforcements back—well, half of them anyway. That was it, of course. They hadn't sent him the reinforcements because they knew that they'd never get them back. Every military governor north of the Guadarramas was jittery—expecting a Gothic revolt out of every tax riot. No one of them would part with troops he really trusted. So who the hell was in charge? Tarik distrusted by Musa. Both of them suspect in Damascus.

Now there was a real emergency and no one was doing anything except talk and send messages back and forth. Five days ago his scouts had brought him news that a large force was moving through the hills to the northwest. They said it was a couple of thousand men but that didn't seem likely. It had to be Pelayo and he only had about five hundred at León a few weeks ago. Beside that, even a good general, and the renegade Goth was that, couldn't feed that many men in that tangle of rocks and pines. Maybe he had a thousand, no more.

As soon as he'd had real confirmation of the report, he'd asked for reinforcements from Zamora, León, and Palencia. Fat chance! At León, five hundred men were working day and night to rebuild the burned gates, palisades and half-ruined walls. The governor at Palencia wanted his western advance post restored.

The only hope was that the commander at Lugo had asked for more men too. Ali knew that because the dispatch rider from Lugo had come down from the hill town through Astorga. Well, if help came back up the road from Zamora, it wasn't going to get past Astorga.

Ali knew that his town was to be the victim. Two days ago the last scout to return said that the Goths had turned in his direction—and no sign of help yet. They'd told him, all those fat slugs protecting their own skins, that the walls of Astorga were the strongest on the frontier. What they hadn't said was how you defend them against odds of five to one or worse!

A sudden slapping of feet in the anteroom brought the commander to his doorway in a minute.

"What is it?"

"Another scout, my lord."

The scout was weaving on his feet from exhaustion. His eyes, however, were bright with pride.

"What news do you have, soldier?"

"They will attack us, sir. They are marching very fast now. They have moved onto the road itself. Goths and Astures. It is Pelayo for sure. Maybe fifteen hundred in all. They might be here tonight but by tomorrow for sure."

The commander dismissed him. Fifteen hundred men, Ali thought. If I could count on the auxiliaries that would be only three to one. The walls are very good. It would be possible to win at those odds but the defenses would be very thin. It would require very careful dispositions.

He looked at his hands on the writing table. In the gathering dusk they looked young, strong. He did not want to die, he thought suddenly. Not yet. He had some good years left still. Not here in this little provincial town. He would take another wife when this was over. A young one and he would have a son who lived yet. Allah give us victory.

"Lieutenant."

His aide entered respectfully, ready.

"Summon all my captains for a council. I want both our own and those of the Goths too. But the Goths will not leave this room alive. See that the palace guard understands that as well as our own captains. Once they are all here I will begin the council. As I begin to speak, I will have their attention and the killing will begin then. The five of them should die quickly.

"When that's done, I'll want another twenty or thirty of the Goths killed. You know the ones likely to make trouble. Get their names together and where they are billeted so that they'll be ready for the guard. It must all be done very swiftly. The rest of the auxiliaries will be told that their captains made a treacherous attempt on my life in council and that the others were privy to the plot. Then I want the rest of them broken up and distributed among our men on the walls. We'll need every one of them tomorrow and I mean to see that they fight. The captains and I will go over the battle plan as soon as the rest of it is carried out."

"Yes, lord."

As his lieutenant turned and left, Ali could see the man's relief in his demeanor and even in his carriage. As a good soldier, he was happy that there was a plan—that the weighing of alternatives was finally over.

Perhaps I should have done this before, he thought. But no, my own men and the Goths could never live together as comrades in a single unit. They might fight together tomorrow to save their own hides in battle but once the siege was over there would have to be more killing. His captains would have to see to it that the Goths took most of the casualties.

It was full night now as he waited. The sun had dropped well behind the western mountains. The bustle of coming and going in the outer office increased. He could see that two of his own captains had arrived and as he watched yet a third. They spoke heatedly to his aide.

"My lord."

His aide entered with the three soldiers. No one of them smiled nor even made the traditional salutations. The tension was palpable but controlled.

"The Gothic chiefs are not coming to the council. They agreed they would but delayed. Now some of them are withdrawing their men to the church near the eastern gate. The others are probably getting ready to follow. It looks like treachery. Should we order an attack on them?"

"Too late for that."

Another of his captains had entered with more news.

"They're barricading the church. Most of their men are already there."

"We can't hold the walls with only our own men," said another of his captains.

But Ali already knew the consequences. Had he not been weighing them for almost a week?

"No," he said, "no attack. Kill any stragglers you can but no general attack. This piece of business has been well planned. For tonight I want a hundred men blockading that church but no attack unless they try to break out and I don't think that they will. The rest of the men will be on the walls. Unless help arrives by tomorrow the city is lost.

"If it doesn't, we'll treat with Pelayo tomorrow. For a bloodless capture of the city, he may be willing to let us march out without weapons by the south gate. Otherwise we shall all be dead heroes in paradise by tomorrow night."

Pelayo admired the gray-brown walls of Astorga, lit by the morning sun. They were as stout as he remembered them. Good, solid Roman construction. He would not care to assault them against an adequate garrison. But Felix had assured him that the Goths of Astorga would not fight. Their captain, Bermudo, had been promised a command in Pelayo's band and a share of the booty for holding his men back from the defense. Even if he didn't join the attack the African commander could not be sure he wouldn't and could not even deploy his whole force of Berbers on those walls. That would mean six, even seven, men on a ladder against each man on the walls. Good odds.

The Gothic chieftain had drawn his full force up in plain sight of the eastern face of the city defenses just out of bow shot. It was the easiest approach and if the defenders wanted to try to make a run for it by the unguarded western gate, so much the better. Hunting them down in the open would be even easier and the story of Africans fleeing in disorder before the city was even attacked would make his fame greater and undermine their reputation for invincibility.

The four divisions of his Goths and the three of Astures bristled with weapons and scaling ladders. They must make a brave sight, in the morning sunshine, from the walls. Pelayo had made no attempt at surprise or concealment. He wanted the defenders to know that they were going to die. Men who knew that they were doomed might fight bravely but they would not fight well.

The tension had been heightening in the last few minutes since the little party of three had issued from the eastern gate. On foot, they carried no weapons. The standard one bore was reversed. Clearly they wanted a parley. But Pelayo had forbidden a response. He had instructed Walla that, if they came within bowshot, they were to be killed.

The little group had not. Something in the steady impassivity of that host before them warned against venturing so far. They stood now, irresolute and unarmed, waiting for some sign from their enemies of a willingness to talk.

Pelayo could feel the sweat coursing down his sides. It was always like this just before battle was joined. The sun seemed unbearably bright—the morning breeze especially cool. The horse under him could feel the nervousness of his rider and shifted in turn. A sword struck metal somewhere behind him.

On the plain by the gate, the dejected emissaries began to back away. They had waited long enough to have done their duty. They despaired of a response.

"Now, now! Attack!"

The long line erupted into movement and swept forward toward the wall.

"Rodrigo! Rodrigo!"

Chapter XIX

The September sun filtered through the pines of the little glade, touching the summer growth of scraggly weed with false promise of sustenance. A giant horned beetle worked patiently at the decaying substance of a fallen limb, at home in the humid world of rot. As the persistent breeze stirred the evergreens the changing pattern of golden light shifted back and forth on the massive bulk of the priest, Paternus. In his rough gray cloak he seemed almost to be another of the stolid gray boulders which everywhere broke the scattered soil and its vegetation, oblivious to the hungry roots that searched their surface and probed their seams.

"How comes the arm, Sunna?"

This personal turn in the conversation annoyed the young Goth. It was just to avoid his own brooding over that wound that he sought out others for talk, however idle. The purple and red of the ugly weal across his right forearm were fading now but the arm was weak, too weak. He feared to think that the strength would not come back. He told himself to be patient, to wait, but his heart suspected that he was a cripple—a woman! Should he be glad to be alive? He knew he was. Dead heroes were glorious only to those who had not smelled them. They had almost been caught there at Astorga. The assault on the walls had been brief, furious, but never in doubt. The Berbers, caught between the overwhelming numbers of the besiegers and the revolt of their own Gothic auxiliaries had died swiftly—to a man.

But who would have expected that Musa would have been so swiftly victorious at Zaragoza. They had scarcely had time to bundle the loot on pack animals and fire the city. As Pelayo had led them back up into the hills to the northwest of the blackened city, the Africans' advance guard entered the ruin. It had taken all of his chieftains' skill to get them back into the safety of the mountains while preserving their precious winnings.

On the withdrawal, the hunters became the hunted among the little valleys and passes of the foothills. Only Pelayo could have managed the ambuscades, the sudden marches, the changes of direction, the counterattacks at night which gave them time, which prevented the retreat from disintegrating into rout. Even then it was lucky that the Africans had no scouts who really knew the country.

How many dozens of fights had there been? On one of those times when an enemy force had briefly found them, he had almost died. In the thick of the sudden fight, a glancing blow had caught his sword arm. As his own weapon slipped from powerless fingers, he had seen the ferocious grin of his opponent. Even now he could remember the numbness of his body as cold despair had gripped him. Had he screamed in terror? He had heard brave men do it as they died. He could not remember.

But he had been crushed to the ground. Flung down like a child from behind as Pelayo himself crashed into his enemy of a moment before. The man, driven back by that superhuman energy, never had time to recover. Battered by blow after blow, his guard had finally slipped and Pelayo's sword stabbed entirely through his body just below the ribs.

Sunna knew little more of the retreat. Lashed across a donkey, he had alternated between delirium and utter blackness. Miraculously the arm had not rotted.

Bitterly, smilingly, he replied.

"It's like a chicken wing, Paternus. I can flap it but it's not good for anything."

"So it is a blessing," responded the impassive mountain.

Sunna was shocked. The bluntness of the priest touched something beyond his soft self-pity. It awoke his caution.

"Blessing?"

"Yes, blessing. If it had not been the arm I think that you would have lost something else—your life perhaps. I think you have no heart for fighting."

"You mean I am afraid of it. It's true, I am. But every man is. Pelayo himself sweats like a bull before the battle. Wala squats down tight on his haunches, draws himself tight, to control the trembling. Everyone is afraid before a fight. No one wants to die."

"Don't take me for a fool, boy. I'm no warrior but I know them. I know they're afraid. But Fruela loves to kill. He likes it more than wine. Pelayo needs it. It chases his demon. For Masona, it's a business, part of life. You are not like any of the three. So you are not a warrior. You could kill ten men, a hundred, and you still would not be a warrior."

"So what then am I? A farmer? A woman?"

"Shut up, boy, and listen to me. I have no patience for child's babble. You know what you are. You have a vision. You want more than any of those fools. You want something better and I can help you get it."

Now Sunna was afraid. But the black eyes of his tormentor held him. He fell back on bluster.

"What can you get me?"

"You already know, boy. Shall I draw you a picture then? Your blood is good, a Gothic nobleman's blood. Your father was careful with you. He gave you an education like no one's in this camp. You can read, write, know the old language and some of the authors. But he could never give you a warrior's heart, could he? And now you have a right hand that will never swing a sword. It's a sign, boy. God's blood, it's a sign! You're to be a priest."

A vagrant cloud had drifted over the fall sun. The young man was suddenly chilled. Far off, the chatter of birds was mocking, unreal. He felt sick. His response was neither question nor challenge but a whisper that escaped like a sigh.

"A priest."

"Just so, Sunna. And I can help you. The wise ones your tutor never set you, Origen, Augustine, our own Isidore, I know. I can be your tutor. And I can teach you the sacred words, the way to say them, the way to hold yourself when you do. And more, I can get you the laying on of hands. More than one bishop knows me.

"Think of it. There will be more than one power in these hills—a power that Pelayo himself will have to reckon with—God's power, your power, Sunna. Me they despise because I'm a refugee like them but you came with them first as a captive—against your will. They tried to make a soldier of you and they could not. But I knew that the Spirit was at work in you and I can make you fit to show these dogs the Spirit's glory."

The young Goth's head reeled. Somewhere inside himself he felt a release—a small drain of tension, a beginning of assent, but his mouth was dry. The prospect that the priest had presented was too new for him to grasp it. He could not imagine himself in such a role.

"How can you be so sure, Paternus, when I am not? How can one know about such a thing? How did you know, in the beginning that you yourself had such a call?"

"The picture I've drawn you moves you, doesn't it boy? That's how one knows. The word is spoken and something inside you says yes. But there are things you must do to prove yourself worthy. Especially you must help me now for I am to help you. I will be your master, your tutor until you are ready."

"What must I do? How should I help you?"

"A little thing for you but a great and necessary thing for the both of us, boy. You know the chalice and the cross that

Pelayo took as part of the spoil at Astorga? The golden ones? They are not broken up yet like the ones from León but that is what he will do with them. He'll turn them into barter stuff for food in the winter. He'll turn them over to that thief, Felix—the furniture of God for pig's food.

"You have to go to him now. Ask him for them as your share of the booty. You have that right. You fought at Astorga. You've claimed nothing so far. You gave an arm for him.

"Besides, he saved your life. That means something to him, boy. He gave you life. Even if he'd hated you before he loves you now. You're his son, boy—born in battle. He'll give them if you ask. Me he'd laugh at but you he will not refuse. And I need them. With them any hut I choose becomes a church. It is time to give some order to this gang of bandits."

"No!"

The same revulsion that forced the reply from his lips also moved Sunna to rise and take an involuntary pace backward without even being conscious of his doing so. Paternus wanted to use him! The priest had been flattering him—talking about his birth and education. What he really wanted was his precious vessels. He wants me to humiliate myself, to take my crippled arm like a relic and use it to barter with Pelayo. Hot shame swept over him at the thought. I'd have to tell Pelayo the whole thing. Have to ask his permission to separate myself from the whole war band. I'd have to tell him that I've no wish to be a warrior—that I'd rather be an apprentice to this great lump of scheming fat. He'll think that I'm a coward or a fool, or both. He'll think that this shrunken arm has unmanned me—that I'm ungrateful for his saving my life. Even if he granted the request, he'd despise me for it.

"I can't, I couldn't," he gasped, half-strangling on the words. The priest opposite displayed not a flicker of emotion. His eyes glinted in the random sun but he did not stir. His voice, when it came, was flatter, more matter-of-fact. It did not seek to argue or cajole.

"It is already decided, boy. Your future is set. You will go to Pelayo, now or later, but you will go."

The words echoed behind Sunna as he fled the spot.

Days later he could still hear them. He was wrestling anxiously with their threat when he entered the grove by the river and came suddenly upon Amalsuntha. The tall blond sat in the sun upon a large flattish boulder. Her hair, freshly washed, fell down about her shoulders in still damp ringlets. Her head was slightly thrown back to catch the sun as it worked at the drying of her hair, accentuating the long, white curve of her throat and the sharp, straight line of her nose. Her profile seemed to him like that of an eagle unawares.

She was alone and he would have withdrawn softly but the faintest motion of her hand betrayed that she had already seen him. Almost without disturbing her motionless repose, it signaled that he was to sit beside her. It was a command, he knew.

For long minutes they sat there silently. Sunna knew that he was not to begin the conversation. Amalsuntha continued to sun her hair, head thrown back and eyes closed, her hands braced upon the flat surface of the rock behind her. The immaculate white wool of her tunic hung caressingly over the high mounds of her breasts and folded slightly at the fullness of her hips. The whiteness of her calves glinted slightly with the gold of their downy hair. Her feet, by their discarded sandals, flexed slightly in the deep, green moss.

Strong feet, he thought, and strong hands as well. For all her beauty, there was about her a vital strength which betrayed a purposefulness and a never absent control. She was enjoying, he knew, the warm play of the sun upon her head and body and the stored warmth of the rock which flowed into her palms, pressed against it. He knew she was enjoying, as well, the fascinated play of his eyes on her face and long body. She is a dangerous woman, he thought, a lioness basking in the sun.

"You know, Sunna, that of all the people in this camp you alone are the equal of Pelayo and I in birth."

She spoke throatily and without turning her head or opening her eyes.

"Yes, my lady, but birth does not count for much in these mountains."

Now she opened her eyes a bit, half-squinting against the sun, and surveyed him briefly without turning. A trace of indulgent smile played upon her lips.

"That," she said, "is why the mountains are such a stupid place. I do not see what your chief can hope to achieve by keeping us all here."

Sunna simply did not respond. She had not called Pelayo her chief but his. He had no wish to defend her brother against her. From somewhere a shout sounded dimly in the silence of the clearing. A bird fluttered busily, alighting home in its nest in a tall pine. Beyond and above the tree a few thin strings of insubstantial cloud fled the sun across the sky. Shaking her head to spread her hair in the sunlight, the Gothic princess continued to speak, once again behind closed lids.

"Have you ever missed your father's palace in Palencia? You must."

"Sometimes, but not very often, my lady. I was very young and not often out of the women's quarters. It was a great, cold stone pile and frightening for a little boy. Really I miss much more my tutor's house in Sevilla where I was sent to study. It was warm white clay and he was a warm person. My father was as cold as his palace, I think."

"But at least you will remember the fine, soft clothes and the splendid food—and great jewels on great ladies?"

At this last she turned her head and gazed at him speculatively. Smiling at him, like a conspirator in mischief, she continued.

"You will remember your mother. She was a great lady. Did she look at all like me?"

"She died when I had but four years, Amalsuntha, so my

recollections are very faint. But I think that she was not so fair nor beautiful as are you."

Pelayo sister's smile broadened ever so slightly at this last and it almost seemed, for an instant, that she might be about to laugh. Instead, she continued on the playful tone which she had already adopted.

"Ah, there is something of the courtier in you, Sunna. You have not forgotten the training of your boyhood. This rough, soldier's life has not completely corrupted you. You could grace a court yet."

"Tell me," she continued, "is there no one of your family left. I know that your father is dead but had he no brothers, sisters? Is there no one in that civilized country that we have left behind so abruptly who could ease your way if you went back some day? No one who could find a fitting palace for a young noble of the Goths?"

"There was my father's uncle in Sevilla. He was the one who found a tutor for me there. But that was eight years ago and I haven't seen him now in three years. Even if he has not been killed in the wars, he was an old man then and not in good health. He did have two daughters, both married and not living in Sevilla, so I didn't even meet them. I suppose that they could be alive somewhere if one could find them."

"Then there would be a chance for you in the great world," she seemed to muse. "It might be a difficult search and some explanations would be awkward but you could have a chance. Living here among these Asturian barbarians is not the only way you could enjoy your young manhood."

She gave a particular, enigmatic emphasis to the last few words and her smile took on a brilliance that almost dazed him. He was aware of now, a slight pressure, the faintest hint of warmth where carelessly her knee had strayed along the side of his hand as it rested on the rock's edge. The lightest of contact continued.

"Have you thought," she asked more quietly now, "since you have become a young man in these last two years who you might marry in a camp like this? Do you find these young Asturian girls herding their goats attractive?"

The warm flesh against his hand had become more insistent now. It pressed slightly, fell away, and pressed again. He was distracted by the repetition.

"I have not thought of marriage," he said lamely, for want of the ability to concentrate fully.

Amalsuntha laughed huskily now.

"There are other uses for manhood than marriage."

His hand was on her leg. He could feel the soft down of it burning against his palm. What else could he do. She was leading him he knew but her face gave no reflection of her purpose. She put her head back again and he could feel the movement in the muscles under the creamy skin.

"Think of the perfumes of a proper court, Sunna. Try to remember for a moment what it would be like to have a rich wine rolling on your tongue. Think of a roast all dressed in spices and cooked by a proper chef. Young girls all bejeweled and finely clothed in dyed stuff of the east."

She inhaled deeply and released her breath in a long, lingering sigh, her eyes closed now again. Her splendid breasts had risen with the inhalation and now ran slightly down and away from her garment. That this effect was not lost on him she knew. At the same time she had slid forward slightly, almost as if stretching, and his hand had reached her lower thigh. Eyes still closed, she smiled dreamily up into the sky.

"Imagine, Sunna, what a figure you would be in such a setting. Your birth would make you a prince. Power, wealth, love—there would be nothing beyond your reach."

At this last, he could feel the ripple of the muscles of her thigh. She could do that—carelessly but quite deliberately. It was an invitation that pounded in his veins. His throat was tight with full desire and he was stiff and erect beside her. He was afraid that she would open her eyes and seeing him, swollen with passion, laugh.

Instead, she looked straight ahead—into the trees. Her voice came from deep in her chest now. It was almost a whisper but a whispered command.

"Go ahead, boy. Touch the golden fur. Don't be timid, stroke it, gentle it. Make me moist. Prepare me for you." The edge of her tunic had drawn back somewhat before the progress of his hand upon her thigh. Her legs were cream against the gray of the stone. The slightest of movement now would—.

"Amalsuntha!"

Neither of the pair could have said at what moment Pelayo had entered the clearing.

"Amalsuntha, I need your counsel."

Even without the anticipated inflection, the sarcasm of the words was like a whip. Sunna was speechless. Never had he been such an obvious fool. Caught playing the dirty little youth with the sister of the chief whom he loved, what could he say? How explain? He could not even look at the big warrior but sat in perfect misery upon the rock, staring at its seamed surface, with his mind racing wildly.

Amalsuntha rose quietly, her garment slipping down about her, and retrieved her sandals from the base of the boulder. Her face was hard, set, and her body rigid. Only the red flush which crept up from her neck and suffused her cheeks betrayed her mixed fury and embarrassment. Without a word she joined her brother and they walked together into the trees and towards the river. Sunna, mercifully, might not have existed.

"By God, sister, do you have to flaunt your body for everyone in the camp? Must you seduce even the boys not yet in manhood?"

The chieftain was in a white rage but he kept his voice low, as they began to walk along the riverbank. Some women were doing laundry, others washing, and some of the men polished weapons or simply lay about in the bright sunlight.

His sister, in defiance, spoke in a normal tone. The edge to her voice was quite as biting as was Pelayo's.

"It seems to me, brother, that the boy may be of some use. He might be the one, not you, who furnishes a way back to the civilized life—out of this pigsty in the mountains you seem content with."

"Him? Sunna couldn't even reach the plains alive. Even if he did, he'd be the prisoner of some chief within a few days. The privileges the old world would have offered him are swept away with it."

Amalsuntha merely shook out her hair.

"But my advantages I carry with me, brother, and I use them as suits my purpose. I would be appreciated in that world no matter who runs it, don't you think?"

She swayed her body so as to make her meaning unmistakable. Pelayo regarded her coldly. Bitch she was, if beautiful.

"I think, sister, that you would be a danger to me no matter in whose hands."

"And you are not a danger to me? You will turn me into one of those," she said, with a contemptuous toss of her head towards the women pounding clothes at the stream's edge.

"What has happened to your fine dreams of the spring? You took two towns, mighty general, but the Africans almost caught you. You and your rabble had to run for their lives. Musa swept all across the north and into Galicia itself. He'll be into these hills next, hunting you down. Who of the Gothic leaders of the plains will join you now? Even your grubby Asturian friends are not sure that they haven't sided with the loser."

"You are always too quick to change sides, Amalsuntha. One campaign, one year, does not end a war—not unless one surrenders."

"There will be no war, Pelayo, and you know it. How will you wage war? With what? Because you have held this motley gang of bandits together, now you have 1,200 men. More refugees will come in. But how will you feed them through the winter? Unless you march out of here, the more men you have the weaker you are. The spoil you took at León and Astorga is not enough to buy them food for a winter even if Felix could find it. The raids you made on the plains people this fall had brought in less grain and livestock than you expected. How long will your fine army agree to live on flour made from acorns and the meat of goats? How long before they start looting among the Astures? The only war you may really fight is one with this year's allies. That greasy little lump, Bodo, will desert you fast enough."

Pelayo was chastened by the vehemence of his sister. No, not her vehemence but the truth she spoke. Her assessment of their situation was the same as that which he had turned over in his own mind. How many times? She should have been a chief. Bitch or not, she was bright enough.

What she did not know, he could not tell her. Even when they were little together it had been like that. She had always laughed at his hopes, his dreams. She had a mind like a wolf after sheep—all blood and power and lust. A she-wolf, he thought. Her death will be an ugly thing.

Amalsuntha knew that, for the moment, she had the advantage. Bullying Pelayo was easy, really. He would always stop and think when he should strike. There was no manhood in him but only a kind of stubborn ass—and a pathetic fairness—and a great well of self-pity. What an oaf!

"Look, brother, you have fought manfully and cleverly. You are famous throughout the kingdom. But now it is time to come in. Reap your advantages.

"You have a war band now. It is as good as any in the land. But by spring, after another winter in these mountains, they will have degenerated into a mob of bandits. No one could hold them together. It's no disgrace. When they get hungry enough they will kill the Astures and one another for scraps. They would kill you for the ransom.

"But if they don't, what will they be worth next summer? The Africans won't forgive us. They'll come into these mountains and hunt us down like rabbits. They are too strong. And when they catch us, they'll crucify us like common thieves. I don't want to die like that—or go back, Pelayo's sister, on the end of a rope.

"Now is the time to go down to them. March down with your men. They expect you to do that. You can sell your sword, and theirs, at a handsome price. We can be great figures in the land. The Africans will offer good terms, fall all over themselves to do it.

"And we can be more than mercenaries. You have a treasure buried down there somewhere and they don't know it. When the proper moment offers, we too can hire swords. We can be princes, you and I, together."

She was panting with the effort to persuade him. Her breasts heaved and the words poured out of her. She could see the whole glittering prospect that her greed flung out. She disgusted him—a wanton intent upon her tawdry triumphs.

Nor had she forgotten the treasure—not her. The merest mention of it now brought back to Pelayo all the shame of his flight. She could not know of his desertion of their brother but she knew something. She must stay in these mountains as he must also.

"There is nothing at all for us on the plains, sister. I have sworn to kill the Africans, not to serve them. The old life is dead and best buried. We shall live or die right here.

"And leave that boy alone. Leave all the men alone. If you want a husband, ask me and I'll think about one. But I won't have my sister whoring around the camp. You shame us both."

"Really, my brother? I have not known you to be so fastidious. How many nights did I know you, in the old days, to sneak out of our father's house to grace some prostitute's bed."

Amalsuntha's control broke. She had lost him then, the great, redheaded pig.

"Where were your scruples then? Oh yes, oh yes! I understand, I think I understand."

She was almost shouting at him now.

"You fell in love back there somewhere didn't you. That's it. A stupid native girl—I could bet. That's why your precious concern for the peasants—not your fine sense of justice. Did she tell you she loved you? Tell you while you pumped your seed into her black belly? And what happened—."

The blow caught her full in the mouth. Arms struggling for balance, she reeled backward. She fell and then struggled furiously to a sitting position. Blood dribbled generously from her mouth.

Pelayo was dimly aware that his knuckle bled too, yet he could not take his eyes from her mouth. A sadness caught him suddenly. Hellion she was, but beautiful and now a rent, a gap, had appeared in that beautiful line of teeth, a jagged break. She would never be perfect again.

As he watched, Amalsuntha realized what had happened. Her tongue sought out the rough stump. For a moment he thought that she was going to scream, such was the pain in her eyes. Then the hurt was gone. Instead a look of pure hatred replaced it, of such intensity that it chilled him.

When she spoke, not bothering to rise, she had completely regained control of herself.

"I shall have old Anna draw the pulp. Then you will give me some little of your gold to make a new top.

"But I shall kill you, brother. Do not sleep. Have someone taste your food. I shall find a way to kill you. If I can, I'll have your guts pulled out of your living body and I myself will sprinkle the salt on them. You will remember this at your dying."

She rose and left him without another word. She did not deign even to hold her bleeding mouth.

Chapter XX

The wind off the snow fields of the peaks drove cold in his face with the brisk threat of approaching winter. September had been colder than anyone could remember. For a moment Pelayo considered returning to the lazy warmth of the fires of the camp. But the thought of that ease and careless relaxation returning then drove him higher up the hill as it had just before driven him out of the camp. The campaigning season was just about over.

The pickings had been slimmer than he expected but few of the men in the camp were bothering their heads about that tonight. For the present there was plenty of bread and plenty of wine, even good cow meat. But a fool could see that it would not last the winter. It was going to be a lean one with sixteen hundred men to feed. Impossible! They would have to break up—spread out. But then the discipline would go. They would start cheating the Astures—or simply plundering them. Fruela's division would probably be first at the game.

And the Astures were restless already. The campaigns had formed a certain bond, even a number of friendships. But how long would it survive the fighting over food stocks once that began? Or the fighting over women? Few women had come into the mountains as refugees. Among the hill people there were plenty. They seemed to outnumber their men by two to one. Still the tribes were touchy about blood lines and the claims to forest and pasture that ran with them in a great, weary tangle. We had rapes enough even during the fighting season. What will happen when there's nothing to do but hunt a little? And if the fighting starts, Goth against Asture, what will be left by spring?

No more than the dozens of other times he had set out the problem for himself could he see a solution. As long as the campaigning had been still going on there was the hope that—.

Without thinking he had stopped, poised, hand to his knife. Ahead, face to the moon, was a man, not another tree among trees. That figure now, unaware of his presence, broke its stillness and moved off. In a few paces it had reached a small open space below a cliff face and entered a small patch of moonlight.

Sunna! The boy had not been seen in the camp for better than two weeks. Like a damn fool he had run away right after Pelayo had blundered upon his near seduction. At least he hadn't gotten his throat cut but he must be good and hungry by now, Pelayo thought sourly. Slowly, like a stalker, he advanced on the boy who had slumped down wearily against the cliff.

"Sunna."

At the sight of his chief the young man started, half up, he sank down again. He would not run. Let him kill me then. I've been disgraced enough.

"Sit quiet, boy. I'm not going to eat you."

Even in the faint light Pelayo could see the humiliation of the young Goth. Christ, what a mess. It was just as well that so few women had come into the hills if they had Amalsuntha's capacity for mischief.

"You are a great fool, Sunna. Do you really think that you are the first young man in the world who was coaxed into bed by an older woman? If boys were killed for that there wouldn't be a warrior left in camp. And my—Amalsuntha is no better than the rest."

He kept his tone light, close to banter. There was no need to shame the boy further.

"But she is your sister, Pelayo. And you saved my life after Astorga."

"And would again. We are comrades, Sunna. And do you think that I do not know my own sister? God, how well I know her! "

With a lightness that belied the solid bulk of his frame, he sat himself beside the young man. Wordlessly the two watched faint tendrils of cloud trail themselves across the moon. An owl's hoot carried to them on the thin air. The rhythm of the night echoed round them, insubstantial as a dream. Sunna finally broke their silence.

"But I'm not your comrade. I'm not a warrior."

Pelayo could sense the trembling in the young figure beside him. More carefully, more seriously now, he took up the thread.

"No, a Fruela you're not—nor a Masona either. But they're veterans, Sunna. They've seen a thousand fights, a thousand dead men. Give yourself some time, boy, you're very young.

"Remember that night before Ávila? I almost killed you that night myself. Then there didn't seem to be time enough to let you grow up. But it passed. And you fought. Ávila, Salamanca, the march, León, Astorga. It's been almost two years and you have learned. That's something. Your arm will heal. Give it time."

Sunna broke in, passionately, angrily.

"No, Pelayo, that's not it. It's not my arm. I don't want to be a warrior. I remember well what you told me that night on the hill before Avila. You said I had no choice. You said that the old, soft world was gone, that warrior or slave were the only choices left. I listened and, after Euric was killed, I hated the Africans. I fought. But it's no good for me. I'll never kill another man—even an African."

The words fell into a silence that hung on and on as the chief turned in his mind the young man's words and the heat with which they had been uttered. He hadn't, himself, believed what he'd said about the boy's arm healing. Wounds like that, which touch the cords of the bones, never did. He had known from the time when he'd first dressed that great gash—during the retreat from Astorga—that he'd a cripple on his hands.

Still, there was a warmth in him for the young man fighting to be born out of this boy. Of all those in the camp, Pelayo thought in a half-surprised recognition, I love only this stripling. If I had a son, the son that died with Elena—smothered in her womb—.

He broke off the thought but said to Sunna with gentle weariness, "It's still the same world, boy. What will you do then? Become a trader? Travel with that rogue, Felix? Take up goatherding? Scratch these rocks for acorns and run pigs in the hills?"

The young man seemed to be gathering some muscles within himself. He will go mad, Pelayo thought helplessly. He'll jump out of his own skin and be lost in the flittering moonlight.

"Why do you do that, Pelayo?" the youth broke out suddenly.

"Why do you despise yourself? Why does Amalsuntha adore her own body and hate her own soul? Why are men— why are we all—like black bears who claw the bark off trees to search for rottenness and scuttling beetles underneath? Is no one to be allowed to be simply good—to be simply kind? Do we fear that so much that we must crush, kill, anyone who even tries to be?"

No answer was possible. Pelayo sat silent, feeling the cold entering his bones. If he could tell anyone of his desertion of his brother back in far away Toledo, he could tell this boy. But he feared to do that. He had never even told Elena— though perhaps she'd known. What had he babbled in those nights of fever and sickness? What a long, weary time ago that was.

Lost in that memory, he almost missed what the boy had said.

"What?"

"I am going to be a priest," Sunna repeated, almost in a whisper.

The redhaired giant felt the warmth and the blood spreading through himself. Yes. By God, yes. That was the answer. Someday when this youth was indeed a priest, he would—could—tell him about his brother. It was right that way. For the first time in more than two years the cold hate that ruled him retreated a little. There was a tiny flame of hope that played in the center of his brain. A smile broadening in the moonlight, he half-turned towards Sunna.

"It's right! It's the right thing!"

Incredulous, unbelieving, the young man asked, "Do you mean that you approve?"

"Yes. Yes, of course. Someone must do it for us—for all of us. You are the one."

Trembling with surprise and relief, Sunna continued hesitantly, "I shall have to study—to prepare myself. Paternus will help."

At the mention of the fat, stolid priest Pelayo tensed.

"Paternus? That sly mountain of—."

"He's a man like us," the other broke in. "Like us he's done what he's done. Perhaps what he had to do. It doesn't matter. There isn't any other here."

The chief regarded him sharply, with sudden suspicion.

"This is Paternus' idea?"

Sunna looked directly and steadily at him. He was calmer now and more confident. His voice was strong and clear as he replied.

"Yes, it was Paternus' idea. But it is my own decision. You have said that it was right."

Pelayo stared long at the young man before him. Their eyes held steadily.

"You won't let him castrate you?"

A rich, deepening smile graced the young man's face. He relaxed in the strength he felt dancing within him.

"I am not a warrior but I am a man. For better or worse, I am a man. With your help he will not castrate my body or my mind."

Gradually at first, then with a rush, the chief's smile answered his son's. His hand found the other's elbow, felt the other's hand find his, their forearms lay together.

After a long pause, Sunna spoke, half-reluctant to lose the minute.

"Paternus had his price."

"Of course. That mountain of deceitful fat would have."

"He wants the golden vessels and the cross you took from the church at Astorga."

Pelayo threw back his head and laughed.

"So little. He shall have them, Sunna. But he will get a pupil who will be such a priest as he will never be. And so he will pay himself such a price as he has no mind to imagine. And I shall see that he pays every penny of it. He will, despite his sour self, become my companion in fashioning such a thing as the world has seldom seen."

Pelayo was up now. His loins were drawn tight. An excitement danced along his veins as in the moment before a battle was joined.

"Go down to the camp now, Sunna. Find yourself a meal and a place to sleep. Leave me alone. You have started a vision in me—dream perhaps. I will pursue it now—alone."

Not understanding, Sunna arose. The words were those of a chief again. Thanks would be wrong now. Happily he moved downhill in the moon's glow.

The valley bottom along the little river lay just to the north of two peaks which formed a natural funnel. From it October's wind roared in a flood over the plain and its packed ranks and fanned the three great fires on either side of the assembly into roar after roar of yellow-red flame. The night promised cold aplenty but just now the heat from those pyres drove the mixed crowd in upon itself, away from the scorching pines. Men in bearskin and mountain pantaloons, women in grayish tunics festooned with bits of amber jewelry, some few with gold, more bedecked with necklaces of seashells and polished stones, mingled with the polished bronze and steel of chestpiece, helmet, and sword. The squat browner Astures had their hair restrained by headbands while the taller Goths pulled their own back into a single tether or plaited it on either side of their heads. An excitement compounded of anticipation and apprehension moved the mass to occasional jests but more often held them silent. The acrid stench of sweating bodies now and again bettered the perfume of burning pine.

Pelayo saw the show with pride. His warriors had not stinted in the preparation of their arms and armor. Still, the most splendid figure of all was that of Paternus seated at the front. The huge, bald pate of the priest sprouted little rivers that ran, unregarded, down his face and neck and then disappeared beneath his robe. That great cope of deep reds, purples, and blues, interworked with threads and festooned with knots and buds of silver and gold threads, was so heavy in itself that it scarcely moved despite the strength of the night wind. Its bearer moved not at all, heavy-lidded and impressive before the crowd, the little three-legged stool that bore him invisible beneath the bulk of man and garment alike. The slight, white-tuniced figure of Sunna and his small cropped head looked more than ever boyish at the priest's right.

On Pelayo's right, facing the assembly and seated like the redhead himself on a forked chair, the Asturian chief of chiefs, Bodo, sat in half-drunken amusement but sharp-eyed and lecherously possessive, his hand upon the thigh of Amalsuntha. Pelayo could smell the oil on the man's body mixed with the odor of the half-tanned skins which the little man wore in careless abundance. Had he not known his sister so well he might have pitied her. But she had given her splendid body to meaner than this when it served her dark will.

She was a marvelous gift. The rich dark green of her tunic showed, in the firelight, to perfection the gold of the jewelry with which she was so heavily laden, belt, bracelets, rings, three necklaces alone. The jewelry had been her brother's gift of plunder but the tunic, like Paternus' cope, had been wrung from the protesting merchant, Felix. God knows, both had come a long and devious route to bedeck this occasion. Spoils, ultimately, of some theft or plunder in the south, Sevilla, or even across the narrow sea from Africa. Even Felix probably did not know for sure.

The Roman trader's reluctance even to admit that he possessed either, much less to part with them, had been funny. Not so amusing at all though had been Amalsuntha's ferocious resistance to the idea of the marriage.

"He is a pig, brother," she had said, spitting out the word *brother* like a bad nut. "The greased body of a pig with its stiff, prickly hair and the mind of a pig within the body."

"Bodo is," Pelayo reminded her, "the greatest of the chiefs among the Astures. That mind holds more than pork fat. He knows his people and his will is as strong and bright as yours, dear sister, to have led them so long. Nor is he a mean warrior."

"A leader of goatherds and acorn grubbers," she had screamed at him. "A princess of the Goths does not marry such offal!"

"Such garbage," he had reminded her with quiet sarcasm, "more than once cut up Gothic armies sent into the mountains in the old days to try to punish their raids. Besides, as I have told you, there will be no more Goths. We shall, all of us, marry and mingle our blood with the Astures and the Romans. We will become a single people and our strengths will blend against the Africans and all those they hold subject on the plains. You and I will lead in this and you shall become the wife of a great chief."

"You mean I will grow great of belly with black mongrel babies which will run naked about the huts of this miserable hill country and forget who their parents were! What will such dwarfish, stunted people rule—or where? The Africans will rightly despise such degenerates. The meanest of them can recite the list of their ancestors back to ten generations."

"And that narrow pride will be their great weakness! What your children become, Amalsuntha, will be yours to decide. But do you think that the conquered Goths of the south will throw off the yoke of the conquerors? Reduced to subjection, do you think that they will not marry with the better sort of the Romans, their companions in slavery? How many half-breeds were there even in the days before the Africans came? One people we will become and, as one people, we shall possess and redeem the land. Sooner or later, the Africans will find they have as many enemies in the south as in these hills."

"Your dream, this nightmare," she hissed at him, "was born upon a black belly. It is a private dream, brother. It will bring our name to shame and nothing else. Are you afraid to go and get yourself killed as a Gothic warrior should? Did she drain so much of manhood's juice out of you? Leave the rest of us alone. I would die before I would accept such shame!"

Pelayo regarded her then, perhaps for the first time, with a hatred equal to that she felt for him.

"No sister," he replied. "You are not the kind that dies—at least, by your own hand. You will do anything to live, and plot, and corrupt. You are a walking cesspool, sister, despite the beauty of your body. But I will tell you what your choices are. You will marry, as I tell you, and with every appearance of acceptance and of joy. Then I shall shower you with plunder and dress you in such fashion as a queen would envy.

"Or you will refuse. Then I will have you shut up, naked, in a cage in the middle of the camp. Do not think that you have such loving friends as would rescue you. There you will live amidst your own excrement, alone and without food, prodded with sticks by little boys, until your skin lies upon your bare bones and every man despises your gift.

"That is your choice, sister. By God, I will do it!"

She would have killed him then if she had been able. But as they stared hatred at one another, he had seen the fear flow slowly into her face. Finally, she dropped her gaze, bowed her head.

Now Amalsuntha sat, regal, beside Bodo. The chief of the Astures might take any liberty with her here and she would endure it but he did not understand that nor, indeed, anything about the nature of his bride but that she promised the fullest delight of womankind, was the sister of a great chief, and had one magnificent gold tooth among the ivory. Pelayo felt some pity for the tough little warrior chief beside him.

After his sister, the others had been easy. Once Bodo had had the chance to reflect on the scheme, he had come around for his own reasons. That the Goths should intermarry with his people, scatter throughout their villages, share their land, would dilute if not break the bonds of kin and share out strangely the sacred, ancestral lands. Still, the alternative was to retreat to the uplands for two, perhaps three, years. It would be to live as animals in their own lands while they harried the Goths to death. But the southerners were formidable warriors and desperate as well.

For a few hours he had thought that the best thing would be to seek out the Africans at once. Reluctantly he had rejected the idea. It was too late in the season. They would be already fortifying their burned-out camps against the winter. Anyway, these Goths knew hill fighting as few others he had fought in a long career of running skirmishes.

Gradually Bodo's thoughts had brightened. Pelayo was a great war chief. He had proved that in the full view of the Astures the past summer. The marriage would bring a full sharing out of the campaign loot—presents for all. It would also strengthen his own, always precarious, supremacy among the other Asturian chiefs even if he would now have to share that position with the redhaired one. Pelayo himself seemed a fair man, a man of impartial justice, if a cold, hard one. In any event, the Goth might not live overly long among these mountains. Accidents happened and then much could be changed back towards the old ways.

Finally, it was the thought of Amalsuntha which overcame his last, lingering objections. By the gods, she was ripe! What a bedding she would be. She stirred his blood as no woman had for many winters. The blond's hips promised to be good for three sons at least and they would lack no suck at those breasts no more than he!

The little chief could not know that less than four years hence he would die on Amalsuntha's knife. But even that night, his bride knew that she would kill this greasy little man—kill the father of her two daughters and her son. But for now she would wait, and smile, and caress. The time would come when she would free herself of him and of her brother alike.

The captains of the Goths had been even easier to persuade. They were used to his orders. All of them understood the necessities of winter camp in a strange land that could not feed them. A dispersal was the only way to survive till spring given their present numbers. But the land would have to be made theirs to share, by marriage, or they would be at the mercy of the hill people once they broke up.

Wala was the only one of them genuinely enthusiastic at the idea. But the others were soldiers who had lain before with native women of many kinds. Pelayo was right though. This time marriage was necessary—at least till spring. Masona, typically, had sounded the caution.

"Bodo will have reasons of his own for agreeing to this, Pelayo. With all of Amalsuntha's charms, these matches will force the blood lines and the property claims of every clan in these hills. Watch your back every minute."

The one-handed Huneric seconded the thought. "And the

old men who still fear the old gods will call these Christian marriages sacrilege. They will not love us as kinsmen."

"All of this is true," Pélayo had answered them. "But they must fear us more. For now they will appreciate the loot of the past summer. Each of you must see that your men don't spend the winter in bed—at least not all the time—though the fathering of new children is important.

"Their young women must be full of new life to think about by the spring. But the young men must be trained in some of the ways that we make war. Keep them at it this winter. Share out the captured arms. They will not break lightly the hope of even more successful raids next summer. When you rally to me in the spring I will expect that your war bands will be swollen, mixed, and every man fit for the field.

"That will leave the old men to grumble by themselves and to watch their granddaughters' bellies swell. And even they will be slobbering for the good meat and the rich wine which we shall bring back from the plains. By next autumn more recruits will mean more marriages. Together with the new babies, they will make this new people harder yet to break.

"As for Bodo, trust my sister to tire him out through the winter. Every honor must be paid to my new brother—as to the other chiefs whose daughters you are marrying. But we, and someday our children, must remain the masters of war. The bands will be jointly led but be sure that all the men, Goth and Asture alike, know who is the real slayer of men and sacker of cities.

"Bodo's sister, whom I am to marry, will be my proper wife and my ally by springtime, I promise you. Her brother will see in her loins a nephew of his blood. It will make it easier for him. He will have hopes, I know, to rule the land alone again through his sister's children and through his own, gotten on Amalsuntha. But he is fifteen years older than I and may not himself survive many seasons.

"No, we shall be one people, in possession of these mountain lands as no mere Goths could ever be, and we shall speak to all the conquered people of the plains with one voice. At such a time, the Africans will not stand against us but we will put them to the knife. It will happen. You have my word for it."

In the silence which had followed his words, only Fruela spoke—boomed rather.

"Christ, what a spreading of legs this will be! Blood on everybody's straw. Even our great Pelayo will lie with a woman."

Now, as the waves of heat and light swept unevenly over them from the roaring fires, Pelayo glanced for a moment at the dark, stocky woman seated to his left, her large feet splayed outwards even in repose. Then briefly his eyes caught Sunna's, held a moment, and then passed onto the gorgeously coped Paternus. At last, at the chief's nod, the fat priest rose slowly, a column—a wall almost—of shining gold, silver, purple, red....

Together with the Asturian woman at his side, Pelayo rose from his chair for the beginning.